FRANCE

A SHORT HISTORY

by

ALBERT GUÉRARD

LONDON

GEORGE ALLEN AND UNWIN LTD

PRINTED IN GREAT BRITAIN
BY HENDERSON & SPALDING
LONDON, W.1

À CEUX DE LA RÉSISTANCE
ILS ONT PRÉSERVÉ
LA FRANCE QUE NOUS AIMONS

Foreword

THIS little book is my testament. For fifty years I have studied, for forty years I have taught in American universities the tragic and magnificent history of my native land. I have never been a propagandist for any class or party. There is no thesis in this book; there are. however, two guiding thoughts, both familiar to the point of triteness, both too often disregarded. The first is that France is a collective achievement without which the world would be darker. The second is that France and the United States, more perhaps than any other major nations, are founded upon the same principles. The two countries have diverged only when they went astray. As soon as they return to their deepest tradition, they are bound to meet. These two thoughts might help us in the difficult problems of today: it is the historical sense that creates a difference between mere politics and constructive statesmanship. But these thoughts were already clear in my mind when I was writing my first historical books, before the first world war.

The book, I feel, owes much to the indefatigable care of the editor, Addison Burnham. I am particularly grateful that the manuscript was read with critical attention by Professor Geoffrey Bruun, whose scholarly work I have long admired. A survey of this kind is bound to be an interpretation; for the opinions expressed in these pages, I alone, and not my kindly critics, must accept the full responsibility.

ALBERT GUÉRARD

Contents

Part Three MODERN FRANCE

List of Maps

PART ONE

The Foundations

CHAPTER I

The Living Past

1. THE HISTORICAL vs. THE EPHEMERAL

FEW MEN are austere or dull-witted enough to scorn the pageantry and romance of history. Froissart, Sir Walter Scott, Alexandre Dumas will eternally appeal to the eternal boy in man. And there are no annals so full of romance as those of the French. We bow courteously before the mighty personages of other traditions—the Emperors Barbarossa and Charles V, Philip II of Spain, Gustavus Adolphus and Charles XII of Sweden, Peter and Catherine of Russia, Frederick II and Bismarck. But it is about Saint Louis, Joan of Arc, Villon, Henry of Navarre, Richelieu, Marie Antoinette, Napoleon, that we love to read. The greatest figure that emerged out of the Dark Ages is best remembered as a character in French epic song, not as the leader of Teutonic hosts, as Charlemagne, not as Karl der Grosse.

The appeal of France's annals is not that of a success story. The record of that smiling land is strangely somber. The earliest heroes are heroes of defeat: Vercingetorix, Roland. Saint Louis dies in failure, Joan of Arc suffers martyrdom, Henry IV is stabbed, Napoleon is chained. But the story is shot through with episodes of unequaled magnificence. Brief and few were the eras of safety first and stodgy comfort. There were for instance the lenitive rule of Cardinal Fleury under Louis XV, and the bourgeois regime of Louis Philippe a hundred years ago; in both cases, "France was bored." It has been the destiny of France to live dangerously. Curious irony, that such a fate should be meted out to a people essentially moderate and cheerful, fond of honest work and of good living, cautious and thrifty almost to a fault, praising and practicing reasonableness as the highest virtue, a people whose favorite sport is the most placid of all human occupations, angling in a quiet stream. The French, in their millions, are shrewd, plodding realists; out of that drab multitude France arises, a romantic flame.

I should have liked this little book to be an epitome of that colorful drama; best of all, perhaps, an album of famous characters and scenes, with a text borrowed from the most vivid, the most ardent of French historians, Jules Michelet. If I gave up the thought, it is not because I despise glamor. The term has acquired a vulgar tinge, but even the realist must acknowledge glamor as a fact, and a fact of the utmost potency. It is rather because I can safely take that romantic prestige for granted. Everyone has in his mind pictures of the French past, distorted perhaps, legendary rather than historical, but intensely alive. I shall attempt to present them briefly, in their proper sequence; but my chief task will be to seek their underlying unity.

For the fascination of France is not a mass of disconnected incidents. Under many regimes, through twenty centuries of splendor and trial, a complex, tormented, vigorous entity has grown: *France,* the France that is with us today. France has never ceased to seek, and thus to create, herself. In hours of triumph, she was unwilling to rest on her achievements; in days of humiliation, she never accepted defeat as more than a temporary check, a spur to *revanche;* and *revanche* never means spite, but vindication, rehabilitation, another chance.

Personality is not a welter of primitive impulses; it is an achievement of the conscious will. In France, the self-creating effort has been unremitting, and that is why Michelet was right in saying: "France is a person." Germany, Italy, Spain gave up for centuries; France never did. And France was spared the temptation that comes with security, the temptation to say: "Let us not think, it might break the spell. The ways of our fathers are good enough for us. We shall muddle through somehow." The thought of France has often been wrong, but hardly ever timid or sluggish.

Here again we find the odd contrast between France and the French. The French, as individuals, want to retire early, on a modest competence, and cultivate their garden. For France as a nation, this is an unattainable dream. In the *Song of Roland,* Charlemagne returns from his hard expedition in Spain, and finds a new, harder task ahead. He sighs: "What a life of travail!" and buckles on his sword again. Such is the fate of France. She had never rested and can never rest. The tradition that impels her is revolutionary. I am not alluding merely to the upheaval of 1789. The Capetian kings represented a constant struggle against the force of custom as embodied in the liberties of provinces and the privileges of feudal lords. No sooner had the kings won their long battle than the bourgeoisie took up the fight—against the kings. And the bourgeois had not yet completed their citadel of vested interests when it was assailed by the common people. France has never been able to turn a revolution, as England has done after 1688, into a reason for stopping the clock. For her, the eternal verities are not a refuge but a challenge.

It will be my endeavor to present that very active reality, the France of today, as it was slowly created by the obstinate will of the centuries. Note the insistence on *will.* The historical sense is not, as Maurice Barrès defined nationalism, "the acceptance of a determinism," it is the acceptance of conditions. The past that created us does not absolve us from all responsibility. Ancient wrong does not mellow into right. It is for us, not for our ancestors, to think, to choose, to act. No creature can belong wholly to the past and be alive.

But on the other hand no creature can belong wholly to the present. The one great service that history can render us is to deliver us from the delusion of the ephemeral. There is a fourth dimension, which is time. An instantaneous object is an absurdity; to exist at all, a thing must have duration. And the longer the duration, the more certain the existence. An isolated snapshot does not tell us the candid truth. It does not tell us whether a man is laughing or crying, yelling or yawning, stumbling or running. Or, to change the metaphor, a chance glimpse of a stream may be utterly misleading. We do not know whether the stream is in full flood or at a low ebb. What we are watching may be a minor fork or it may be the main channel. A few miles below the placid pool, there may be rapids. We do not even know in which direction the stream is permanently flowing; the current may be reversed by the tide, like that of the Thames in London. In order fully to understand a stream, we must follow it for the greater part of its course. The life of an old nation is such a stream.

This contrast between the ephemeral and the historical is too crude to be accurate. Between the evanescent and the permanent, there are innumerable degrees. Certain things disappear swiftly and altogether, like the best sellers and the smart politicians of yesterday; others melt slowly away; others still are fresh and strong after centuries. In the same way, from the window of a speeding car, bushes and telegraph poles dash past, each a glimpse and gone forever; bolder and more distant features stay within sight for an appreciable time; and Mount Shasta remains our companion for hours. This is what we may call historical perspective, or the sense of history; and we need to take it into account if statesmanship, not mere politics, is to be our guide.

On this vaster stage, what is of greatest import is not the *moment* but the *momentum*. The true "inside story" is not backstairs gossip, but history. The latest news is but an infinitesimal part of the truth. Recent events offer a striking illustration of what may be called the journalistic delusion.

In June, 1940, the armies and the government of the Third Republic collapsed. The Walter Winchell school of history explained the catastrophe by naming the lady friends of French cabinet ministers. It never crossed their minds that the disaster was due to the coincidence of two age-long conflicts. The first is the contest between France and Germany, as old as the treaty of Verdun in 843, and virulent ever since 1795. The second is the struggle between the Ancient Regime and the Revolution, which has never abated since 1789. The French could cope with a crisis in either field separately, the Dreyfus Case for instance, or the first world war. When two crises happened to synchronize, the breaking point was reached.

France, divided, betrayed, abandoned by her natural allies, ceased to exist, not merely as a great power, but as a sovereign state. And the journalistic mind concluded: "France is through." The historical mind viewed the plight of France as a sorrowful picture in a series which had been unrolling for at least a thousand years. In 1422, the king of England ruled in Paris and there were many collaborationists who accepted his new order. The legitimate king was an object of derision; he was called the king of Bourges. A few years later appeared Joan of Arc. In 1589, France was rent by religious strife. The rightful sovereign, Henry of Navarre, was an adventurer in his own kingdom, the leader of a small desperate band. Paris was in the hands of his enemies, collaborating heartily with the new order of those days, the European leadership of the Spanish crown. But Henry IV opened for France an era of unprecedented splendor. In 1814 and 1815, Russians, Austrians, Prussians, Englishmen, united against France, occupied Paris, and forced upon the French a government of senile ghosts. Once more, there were collaborationists who welcomed the new order, the Holy Alliance, and shouted: "Hurrah for our friends the enemies!" But France found herself again, and resumed her rightful place in the van of liberal powers.

Whoever had felt the tremendous momentum of French history knew in June, 1940, that France was down but not out. The fruit of much patient labor might be destroyed at one blow; but the soil and the people were not exhausted. There was fruitfulness in reserve, and fortitude, and lucidity, and will power. The France of Léon Blum might be stabbed in the back, and the France of the Cagoulards might be eager to capitulate; but political quarrels, for all their violence, are the merest eddies. The increasing flood that had carried saints, heroes, thinkers, workers for so many hundred years did not suddenly disappear into the tiny gulf called Vichy. When in August, 1944, our men entered liberated Paris, they found, with all its charm and its failings and its heroic tenacity of life, the people of the Bastille and of the Marne. History had given the lie to journalism.

There is more than weary scepticism in the familiar phrase, *plus ça change, plus c'est la même chose,* the more things change, the more they remain the same. On the surface, the epigram is a denial of progress; but it is also an affirmation of historical identity. With an ironical twist, it is synonymous with the expression which Victor Hugo turned into a household word, and which President Roosevelt repeated at a solemn hour: "Eternal France." It means: "We may freely experiment and explore; such is our destiny. But the more we do so, the more profoundly we are ourselves." A Frenchman challenging the authority of Descartes, like Jacques Maritain, knows that in so doing he is true to the Cartesian tradition. The Encyclopedists were consciously the heirs of the crusaders. The Jacobins completed the work of Louis XIV. When General de Gaulle broke away from the official leaders of the French army, he felt himself one with Clemenceau, Gambetta, Danton, and Joan of Arc. History is no mere remembrance of things past; it is, as Michelet put it, resurrection. It is the realization that time is the essence of our being, and that the past is alive in us.

Other lands in Europe have a longer history than France, for instance, Greece and Rome. But they do not present the same continuity of purpose. As organized nations, they are of yesterday; and now they have to start anew. England alone has the same historical depth and density as France. However, England is somewhat younger: France was already called *douce France* by the time of the Norman conquest, that is to say before England was born. England is more ostentatiously attached to the forms of her past, while in the last century and a half there has been a kaleidoscopic effect about French political life which has often bewildered foreign observers. Yet the difference is superficial. France is no less deeply rooted in the past than England. Trappings should not mislead us; without paradox, it may be said that the antiquarian spirit is not the truest form of the historical. The antiquarian would have fossils sit at the council table by the side of living men; the true historian is concerned primarily with forces, not with monuments. When ancient forms—abuses, privileges, superstitions—clog the stream of national life, they become antihistorical and have to be swept away.

2. FRENCH NATIONALISM: ITS EUROPEAN AND HUMAN CHARACTER

In claiming for France this high degree of historical consciousness, I may seem to be pleading the cause of nationalism. Now nationalism is a narrow and dangerous creed. The French version of it, as expounded by Maurice Barrès and especially by Charles Maurras, is to me as objectionable as any other. *France d'abord!* is no better than *Deutschland über alles!* But what I have in mind is not a Gallic form of *Sinn Fein*— ourselves alone—or of *sacro egoismo*. It is rather the fraternal feeling, within the nation and among the nations, that prevailed in 1789 and 1848. The national spirit may be defined as collective personality; but a personality, whether man or country, need not be brutal and selfish. It is possible to be conscious of one's identity without desiring to snub, bully or enslave others. The highest exponent of historical nationalism, Jules Michelet, actually loved Italy, Poland, and Germany.

Through no mystic virtue of their own, but simply as the result of natural conditions, the French have never been able to isolate themselves from European civilization as a whole. They are not a race, and have never believed themselves to be a race; anyone who lives in France and feels himself a Frenchman is a Frenchman. Their land is an integral part and an epitome of Europe. It belongs at the same time to the Mediterranean zone, and, more intimately still, to the northern world. It opens wide on the Atlantic, and is solidly linked with the mass of the continent. Vast migrations are rare accidents in history; but infiltration has been a continuous process for over twenty centuries; in every generation, there were excellent Frenchmen whose families had come from across the Alps or the Rhine. At no time in her long career could France find pride, joy or even safety in aloofness. Isolation for her never was splendid, as England professed to find it; it was a morbid condition to be cured. When France erected a Chinese Wall named the Maginot Line, she soon discovered that Prague and Danzig were of no less concern to her than Dijon or Poitiers. France cannot ignore the continent, and the continent cannot ignore France.

Hence this essential paradox: the highest achievement of the national spirit, in France, is the cosmopolitan. Geography has made her a meeting ground; history has made her a common denominator. That is why people throughout the world enjoy France not as a land of strange exotic charm, but as an extension of their home. That is what Jefferson meant when he proclaimed France the second choice of every traveled man.[1]

---

[1] The phrase: "Every man has two countries, his own and then France" is often ascribed to Jefferson; it is not untrue to his spirit.

Matthew Arnold's sneer, "France, famed in all great arts, in none supreme," is a grudging admission of the fact that everything of European value is worthily represented in France. Her originality consists in being a composite picture. In the process, the bolder features of other lands may lose something of their sharpness; yet the result is neither lifeless nor commonplace. If there were a French type, it would have to be described as "of medium build and intermediate coloring." Yet *Frenchness* (I do not mean *Frenchiness,* a mere caricature) is a clear-cut and unmistakable attribute. The French have achieved raciness by denying race and originality by spurning the eccentric.

I do not claim that French nationalism and European civilization are identical. If it were so, there would be a Europe today. The French—like ourselves—have repeatedly been untrue to their destiny. They have relapsed into a "sacred egoism" adverse to their permanent interests. Under Louis XIV and Napoleon I, in particular, they tried to coerce when their mission was to welcome. They made their country the barracks of Europe, while it should have remained its salon. No tradition, no institution is pure and in the prestige of France there are equivocal elements. Perhaps it is better for the soul of France that her periods of insolent pride ended in humiliation. Louis XIV and Napoleon had to acknowledge defeat; the elder Pitt, Frederick II, Bismarck did not. As the relative numerical strength of France declines, the temptation to imperial sway recedes but France's true mission will appear all the more clearly. It does not take power to offer a meeting ground, it only requires intelligence and courtesy.

The central position of France in European culture is not an empty boast but a plain fact. It has been generally acknowledged not once, but many times. No other European country except Renaissance Italy ever attained the same degree of leadership. Although the nineteenth century was a period of English triumph in every field, the London of Queen Victoria never had the magic appeal of Paris under Louis Philippe or Napoleon III. This freely accepted leadership of France, not political, not military, not economic, was manifest in the Middle Ages. The Crusades swept the whole of Christendom; but the crusaders were known in the East as the Franks; the kingdom of Jerusalem, in its language, in its institutions, in the style of its churches and of its fortresses, was an extension of France. Gothic art spread from Ile-de-France to the utmost confines of medieval Europe. The thought of the time was crystallized in the University of Paris, Latin of speech, made up of many nations, and withal as French as Peter Abélard himself. Dante's master, Brunetto Latini, wrote his *Treasury of Wisdom* in French, because, "of all languages, it was the most delectable and the most common among men."

Again in the seventeenth century, France set a European pattern. It was not because of Louis XIV's victories that princes and bourgeois throughout Europe followed the fashions and adopted the speech of Versailles and Paris; it was because the French elite had evolved a style of living, of thinking, of writing, which satisfied the desires of the continent. The salon of Madame de Rambouillet, the dramas of Molière and Racine, the poetic rules of Boileau, the palaces of Mansart and the gardens of Le Nôtre did more for the prestige of France than the armies organized by Louvois or the victories of Condé and Turenne. In the eighteenth century, that glamor grew instead of waning although the armies of the French met with repeated defeats. Kings felt exiled on their thrones in Sweden or Poland, and sighed for "the kingdom of Rue Saint Honoré," the salon of *Maman* Geoffrin. The enlightenment, born in England, won Europe through Montesquieu, Voltaire and the Encyclopedists. Frederick II spoke French by preference, and the Academy of Berlin offered a prize on the subject: "What are the reasons that have made the French language universal?"

The fundamental reason for the privileged position of

France was the renunciation of privilege. At their best, the French did not divorce nationality from humanity. The medieval Sorbonne attempted to formulate *Catholic* truth. Descartes sought the rules for the conduct of *universal* reason. The *philosophes* consciously thought and wrote for the world. Paris was their tribune not their intellectual prison. The revolutionists proclaimed, not special liberties based on ancient charters, but the rights of man; and for that reason, the fall of the Bastille roused even the unworldly Kant in his remote Königsberg.

Pride and greed corrupted the international ideal; dominion took the place of leadership; and in 1814–1815, France was punished for having strayed from her appointed path. Waterloo was not the bitterest defeat; the worst was to see the legitimate prestige of France suffer an eclipse, and with it those European ideas which had once radiated from Paris.

But France continued to "fulfill herself in many ways." By 1848, the great romantic apostles of democracy, Lamennais, Lamartine, Michelet, Hugo had evolved a new synthesis: ardent Christianity with the utmost freedom of thought, nationalism reconciled with brotherhood, social justice inseparable from political liberty. Realists sneered; Bismarck, not Lamartine, was to provide the pattern for the new era; and the possibility of a free harmonious Europe was held back a hundred years. Chartism disappeared in England; the best of the German "men of forty-eight" emigrated to America; the Mazzini spirit in Italy was superseded by the shrewd bargaining of Cavour; liberal Hungary went into exile with Kossuth. But in France, although there was a sharp reaction, the disruption of the European ideal was not complete. Even the sovereign who represented material power, prosperity, realism, Napoleon III, was still, in his baffling hesitant way, a "man of forty-eight" and a good European. The republican opposition was much more definitely committed to a united democratic Europe. The defeat of 1870–1871 caused a narrowing of the

French horizon; but the people had not lost their faith. The funeral of Victor Hugo in 1885 was a spontaneous tribute of the masses to the man who had prophesied the "United States of Europe." The thought never was absent from the mind of Jean Jaurès. When Aristide Briand took up the idea in 1929, he was strictly in line with the French tradition.

Of that tradition, Georges Clemenceau may be considered a crucial example. Old "Father Victory" is often cited as the perfect pattern of fierce militant patriotism. No one could have a more single-hearted devotion to his country. But Clemenceau's "country" was not a territory, it was an ideal of freedom. As long as France was the chosen instrument of the human cause, he served France. But he told Pershing, in an hour of severe trial, "Above Paris is France and above France is civilization." [2] So, in the moment of triumph, he who scorned empty phrases spoke quite naturally of "France, yesterday the soldier of God, today the soldier of humanity, ever the soldier of the ideal." [3] Rhetoric? No, but a lucid conception of France's living past.

Nor was this a naïve egocentric delusion. The words of Clemenceau were soberness itself compared with the tributes of Walt Whitman [4], George Meredith [5] and Friedrich Nietzsche.[6] D. W. Brogan, a sharp realistic mind, prefaces his history of *France Under the Republic* with the weighty words: "Of that Western civilization (of which with all its faults we are unescapably the children) France has been, since the time of the *Chanson de Roland*, the main sword and the main shield." Patrick Geddes, also a man of cosmopolitan experience, who labored in Scotland, England, India, America, shared the same conviction, and offered a proof which many,

[2] J. J. Pershing: *My Experiences in the World War*, II. 93.
[3] Speech before Chamber of Deputies, November 11, 1918.
[4] "O Star of France," 1870–1871, *Leaves of Grass*.
[5] Odes in Contribution to the Song of French History, particularly "France: December, 1870."
[6] Most tersely in *Beyond Good and Evil*, Ch. VIII.

at the time, thought paradoxical: the world-wide indignation caused by the Dreyfus affair. No country is free from miscarriages of justice; France alone could transmute a mere scandal into a moral issue which probed the conscience of mankind.

Even during the tragic twilight between the two world wars, the central position of France was manifest. So far as home and foreign politics are concerned, there are few more discouraging periods in the story of the country. But the indomitable vitality of the French asserted itself again in other ways, when with very little help they repaired their ruins and equipped their vast empire. In the domain of the spirit, it was one of the brilliant moments in France's long career. Not only were there great artists, writers, and scientists of French birth but France attracted and assimilated refugees from all the lands blighted by dictators. More strangely, she was a haven for English writers as well (D. H. Lawrence, James Joyce), and Paris became for a decade the literary capital of America with authors as diverse as Gertrude Stein and Elliot Paul. This was no new development; as Van Wyck Brooks notes,[1] "many American books have been written in Paris, from the days of Franklin, Jefferson, and Joel Barlow to the days of Hemingway, Dos Passos, and Scott Fitzgerald. There Cooper wrote *The Prairie* and Irving *The Tales of a Traveller*, and John Howard Payne wrote *Home, Sweet Home*. Henry Adams followed the precedent of Jefferson's *Notes on Virginia* when he had his *Tahiti* privately printed in Paris, where Stephen Vincent Benét wrote *John Brown's Body*. Writing in Paris is one of the oldest American customs. It all but antedates, with Franklin, the founding of the republic." In the nineteen twenties and thirties, the University of Paris became as cosmopolitan as it had been in the thirteenth century. It had literally thousands of foreign students, and the University City at Montsouris had a score of residential halls built by friendly nations. At the very moment when France

[1] *The World of Washington Irving,* 256 n.

was going through her great ordeal, in 1939 and 1940, the French Pavilion in the New York World Fair offered a unique blend of tradition and daring. And already the irresistible momentum is felt in the liberation and the reconstruction of France, as the indispensable nucleus of a free and united Europe.

This, I firmly believe, is the lesson of the living past. France exists in historical depth. She is a cemetery, and a museum, and withal a plaisance; but she is above all a laboratory.

More daring experiments are performed elsewhere, in the United States and in the Soviet Union; and we do not grudge our admiration and gratitude to these gigantic efforts. But the less sensational endeavor of the French possesses a quality of its own, which is of inestimable value. It is the slowly ripened result of history: measure, balance. This virtue—like all virtues—is a handicap. It precludes France from accepting the ruthless sacrifices, the spiritual mutilations, that inevitably attend certain forms of pioneering. The most revolutionary among the French cannot forget their sense of delicate values. Voltaire the iconoclast was fond of exquisite luxury. Renan and Anatole France were conservative in their artistic taste. Jean Jaurès, Edouard Herriot, Léon Blum took literature seriously. For the French, civilization is continuous and can never be served by a relapse into barbarism. There is no reason why the truth should be crude.

The result of this balance is not timidity, but freedom. French culture is so consciously many-sided that it cannot surrender to the tyranny of a single principle. It rejects the autocracy of any man, race or dogma. It cannot brook the dictatorship of business, or the dictatorship of the proletariat. It even spurns, in the name of history, the absolute authority of tradition: tradition is a possession, not a rule. Against every form of superstition and fanaticism, French irony remains a unique weapon. In no country have thought and speech been so utterly free. If the world of the Four Freedoms is to be established, it cannot be on the basis of power or of clashing ideologies. Intuition may be madness, heroism may be wrong-headed; a civilized commonwealth needs common sense, and the smile that is the badge and the reward of fearless appraisal.

CHAPTER II

The Land and the People

1. GEOGRAPHICAL SURVEY

FRANCE is a country of western Europe, in the heart of the temperate zone, exactly halfway between the North Pole and the Equator. Its area as it was before 1870 and after 1919, that is to say including Alsace-Lorraine, was roughly 212,000 square miles. Compared with the world giants—the British Empire, the Soviet Union, China, Brazil, the United States, India—France is of small stature. But it is the largest unit in Europe west of Russia, and Russia is a world apart. In American terms, France would cover barely one-fifteenth of the union; it is considerably smaller than Texas, and only a third larger than California. It would compare in area and population with the New England states, New York, New Jersey, Pennsylvania, and Ohio combined—not an inconsiderable portion of the United States. Before the war, France had some forty-two million inhabitants, a little less than one-third of America's numbers. Greater France claimed over four million square miles and a hundred million inhabitants; but the vast French Empire is still in the plastic stage. These elementary statistics suggest that, physically, France is a sturdy medium-sized country, which can neither impose herself nor be imposed upon.

The meridian that passes through Dunkirk and Paris may be considered the country's north-south axis: the distance between the North Sea and the Pyrenees, on this meridian, is about six hundred miles. The easternmost point, Lauterbourg on the Rhine, and the westernmost, beyond Brest, are approximately equidistant from Paris and on the same latitude. This east-west axis likewise extends over some six hundred miles. The geographical center is near Bourges, one hundred and thirty miles south of Paris.

The shape of France is vaguely hexagonal. Three sides border on the sea: the North Sea and the Channel, the Atlantic (Bay of Biscay), and the Mediterranean. Two sides are formed by ranges of mountains, the Pyrenees in the southwest, the Alps in the southeast, continued by the Jura; still in the east, the Rhine is the moat, the Vosges the bastion, and Alsace the glacis, of the French fortress. The sixth side, from Lauterbourg to the vicinity of Dunkirk, has been fought over for two thousand years. The Rhine itself has never been a "natural" and hardly ever a political boundary. The historical frontier, a weary compromise, cuts across the valleys Sarre, Moselle, Meuse and Scheldt.

The mountains of France are found mostly southeast of the diagonal Dunkirk-Hendaye. In addition to the ranges on the periphery, there is a great mass of mountainous country in the center, extremely varied, and partly of volcanic origin. The core of that *Massif Central* is known as Monts d'Auvergne. Sloping gently westward, the Central Mountains drop abruptly on the Rhône valley, forming the long range of the Cévennes.

The rest of the country is by no means level. There are hills in Normandy so picturesque that they have been called with an affectionately indulgent smile Norman Switzerland. And although the primitive Armorican peninsula (Brittany) has been worn down by erosion in the course of millennia, it retains an austere mountainous character. The typical landscape of France below the six hundred foot level is gently rolling. Flat expanses, fertile like Beauce, marshy like Sologne or Dombes, sandy like the Landes, are the exception. Only in Flanders does one reach the lowlands that stretch interminably through Belgium, Holland, Germany, Poland, Russia, as far as the Urals.

Alternating with the mountain regions are found three main basins. The first, squeezed between the Cévennes and the foot-hills of the Alps, is the narrow corridor through which the Rhône rushes to the sea. The second, more ample, is the Aquitanian basin, between the Central Mountains and the Pyrenees. Its central stream is the Garonne, with Toulouse as its inland capital and Bordeaux as its Atlantic port. The largest of all is the Parisian basin, a series of concentric geo-logical layers piled up like smaller plates within larger plates. Paris is the actual center of the region; there the Seine and its affluents converge; and from that low point (seventy feet above sea level) the river has to meander its way to the Channel through the hills of Ile-de-France and Normandy. It will be noticed that the longest of the French rivers, the Loire, has no distinct basin of its own. Its upper course is headed toward Paris, and is deflected only by a rising plateau near Orléans. In its lower reaches, it cuts off the southern corner of the Armorican block, which includes Brittany and extends from Cotentin to Vendée.

From this rapid survey, a few simple conclusions may be drawn. The first is the extreme variety of France. In many minds, the word France evokes exclusively the Parisian region, Normandy and the Châteaux country of the middle Loire—a gentle smiling land, not very different from southern England at her sunniest. France is also a country of rugged desolate landscapes. The Brittany coast is a hard-fought battlefield between primitive rock and furious sea. The Pyrenees, on the French side, fall abruptly, a stupendous wall; and the *Cirque de Gavarnie* [1] is one of the most impressive sights in Europe. In Savoy, and even more in Dauphiné, the Alps rival the wildest aspects of Switzerland; the highest peak of the whole range, Mont Blanc (16,000 feet) is in French territory. And in

[1] A gigantic terraced amphitheater.

the Central Mountains, away from the beaten paths, there is an extraordinary wealth of weird picturesqueness. The Tarn with its canyons is a Colorado on a reduced scale. Some extinct craters, with a vast circle of debris, have a lunar appearance; they look like the shell holes of a cosmic bombardment. In the city of Le Puy-en-Velay, enormous rocks frown above the plain, witnesses of a lost world; one of them, needlelike, is capped with a quaint and beautiful little chapel, like the flower of an enormous petrified tree. The Rhône dashes against mountain spurs, less rich in legends than those of the Rhine, but even more strangely romantic. With its Alleghenies in the Jura, its Rocky Mountains in the Alps, its Sierras in the Pyrenees, and a Riviera which surpasses the California coast, France offers almost as much variety as a whole continent. If man were molded by his physical environment, we might expect the French population to be infinitely varied —as indeed is the case. But the influence of geographical conditions should not be overemphasized; in many of their virtues, the Dutch and the Swiss are curiously alike.

Although the country is exceedingly varied, although Brittany and Nice differ as radically as Maine and California in the United States, still it possesses a remarkable degree of unity. The geographer Strabo stated this as an accepted fact in the first century of the Christian era; historians and geographers have insisted upon it over and over again. We may be influenced by long habit; we are so familiar with the traditional figure of France that we take it for granted that God Himself meant it to be "one and indivisible." A closer study makes us less assertive. Brittany might very well have remained a distinct nation; the south had a civilization of its own until the thirteenth century; in the fifteenth, Burgundy was still striving to establish a middle kingdom between France and Germany. Neither Alsace nor Corsica was assigned to France by a special decree of Providence. On the other hand, the upper valley of the Rhône, the lower valleys of the Scheldt or the

Meuse, and perhaps even the greater part of the Rhine region might have been permanently connected with Paris. The France that we know is an achievement, not a necessity.

In France, geography does not compel, it merely permits. Had the physical obstacles been greater, the course of history would have been deflected. If the country could assume its present form, it is because there existed between the principal basins easy means of communication. These therefore afford the key to the development of the country. In the south the Naurouze pass, a gap between the Cévennes and the Pyrenees, is only six hundred feet high; as early as the seventeenth century, a canal was built connecting the Garonne with the Mediterranean. It is because this pass is so accessible that Roman civilization could expand so easily and so brilliantly from Narbonne to Toulouse and Bordeaux. The valley of the Saône, above Lyons, extends the Rhône corridor into the heart of France. Here there is no single pass to the north; but the whole region, Burgundy, astride on the Saône and Seine watersheds, is rich and hospitable. Most decisive of all is the role played by the wide and low Gate of Poitou, connecting the regions of the Loire and those of the Garonne. Had the Armorican (Breton) block and the Central Mountains been linked, southwestern France, behind that barrier, would in all probability have preserved a separate existence. Twice at least, the commanding importance of that gateway was made manifest. In 507, Clovis defeated the Visigoths at Vouillé near Poitiers, and was thus able to create Merovingian France. In 732, somewhere between Tours and Poitiers, Charles Martel turned back the Saracenic tide. In the Hundred Years' War, Poitiers, the logical passage between Normandy and Aquitania, was again the scene of a great battle. But it would be misleading to accept a rigid geographical determinism. By the same reasoning, Belgium should have remained part of the Gallic, Frankish or French community. The sun and the moon at times pull together, at times against each other; so do geography and politics.

It was then not inevitable, but possible, for the three great basins to be united. Of the three, the Parisian basin was clearly marked for predominance. The Rhône valley is too narrow to become the nucleus of a great state. The Aquitanian basin is larger, rather more fertile, and decidedly pleasanter in climate. But it is not so extensive as the Parisian, and it is more isolated. It opens on the Atlantic which, until five hundred years ago, was an empty sea. Spain, its only foreign neighbor, turns her back on Europe. A power established in Paris, on the other hand, could at the same time be in close touch with southern France, and with the active nations of the north. Marseilles, Lyons, Nîmes, Narbonne, Toulouse, Bordeaux, were cities of repute when Paris, under the name of Lutetia, was a mere fishing village. But, from the days of Clovis, the possession of Paris has been decisive. When in the tenth century the decaying Carolingians could no longer defend the land against the Northmen, it was the counts of Paris who assumed leadership, as dukes of France and as kings.

Thus the country was fashioned through eight centuries of collaboration between the kings and their capital city. The kings, because of the prestige and power that Paris gave them, increased their domain with the pertinacity of a peasant family rounding out its farm; and, as the boundaries of the realm were extended, Paris grew in population and wealth. It is perfectly true that "Paris is not France." But it is dynasty and city jointly that performed the historic work of nation-building. If there is an undeniable Frenchness about Rennes and Ajaccio, about Pau and Strasbourg, about Nice and Dunkirk, it is because the language of Paris and the styles of Paris have been superimposed upon the local dialects, customs and fashions. Not without a loss, but the creation of France was worth the sacrifice. In 1789, Paris wrenched the scepter from the defaulting king; France today, having reached full consciousness, might dispense with Parisian hegemony, and foster regional cultures without destroying her unity. Paris will not suffer; its sphere of influence, for centuries, has extended far beyond the political boundaries of France. Our age of air transportation and radio is far more independent of the land than the old world was. But, for countless generations, history and geography in France have worked in close unison. Because the Seine, the Marne, and the Oise met in the center of a vast geological basin, there grew a city which imposed its speech, its art, its kings, upon the whole nation.

This unquestionable predominance of Paris brings out a fact which is too often overlooked: France is not primarily a Mediterranean country. Civilization came to her through the mother sea, as it did to the whole of Europe; it came to her earlier, more freely, than it did to the remoter north, England, Germany; Scandinavia; and so France bears an ineradicable Greco-Latin stamp in her language, and to a lesser degree in her thought and in her institutions. But in this case, geography and tradition are at odds. The Mediterranean is in a sense the back door of modern France. The eastern half of the coast is rocky, and its communications with the interior are difficult; the western half is marshy. The only natural harbors are small; the modern installations at Marseilles, including the great canal connecting the port with the Rhône, are costly triumphs of the human will. Between France and her so-called Latin sisters, Italy and Spain, stand the highest and the most impassable mountains in Europe. Between Geneva and Nice, two hundred miles as the crow flies, only one railroad line crosses the Alps. From end to end of the Pyrenees, two hundred and fifty miles, there was not a single line until three decades ago. Far more Frenchmen study German or English than Spanish or Italian. The Latin bloc, almost realized by the

Bourbons on a purely dynastic basis, a vague dream with Napoleon III, a feeble hope with Marshal Pétain, is a delusion. The French center of gravity is not Marseilles or even Lyons but Paris, and Paris is essentially northern. It belongs with London, Brussels, and Cologne not with Naples or Barcelona.

2. ECONOMIC RESOURCES OF FRANCE

What are the resources that nature has placed at the disposal of the French?

André Chénier opened his hymn to France with the lines:

France, thou fair country, thou generous land
Whom the gods in their benevolence had shaped to be happy . . .

and even Grotius, staid, learned and legal, averred that the kingdom of France was surpassed only by the kingdom of Heaven. This hoary commonplace has been repeated in good faith by innumerable travelers. The position of France as a land of Cockaigne is secure in the popular mind. The fabulous splendor of the French court, the handsome residences in every city, the lovely châteaux on every hill, the treasures heaped up in churches, museums and private homes, the arts and crafts producing masterpieces of delicate and costly luxury, the abundance and refinement of the French table, with noble wines and liqueurs as a supreme touch of perfection, all serve to build up the conception of France as an eminently fortunate country; and it would take a drastic dose of surly realism to destroy it altogether.

Yet a more intimate knowledge of French life reveals a slightly different picture, and heartless statistics confirm the less optimistic view. The contrast between fact and legend is not so glaring as in India, land of abysmal distress and incredible glitter. France is not poor; she is evenly well-to-do; but she is by no means wealthy. Her riches like her spirit have their roots in history. The French have worked hard and lived frugally for centuries; and, in spite of repeated catastrophes, their hoard of beautiful things is impressive. Above all, they have built up intangible treasures that war and revolution cannot destroy: unremitting industry and traditional skill. Nature in France is neither niggardly nor prodigal; for sustained effort, it offers modest but adequate rewards. The delightful idler La Fontaine was French of the French when he preached: "Work hard, take pains: that alone never fails." Boileau, a true Parisian bourgeois, advised would-be writers: "Put back your poem on the working bench not once but twenty times; polish it without ceasing, and then polish it again." Voltaire closed the record of Candide's wild adventures with the realistic and courageous injunction: "We must cultivate our garden."

From the point of view of agriculture, France is merely a good average country. It has practically no waste land, except on the high mountains; but a great deal of the soil is mediocre and the very best is not of miraculous fertility. The brilliant successes, such as vine growing, market gardening, or the flower fields of the Riviera, are the precarious rewards of incessant care. Urged by their earthy desire to extend the ground they till, the French have cleared forests and turned pasture lands into fields, with the result that the average yield per acre is lower than in England or in Germany. If French agriculture were not heavily protected, part of the land now devoted to wheat growing would revert to forests and grazing. The balance, to meet world competition, would have to be cultivated in larger units by more mechanical methods. The result of both these processes would be to decrease the number of agricultural workers. We have often heard the complaint: *"L'agriculture manque de bras,"* there is a shortage of farm labor. Under a freer and more rational economy, this would be the reverse of the truth; the fact is that rural France is overpopulated. It could be kept up at its present level only by depressing the standard of living, which in many parts is primitive enough; and by maintaining a high tariff wall, thus creating a great handicap for French commerce and industry. The patriarchal agrarian state envisaged by Marshal Pétain fitted admirably into Hitler's new order; it would have made it certain that France would never again be able to cross Germany's path.

From the point of view of industry, France is not specially favored. She has no precious metals, no copper, and practically none of the modern "liquid gold," petroleum. Until the eighteenth century, France was not ill equipped to meet the industrial needs of the times. Iron was fairly abundant, scattered in easily worked pockets, and the vast forests provided ample fuel. With the machine age, the picture changed. For two hundred years, coal became the unquestioned king and England acquired a supremacy which was not challenged until the end of the nineteenth century. Not only did the French coal fields yield barely one-eighth of what Great Britain produced, but the coal was of poorer quality and the mines much harder to exploit. It is highly to the credit of the French, especially under Napoleon III, that in spite of such a handicap, they preserved a high rank among industrial powers.

The situation was changing again even before the first world war. France had one great asset, her supply of iron, especially in Lorraine. In addition, she had bauxite, and aluminum was then attaining its industrial majority. The French developed water power, which the technicians poetically called *houille blanche,* white coal, and in this respect their country was better favored than England or Germany. Many districts in the Central Mountains, the Alps, the Pyrenees, hitherto either desolate or pastoral, turned into industrial beehives. Modern alchemy, which extracts metals out of common clay or out of sea water, nitrogen out of the air, plastics out of everything that grows, enriches, not the land abundant in obvious raw materials but the one endowed with skill and determination. It must be remembered that in scientific chemistry there has been a curious race between Germany, England and France. If during recent years Germany took the lead, there have been times when chemistry seemed primarily a French science, and the French have never been out of the running. American triumphs in mass production should not blind us to the fact that in every field of engineering—steel and concrete bridges, tunnels, dams, power houses —the French have created masterpieces of moderate size but remarkable perfection. The S.S. "Normandie," which caught our fancy, was only one among many brilliant achievements. Hull and propeller design, turbines and electric motors revealed the highest degree of technical refinement, while the decorative scheme and the bold and graceful silhouette turned the enormous mass into a work of art. France has a good chance of retaining her leadership in the luxury trades, including horticulture; but she may also keep her rank and even forge ahead in the more advanced forms of heavy industry.

Some three generations ago, parts of the Rhône valley had a triple source of wealth: wine, raw silk and a red vegetable dye, madder. Vines and mulberry trees suffered from a blight; madder was supplanted by aniline products. There were hard years, but no despair. The vineyards were reconstituted; new crops were introduced; soon the valley was as prosperous as ever. France's best asset is not the French soil, but the French people.

3. WHO ARE THE FRENCH?

a. IS THERE A FRENCH RACE?

Who are these French then? A simple question to which there is no simple answer.

It will not do merely to substitute another historical name, and say: "The French are Gauls, or Gallo-Romans." As we shall see in our next chapter, the Gauls never were more than a minority in France, and the Romans an infinitesimal minority; and we should find it very hard to give a scientific definition of the Gauls.

As a race, the French do not exist, and are very proud of the fact. If we accept the rough classification of European stocks into Nordics, Alpines, and Mediterraneans, we find that all three are represented in France. And all three together, as pure types, are but a minority; even the most numerous, the Alpines, are by no means ubiquitous. There are in France many families of men, such as the Cro-Magnon, the Basque, the red-haired Kymric, the Semitic, which do not fall under any of these three divisions. The Bretons are, as a rule, short and roundheaded, but blue-eyed. The Alsatians are tall, but often with brown eyes. All these alleged races, be they three or a score, have freely intermingled for thousands of years. There has never been a law or a taboo, or even a feeling, which might preclude a blond from marrying a brunette.

There is nothing so deceptive as human statistics. They deal with lifeless myths called averages. It is a solid fact that the average Frenchman is nearly an inch shorter than the average Norwegian. But there are many Frenchmen who are taller than most Norwegians. So it is impossible to tell the nationality of an individual purely by his physical characteristics. All manners of men are found in France. A tall blond Frenchman like Pétain is no less French than a short dark Frenchman like Foch. A *typical* Frenchman may be as thin as Voltaire or as fat as Renan. The Frenchness of them all is not in the blood, but in costume, education, manners, philosophy; and that kind of Frenchness is easily acquired by negroes from Martinique and Senegal, and even by Annamites and Cambodians.[2]

So we are not surprised to find French generals called Mac-

[2] In this as in so many other respects, the experience of France is ours. I have had among my students Japanese young men who were unmistakably American.

donald, Clarke, MacMahon or Dodds, or a naval minister called Thomson; among ultranationalist leaders, an archdeacon; among writers, a Stuart Merrill, a Julien Green, a José Maria de Heredia, a Zamacois, a Papadiamantopoulos. One of the most fanatical defenders of the purely Gallic tradition was the historian Frantz Funck-Brentano, who evidently was no Gaul. The incarnation of French patriotism, Gambetta, and the voice of the French conscience, Zola, were both the sons of Italians. As for names of German and Polish origin among the French elite, they are past numbering. Racially, France is Europe. This was particularly true of the House of France, symbol of the nation; it was France, indeed, because in its veins there flowed English, Polish, German, Spanish, and Italian blood.

This is very reassuring for the friends of France. Since there is no French race, the French race cannot die. France will have the population she can feed; the French spirit will have the heirs it can win. The French population is not a matter of biology, but of economics and ideology.

b. THE BOND OF LANGUAGE

If the French are not a race, are they a culture group, delimited by the diffusion of its language? We believe that, with reservations, this is a much sounder definition than any based on blood or political allegiance. Race is a myth, and allegiance may be arbitrarily shifted; the frontiers of speech are the only real ones, for we carry them with us. And language is the vehicle of tradition; it might even be said that language is tradition itself, the living past.

So when we meet a man whose native language is French, we feel that if he is not a Frenchman, he ought to be one; and if we meet a French citizen who cannot speak French, we feel that his case is an anomaly if not a scandal. There is a constant effort, obscure or determined, to make language and nationality coincide. Either we want to redraw the map, so that all men of the same speech may be under the same flag, or we seek to enforce language conformity within the national frontiers. Thus did the Hungarians in the nineteenth century attempt to impose Magyar upon Croats, Serbs, and Rumanians.

We have no thought of denying the commanding importance of language; there is good sense in the ancient jest, "The tongue is thicker than water." But here again, we are confronted with the extreme complexity of French problems. In Italy and Germany, the flag followed the language; the true creator of Italian unity was not Cavour in 1860, but Dante in 1300. In France, the reverse was true. Political integration came first; the king's language followed the king's arms, sometimes with a lag of centuries. And the process is not absolutely complete today. The Republic may be one and indivisible; but, after two millennia, France has not yet fully achieved linguistic unity.

The French language is of Latin origin. The number of Celtic and Frankish words it has adopted is small. In the five hundred years of Roman rule, the country was slowly Latinized, even remote Armorica, the Brittany of today. But only the elite knew classical Latin. The masses had acquired their knowledge from soldiers and traders, whose tongue was incorrect and slangy. With the dissolution of the empire, the linguistic bond among the provinces was weakened; relapsing into barbaric isolation, every region evolved a different dialect. Only the church preserved Latin unity; but in Merovingian times, even the church was barbaric. When Charlemagne ordered that sermons be preached "in the rustic Romance language," the disruption of the Latin world became an acknowledged fact. The Oaths of Strasbourg in 842, in which Louis the German spoke in Romance so as to be understood by the soldiers of his brother and ally Charles the Bald, may be considered as the birth certificate and the first monument of the French language.

There were innumerable dialects in "Romania," the domain of Romance speech; and they merged by imperceptible transitions. Gradually, for political and economic reasons, some dialects assumed leadership and served as patterns. It is these superdialects which later became national languages.

The dialects spoken in France were divided into two groups, *langue d'Oil* in the north, *langue d'Oc* in the south, *oil* and *oc* both meaning *yes*. The south had been more deeply impregnated with Latin culture; there the feudal caste was not so completely divorced from urban life as in the north; as a result, the southern dialects had a particularly brilliant life as late as the thirteenth century. But the north conquered, and the south lost its cultural autonomy with its political independence. The *Langue d'Oc* ceased to have a recognized literature, and sank to the level of a patois. But it did not die. When I was a student, I was surprised to discover that there were still educated southerners who, among themselves, preferred to speak their local patois. In the middle of the nineteenth century, a group of poets and folklorists revived Provençal as a literary medium; and Frédéric Mistral achieved international fame with his *Mirèio* (Mireille).

The dialect that finally prevailed was that of the king's court, the tongue of Ile-de-France, *Francian*. It extended with the progress of royal authority but there was no ruthless compulsion. Everywhere, the local elite took up French as a matter of pride and profit. There were opportunities in the king's service that were not to be despised. A striking example is offered by the Bonapartes. The family spoke the Corsican dialect and was taught Italian. But, as the island had become French, a military scholarship was secured for young Napoleon who studied at Brienne and in Paris. He was at first derided for his accent; but he mastered the language as well as the profession, until he became one of the most effective orators in French literature.

The present situation is this: northern French is the official language, and is almost universally understood throughout France, but the local dialects, particularly in the south, have not wholly disappeared. In addition to the descendants of *langue d'Oil* and *langue d'Oc,* other Romance languages are represented in France. In the eastern Pyrenees, the country of Marshal Joffre, Catalan is spoken. In the Nice region, the local language might be classified as Italian rather than southern French; and this is even truer of Corsica.

Furthermore, there are in France populations whose native speech is not Romance at all. In the northern corner of French Flanders, round Hazebrouck and Dunkirk, Flemish prevails; in the eastern tip of Lorraine, beyond Metz, German. In Alsace, the situation is extraordinarily complex. The local dialect is very different from standard German but is undeniably Germanic. Under the Bourbons, the upper classes took up French of their own accord and their example spread slowly down. At the time of the Revolution, Alsace was born anew with the other provinces and acquired a vigorous sense of French nationality. No population ever had such dramatic opportunities for declaring the allegiance it preferred; the protest of the Alsatians in 1871, their explosion of joy in 1918, were the most emphatic of plebiscites. Alsatians feel, think, and fight as Frenchmen; but many of them still speak Alsatian.

There are finally two odd linguistic groups, neither Romance nor Germanic. In the western Pyrenees, the Basques, dominant on the northern coast of Spain, and struggling there for their autonomy, are also represented on the French side. Their mysterious language, unrelated with any other, the delight and despair of philologists, may be a survival of ancient Iberian, once spoken throughout Aquitanian Gaul. But the French Basques are few, and do not create a political problem.

The case of Brittany is more difficult. Armorica, as the province was known under the Romans, had been Latinized by the fourth century; it became Celtic again when many Britons, driven from their island home by Anglo-Saxon in-

vasions, crossed the Channel and settled in the peninsula. The
Celtic language, akin to extinct Cornish and to Welsh, has
not yet disappeared. While the people of the large cities,
Rennes, Nantes, Brest, Lorient, use French almost exclusively,
Breton is heard in the countryside and in the many little fishing harbors. This picturesque survival has been a great handicap for the Bretons. They received no education in their own
language, and found it difficult to master French. So a gifted
minor nation—Chateaubriand, Lamennais, Renan were Bretons—was almost compelled to remain backward. During the
second world war, the Germans attempted to foster Breton
separatism; by so doing, they probably have settled the problem once and for all.

Other languages than French are spoken in France, and
French spills beyond the frontiers of the country; but this
creates no political difficulty. The French do not consider
Wallonia (the southern, French-speaking half of Belgium) or
Romande Switzerland (Neuchâtel, Geneva, Lausanne) as
captive French provinces, to be redeemed from their oppres-
sors.

This complexity of the language situation in France explains
why the French have no mystic faith in speech as the expression of race. They know that they have changed their national
tongue three times in recorded history. They know that to
this day there are excellent Frenchmen who do not speak
French. They consider their language as the expression of
their growth as a people. Its sphere has increased partly as a
result of an unconscious development, partly as the fruit of
deliberate efforts, but most of all as the reward of cultural
achievements. Frenchification never was a brutal process; it
was an opportunity. So the French see no reason why the same
method should not be extended to their vast empire. It seems
to them perfectly natural that Berbers and Malagasy should
become French if they choose, in the same way as Basques,
Bretons, Flemings or Martiniquais. We shall see that one of

the main assets of Greater France, within the colonial empire and beyond, is the French language. Whoever reads French anywhere in the world, whatever his race or flag may be, becomes in some degree a part of the French culture group.

Is there a special quality about the language itself that explains its diffusion and prestige? Let us be true to the French spirit of measure and avoid absurd claims. As an instrument, French has no outstanding virtue. It is less musical than Italian, less sonorous than Spanish, less terse than English. Its nasal sounds are not pleasant, its spelling is almost as perverse as ours, and its grammar is a tangled mass of historical absurdities. It possesses no intrinsic clarity; it is just as easy to be vague and equivocal in French as in any other language. In the phrase: "Whatever is not clear is not *French*," French refers to spirit and tradition, not to vocabulary and syntax. Rivarol extolled "the probity attached to the genius of the French language"; at the same moment, Goethe called French *"une langue perfide,"* and French lends itself particularly to *double entendre*. The probity so highly praised by Rivarol does exist, and is one of the cherished possessions of France; but it is found in the thought, not in the words. It is a discipline to which the French, at their best, consciously submit themselves. Not all Frenchmen master it; and it is freely open to all men.

4. PSYCHOLOGY OF THE FRENCH PEOPLE

What is France then? Not merely a territory, not a race, not a language; France is a traditional attitude of mind, a psychological entity.

I am fully aware that "national psychology" is an absurdity; strictly speaking, France is a myth, the average Frenchman is an abstraction, the composite picture of all Frenchmen is a blur. The differences among human beings are minor compared with their resemblances. These differences are individual; every Frenchman, every man, is unique. Within that great reality, mankind, we may descry, or imagine, any number of groups. But the group *European* has far more substance than the groups *French* or *German*. Within the European family, class and period are more definite than national distinctions; the peasant, the lawyer, the soldier, the merchant, the man of the Renaissance or of the Enlightenment are clearcut figures compared with the Frenchman. The idea of comparing nationalities with breeds—the tenacious bulldog, the high-strung fox terrier, the gentle spaniel—is a poetic but most dangerous fallacy. Bernard of Clairvaux and Madame de Pompadour were both undeniably French.

As for *Frenchiness* in the derogatory sense, it is a form of cosmopolitan frivolity which, while it may find freest scope in Paris, is quietly ignored by the vast majority of Parisians. Under the Second Empire, a period noted for that type of Frenchiness, the protagonists of "Parisian life" were Offenbach from Cologne and Princess Pauline Metternich from Vienna. A few years ago, a friend whom I challenged to name an example of Frenchiness suggested Miss Josephine Baker.

When we are speaking of national traits, we are dealing, therefore, not with solid roughhewn realities but elusive shades. Those who claim that national psychology is a scientific field are indulging in solemn bluffing. National psychology belongs to the domain of art. A people, like a street, a landscape or an individual, has its peculiar, undefinable consistency or style. Each wears his rue with a difference.

That is why the key to the French mind is not to be found by means of physical tests, skull measurements or vital statistics. A far more reliable indication would be a certain quality in the French smile. That smile is not a veil, like Mona Lisa's: it is a light. We find it as early as *The Voyage of Charlemagne to Constantinople and Jerusalem,* in the eleventh century; it is manifest in *Aucassin and Nicolette,* in Marot, Montaigne, La Fontaine, Voltaire, Renan, Anatole France.

Paradoxically, it flickers on the tormented mask of the great mystic, Pascal. It is constant in the learned student of comparative law, Montesquieu. Joinville caught it on the gentle lips of Saint Louis. Joan of Arc had it when she was fighting for her life and for her soul against her ecclesiastical tormentors. Henry IV wore it through long years of adversity; and Clemenceau, when he refused to despair.

Such a smile is not levity; nothing would be more misleading than to label Voltaire a shallow jester. Some of the deepest sayings in the world—even in the Gospels—were uttered with a smile. The French smile is neither benevolent nor malicious. It expresses the joy of understanding, the pride of not being duped, bitter though the truth may be. Pascal speaks of man as greater than the physical universe that may crush him, because he knows he is crushed; the visible sign of that triumphant knowledge is a smile. That smile is deadly to pretenses, and pricks every metaphysical bubble. It is a challenge to the absolute, and to all forms of absolutism: Léon Blum was a Marxian—but with a smile.

It would be most un-French to accept this smile as a magic key, since it is the denial of magic keys. There are few French leaders in action, art or thought who went through life with a frown; but there were many who were steadily grave. There is nothing so French as the unsmiling portrait of Richelieu by Philippe de Champaigne, or those of Louis XIV and Bossuet by Hyacinthe Rigaud. Calvin, Buffon, Guizot, Vigny were true Frenchmen. So—alas!—was Robespierre. So—thank God!—is Charles de Gaulle.

The secondary characteristics usually ascribed to the French do exist indeed; but they are local or superficial. Cheerful, gesticulating volubility is a Mediterranean rather than a French trait; it is aggressively present in Naples, Athens or Alexandria, conspicuously lacking in most French villages. The provincial bourgeois are placid and rather tongue-tied. As for hard work and frugality, they are long habits imposed by natural conditions. They are typical of the *petit bourgeois* rather than of the nation as a whole (and here *petit bourgeois* includes the peasant proprietor). The kings and the nobility were renowned for their extravagance. The urban proletariat is fond of good living and pleasure rather than of rigid economy; the French masses know very well that wine is not a necessity.

Lucidity, courtesy are virtues which the French praise highly and honestly strive to practice. They may result in artificiality—clearness reduced to common sense and elementary logic, politeness shrinking into a code of etiquette. But these qualities are not *national*: they are essentially diplomatic. They are required when people of widely different origins come together. Within the family, you do not need to be clear, and you do not need to be polite; it is sufficient to be natural. Let us repeat that France, land and people, is the epitome of Europe; the social graces, the *savoir-faire*, the *savoir-vivre* which strike us as eminently French, are those of the cosmopolitan, of a Prince de Ligne, for instance.

These social and intellectual qualities are superimposed, and therefore they are superficial. They may veil, they do not destroy, the wild impulses, the passions and the aspirations within. Only the crudest reader would fail to notice that the men and women of Racine are as intense, as ruthless, as primitive as those of Shakespeare. Be sure that even in the bygone days when the French strutted, minced, and smirked, they could also love, hate, hope, despair, and dream after the fashion of all human beings and probably of all the higher animals.

Let us never base a judgment, or a policy, on a certain conception of "French psychology." What is peculiarly French in the French character is but a cloak. The French are rather proud of that cloak, and take good care of it. But they are fully aware that it is a cloak, which they are free to alter and even to discard. They—and we—can best be defined in the words of Terence:

Homo sum: humani nihil a me alienum puto.

(I am a man: nothing that is human is alien to me.)

CHAPTER III

The Origins

1. BEFORE THE GAULS

a. PREHISTORY

THE HISTORY of the French people begins a thousand centuries ago—more or less. For during that enormous period of time, through glacial and interglacial ages, the territory which is now France has been inhabited by man, perhaps without a break. One concrete instance: Amiens, before the second world war, was a great railroad junction and a thriving modern city of nearly a hundred thousand inhabitants. It clustered at the foot of a magnificent thirteenth-century cathedral. In this vicinity, the banks of the Somme had seen Franks, Romans, and Gauls; in the suburb of Amiens, Saint-Acheul, were found remains of the New and the Old Stone ages; and traces were discovered of that infinitely remote age of the dawn (Eolithic) and of implements which, although indicative of human purpose, bear practically no sign of human workmanship. The fact that French names have been adopted to denote the stages of Paleolithic culture is no evidence of French hegemony in the early Stone Age; it is simply a tribute to the pioneer work of archeologists such as Boucher de Perthes and de Mortillet. It does show, however, the variety as well as the antiquity of French origins. Hundreds of centuries ago, even as today, France was a country with a comparatively mild and equable climate; and it was the place where migrating tribes from North Africa and Asia would meet, clash or mix, and pass away, leaving a sediment of culture.

The artifacts of our ancestors are deeply moving in their rough simplicity; but our subject is the living past, not archeology. The prehistoric is still among us, and deep within us, in the form of unreasoning dread or wrath. The fact that man uses robot bombs instead of chipped or polished flint does not mitigate the terible primitiveness of his instincts.

There are two works in modern French literature which give us the sense of that profound historical perspective. The first is a poetic drama, *Cromedeyre-le-Vieil,* by Jules Romains. Romains imagines that in our own times a village lost in the Central Mountains has preserved the tradition of its immemorial past. Before Napoleon, Louis XIV, Charlemagne, Clovis, Caesar were, Cromedeyre was, *is* and shall be. Its low houses, huddled together into a single mass, can hardly be distinguished from the rock. In like fashion, the obscure thought of the Cromedeyre dwellers clings to the silent centuries. Do not explore the Monts d'Auvergne or the Cévennes in the hope of discovering an actual Cromedeyre; Romains' drama is symbol, not history. But many a literate voter in France, accepting without question the tools, toys and tricks of the twentieth century, is solid Cromedeyre at the core.

The second study in historical perspective is *The Inspired Hill* by Maurice Barrès, a novel, or rather a romanced chronicle, of religious life on a Lorraine height. There are places, according to Barrès, where the spirit seems to dwell. They were sacred indeed long before the temples which now crown them were built. Demons and saints, who haunt or hallow the countryside, were the new avatars of the Gallo-Roman gods; and these gods had simply imposed their names upon pre-Celtic deities. Joan of Arc dwelt by a forest of oaks, beloved of the "dames" or fairies; there was a spring in the woods which they claimed as their own and which bore their name. The winged resplendent Saint Michael who bade her help the king in his distress is one with Teutates, the Gallic Mercury, champion of light against the powers of darkness. The bonfires which blazed on the hilltops on St. John's Eve were first lit thousands of years ago. The dweller at Cromedeyre may vote the *radical-socialiste* ticket, and thus endorse "the party of progress"; the worshiper on "the inspired hill," Sion-Vaudémont, may clothe his thoughts with Roman theology or liturgy; but the instincts of community life, the urge to beseech and to placate, were deep-rooted realities before Rome was born.

Among the innumerable prehistoric remains in France, two sets are of particular interest: the Cro-Magnon works of art and the rough stone monuments, the most impressive of which are found at Carnac in Brittany.

In the upper Paleolithic stage of prehistoric culture, there appeared a species very different from the still apelike Neanderthal man. Erect, taller than the average Frenchman of today, this type had a finely developed head and a cranial capacity that would meet our modern standards. These people have been named the Cro-Magnons, from the cavern in Dordogne where their remains were first identified. Their skulls, seen from the top, are long but their faces are broad, a striking peculiarity which makes them easy to recognize. In the cave of the Les Eyzies region (a hundred miles east of Bordeaux), particularly at La Madeleine, not merely Cro-Magnon artifacts, but works of art of striking vitality have been discovered. Drawing, carving, even polychrome painting, were practiced. Frescoes show all the shades of ocher, from yellowish to dark brown; intense blacks were produced by means of manganese salts. The animals depicted reveal how varied was the fauna of western Europe in those days; beasts of the tundra, the steppe, the mountain, the meadow, and the forest, now widely scattered, were all flourishing in the present territory of France. Most prominently represented was the reindeer. This would seem to indicate that Cro-Magnon culture arose in the postglacial age, when the climate was still subarctic.

These animals are drawn not only with great realism, but with extraordinary spirit. They seem to breathe rage, fear or pain. They are caught in motion with a sureness of touch that a Walt Disney animator might envy. It is strange that the Cro-Magnons should have crawled into the most inaccessible recesses of their caves, and there painted these masterpieces, by the light of some animal grease burning in a stone cup. This can hardly be explained except through the association of art with some form of religious worship.

It had been taken for granted that the Cro-Magnons were a fossil breed, extinct for millennia; but skull measurements established that among the peasants who today live in the Dordogne region there are genuine Cro-Magnons. The type also exists sporadically among Spaniards and Berbers. Our Cro-Magnon contemporaries are not noticeably different, in appearance or mental gifts, from the surrounding population. They have not, however, preserved the artistic skill of their remote forebears. Perhaps great artists were miraculous rarities twenty thousand years ago, even as they are today.[1]

France has kitchen middens or prehistoric refuse heaps, like those of Denmark; in Savoy are found lake-dwellers' cities, like those of Switzerland; and in many parts of the country there are mound graves or *tumuli*. But the most interesting of all the prehistoric remains that belong to the Neolithic and to the Bronze ages are the huge stones or megaliths. They were long supposed to be associated with the religious life of the Celts, and for that reason they were called Druidical. It is now certain that they antedate the Celtic invasions of

[1] If the discoveries at Glozel, in the Vichy region, had been accepted as genuine, they would have revolutionized our conceptions of prehistory, for they offered a series of signs which were, almost too obviously, alphabetic. The consensus among the experts is that they are a fraud. But some reputable archeologists were ready to accept them, and some of the official savants rejected them for extremely poor reasons. A layman must hold his peace.

western Europe. As they were found in large numbers and
in a good state of preservation in Brittany, they are still known
by their Breton names—*menhir, dolmen, peulven, cromlech*.
A menhir is a standing stone. The menhir of Locqmariaker
(Morbihan), now fallen and broken, was nearly seventy feet
high, and weighed over three hundred tons. These stones
were probably memorials, unconnected with either burial or
worship; [2] perhaps the Washington Monument keeps up the
tradition of the menhirs. Cromlechs are circles of menhirs:
Stonehenge in England offers the most perfect examples.
Dolmens look at present like large tables, one flat stone lying
on top of two or more standing ones. But the dolmens were
originally artificial caves; their sides were closed with smaller
stones, and the whole covered with a mound of earth. They
were used as burying places, concurrently with natural or
dug-out caves. The most famous assemblage of megaliths in
France is the *alignment* at Carnac in Brittany. But we come
across them in every part of the land. Place names such as *Le
Gros Caillou* (the Big Stone) and *Pierrefitte* (the Standing
Stone) prove that at one time they must have been even more
numerous. The transportation of such enormous blocks, in
certain cases over a distance of several miles, and to a point
higher than their original location, must have involved immense difficulties. This reveals the existence of a society so
strongly organized that thousands of men could be compelled
to toil wearily and long, so that the pride of some chief might
be exalted. Collectivism is not an invention of the machine
age.

Passing from the Lower to the Upper Paleolithic period
and again from the latter to the Neolithic seemed to imply a
break or a jump in the cultural history of Europe. One race
had run its course, one civilization had completed its work,
and now a new element had come in from afar. Whether a

[2] Stonehenge and other cromlechs reflect a knowledge of astronomy and may
have been connected with sun worship.

similar revolution took place at the beginning of the Bronze Age is still an unsolved problem. Bronze implements did not come as a sudden revelation; the transition was gradual. For awhile, bronze and stone were used concurrently and the earliest bronze objects reproduce pretty faithfully the shape of their stone models. But iron, for most practical purposes the more desirable metal, is more abundant than copper in central and western Europe: why did not its use precede that of bronze? The designs on the bronze tools or ornaments show Oriental influences, and the bronze culture seems to have been almost invariably accompanied by the custom of cremating the dead, which is of Eastern origin. It is therefore a moot point whether bronze metallurgy in the West is an indigenous development or a ready-made acquisition from Asia.[3]

As early as the second millennium before Christ, iron began to be used concurrently with bronze. In course of time, it displaced the less practical metal, except for artistic purposes. Iron was first used for the edge of cutting instruments, then for reproducing bronze objects, and finally for direct and original creation; to this transitional stage, the name of Hallstatt (Upper Austria) is given. In the La Tène (Lake of Neuchâtel) stage of culture, bronze is not discarded but iron is more extensively used and is of greatly improved quality. This type of culture ranges in date from 500 B.C. to A.D. 100. Its center may have been southern France or Switzerland. From that point it spread over all the parts of Europe that were not under the direct influence of Greece and Rome. The Germans, still in the Bronze Age, received eagerly from the Celts this La Tène culture, the diffusion of which coincided with the greatest expansion of the Celtic empire. As G. Bloch puts it, "it was the great iron sword of La Tène which, in the fourth century B.C. carried throughout the ancient world the terror of the Celtic name."

[3] Copper was used in the Near East before 3500 B.C. but did not appear in Europe until 2000 B.C. apparently.

b. PROTOHISTORY: LIGURIANS, IBERIANS, PHŒNICIANS, AND GREEKS

Thus we reach protohistory, the uncertain dawn of our own epoch. Of the Pre-Gallic peoples, two have left at least a memory, the Ligurians and the Iberians.

The Ligurians spread far beyond the Italian province which is still known by their name. If geographical etymology can be trusted, they may have reached the valleys of the Seine and the Moselle. But their contribution is not easy to identify.

It is taken for granted that Aquitania, one of the three parts of Caesar's Gaul, was Iberic and not Celtic in stock and speech. It seems that at one time the Iberians had spread over the greater part of Gaul and of the British Isles, as well as Spain and Portugal. They probably belonged to the Mediterranean race of modern anthropology—dark, medium-sized and longheaded. An Iberian ancestry might account for the brunette substratum in the population of western Britain, particularly the "old black breed" in Scotland and a large proportion of the Welsh. The modern Aquitanians are the Gascons; now the word Gascon or Vascon is the same as Basque; and Humboldt claimed that the Basque or Euskarian people were but the racial and linguistic remnant of the once far-flung Iberians. This reasonable but unprovable hypothesis has been vigorously contested.

Even before the Greeks, the Phœnicians had dotted the Mediterranean shore with commercial settlements, some of which can still be identified in Roussillon and Provence. The decline of Tyre favored the expansion of the Hellenes. About 600 B.C., a company of Phocaean adventurers founded Massalia (or Massilia), which is now Marseilles. Three generations later, the bulk of the Phocaean population was driven from its Asiatic home by the Persian conquest; and many of them sought refuge in their distant colony. Massalia fought bitter wars against the surrounding Ligurians, against the Etruscans, and especially against Carthage, daughter and successor of Tyre. Common enemies drove Massalia and Rome into an alliance which proved lasting. Nevertheless, Massalia retained its Greek culture with singular purity; and for a long time it preserved also its political autonomy, with an aristocratic form of government.

Thus the Greeks had colonized French soil before the Gauls or the Romans; but their influence never extended far inland. They remained part of the Mediterranean world rather than of Gaul. Later, Celtic and Gallo-Roman domination gave the Greeks a chance to extend their trade and their culture. The first coins of the Gauls were Greek or crudely imitated from Greek models. Greek was the language of commerce as well as that of philosophy and of the early church. The first Christian congregations in Gaul were formed among the Greek colonies, perhaps through the Hellenized Jews. The "Syrians" who had almost a monopoly of Gallic trade under the Merovingians were Byzantine Greeks. Traces of Hellenic beauty among the women of Arles may be accepted as a pleasing but tenuous evidence that the Greek element was not without influence in the formation of the French people; but on the whole, that influence was limited. We are speaking only of actual Greek settlements; Greek culture, of course, is the glorious heritage of Europe as a whole.

2. INDEPENDENT GAUL

French history textbooks often begin with the words: "Our ancestors the Gauls . . ." With the coming of the Gauls, we are supposed to enter the full light of history. But that light, we soon discover, is "hyperborean" darkness.

According to our present conception, land and people belong together. The Gypsies, who do not obey that rule, are a disreputable oddity; the Jews desire either to be assimilated or to settle in a country of their own. Yet for untold millennia, communities were migratory even as many individuals are today. Driven by poverty or defeat, drawn either by ambition or by sheer *wanderlust,* whole tribes moved restlessly about. The Gauls, for instance, roamed throughout the ancient world from the North Sea and Great Britain all the way to Spain, Rome, and Asia Minor. The great invasions, in the fifth century of our era, were only the most tragic episode in that vast, age-long, unaccountable flow. The invasions of the Saracens and the raids of the Northmen in the eighth and ninth centuries were the last great waves in the west; but in eastern Europe, Tartars and Turks prolonged the era of armed migrations until the sixteenth century.

The wandering hordes did not remain homogeneous. Warriors picked up wives as they went. Tribes coalesced; older units split. The weak, timorous or sedate were left behind; the bold whatever their breed followed the call to adventure, battle, and loot. Languages and faiths mingled as well as blood. We are left without a definite clue. The migrants kept no record; their ancient lore in myth and song has vanished beyond recall.

The Romans who, for centuries, had to deal with the barbarians, could have ascertained at least a few elementary facts about them. They did not do so because they did not care. All peoples between the Ligurians and the Scythians were to them Hyperboreans, an indistinct mass which they dreaded and despised; the term Hyperborean was applied to the Gauls who sacked Rome in 390 B.C. Whenever the Romans caught a gleam of resemblance between the beliefs or institutions of the barbarians and their own, they applied a Latin term without compunction. Thus they called the federations of Gallic tribes "cities" and their aristocratic councils "senates." Thus they considered the Gallic deities the rough equivalents of the Greco-Roman gods. This ruthless assimilation was good policy, for, by insisting on resemblances, the Romans managed to obliterate differences. But it was poor history, for it destroyed the past.

Later a new factor came to distort a picture already blurred. It is a recurrent fashion among sophisticates to praise primitive virtues; thus in the eighteenth century the overrefined Enlightenment extolled the noble savage. In the same way, Posidonius in Alexandria discovered treasures of wisdom in the alleged mysteries of the Druids; Tacitus wrote an apology of the Germans which was, unconsciously perhaps, a satire on imperial Rome.

The Celts established themselves in France in the fifth century B.C. They came from the north—Jutland, Friesland and the Baltic. They did not exterminate the aborigines, but settled among them and mingled with them. There is no reason to consider the present population of France as predominantly of Celtic origin.

Who were these Celts? Today, the term Celtic has a definite meaning in philology. It denotes a group of languages surviving tenaciously on the western edge of France and Great Britain, and resurgent in Eire. But the term is meaningless as an indication of race. The populations which still speak Celtic belong to widely different physical types. The existing dialects bear only a distant resemblance to the hypothetical primitive Celtic reconstituted by epigraphers. The language of illiterate wandering tribes is fluid.

The Romans recognized no differences between Celts, Galatae, Galli. They described all the northern barbarians as tall, fair and fierce—the "blond beasts" of Friedrich Nietzsche.[4] This would fit equally well the early Germans, the early Gauls, and the early Slavs. Indeed, Houston Stewart Chamberlain, a fanatical advocate of Germanism and racial purity, assumes that originally these three groups of people

---

[4] We are informed that in later times, Gallic ladies bleached their hair with limewater. From this odd bit of beauty-parlor information, scholars have deduced that blondness was the desirable sign of a privileged minority.

were of the same stock. The Cimbri and Teutones whom Marius defeated decisively at Aix in Provence (102 B.C.), comprised both Celtic and Germanic tribes.

Pre-Roman Gaul was divided into tribes; these were federated into peoples, which the Romans chose to call "cities." The term is misleading, as in fact the Gauls had no urban centers. Their "towns" were occasional meeting places and emergency shelters. They had a priestly order, the Druids. Theirs was a nature worship; for them, mountains, rivers, and woods were the abode of divine spirits. They had no temples built by hands; only high places or forest glades. The mysteries of the Druids may have been sublime; but we have no direct knowledge of them. All that we know is that the Druids offered human sacrifices and that they considered the mistletoe a sacred plant and a panacea.

Materially, the Gauls had reached the Iron Age. Their political and social structure might be described as feudal. No unity and no stability had been attained. The "cities" constantly fought for supremacy within a limited area; there was no clear notion of *Gaul* as a whole. The masses were by no means satisfied with the rules of the privileged orders. Occasionally, ambitious leaders, demagogues or rabble-rousers of aristocratic origin won the support of the common people against the upper classes. All this reproduces in shadowy fashion struggles which are as old as the world, and which have not yet come to an end.

3. ROMAN GAUL

In the third century B.C., the Romans, in their career of conservative expansion, had conquered Cisalpine Gaul, or the valley of the Po; this was completed by 190. By 133 B.C., Spain had come under Roman sway. Between the two lay the possessions of the Greek city of Massalia, an old ally of Rome, hard pressed by Celtic and Ligurian tribes. Rome intervened;

after her wont, she came to assist and remained to rule. Thus was created in 121 B.C. the province of Gallia Braccata, soon called, after the colony of Narbo Martius, Narbonensis. The eastern part of this region is still known as Provence. It received a number of Roman settlements, and was thoroughly assimilated. Cities like Aix, Arles, and Vienne, and particularly Nîmes and Orange are rich in antique monuments.

About the middle of the first century B.C., the dimly known populations of the north were stirring again; and the Gallic tribes, divided, were unable to check their encroachments. The Sequani, harshly treated by the Aedui, had called to their help the German adventurer Ariovistus. The Aedui implored the support of Rome. While the senate hesitated, the barbarians were growing more arrogant and restless. It seemed as though the Cimbric invasions were about to be repeated.

At that time, Julius Caesar, after a brilliant and somewhat equivocal career, had just struck an alliance with Pompey, the greatest general, and Crassus, the richest citizen in the Roman world. As his share of the spoils, he received in 59 B.C. the government of Cisalpine and Transalpine Gaul, with extraordinary powers. Caesar determined to conquer the rest of Gaul. His immediate purpose was to rival the fame of Pompey, and to forge the military instrument that would make him the sole master of Rome. He checked the wandering tribes, and drove back Ariovistus. He thus appeared in Gaul, not as a conqueror, but as an arbiter and as a liberator. He took advantage of the hostility between tribe and tribe and, within each city, of the feud between the aristocracy and the people.

But, in spite of his diplomatic skill and of his tactical superiority, the subjugation of Gaul proved to be exceedingly difficult. For eight successive years, he had to renew his campaigns, scouring, either in person or through his lieutenants Labienus and Crassus, the whole land from Aquitania to Armorica and Belgium. Under the leadership of a young Arvernian chief, Vercingetorix, supported by the popular ele-

ment among the Celts, there was at last in Gaul a resistance
movement almost national in spirit and scope. The campaign
of 52 B.C. was stubbornly fought out. Caesar captured Avari-
cum, the sole city that the Gauls, in their scorched earth policy,
had been unwilling to sacrifice. He suffered a check before
Gergovia, but he succeeded in besieging Vercingetorix in
Alesia. All attempts to break the elaborate investing lines
failed; an army of relief was driven off. Vercingetorix surrendered, and five years later, the hero of Gallic independence
was executed by order of the merciless victor. Fifty-one B.C.
saw the final and ruthless subjugation of Transalpine Gaul.
In Caesar's own lifetime, the romanization of Gaul was already under way, and the Gallic legion, the Lark (*Alauda,*
a Celtic emblem), served in the ranks of the conqueror.

The process of assimilation was rapid and thorough, at least
among the upper classes. Remote districts, however, preserved
their Celtic speech until the fourth century. Romanization
was not due to any large influx of Roman blood. Only Narbonensis received a fair number of Roman settlers. The
veterans established in other parts of the country were by no
means of pure Roman ancestry. As a matter of fact, military
colonization introduced into Gaul far more barbarians than
Romans. The few higher officials sent by the central government did not form a permanent element; the trading class was
cosmopolitan, and less Roman than Greek.

The true secret of the assimilation is twofold. First, there
was the immense prestige of the imperial city. The Gauls had
reached a stage of development when they could appreciate
the superiority of Mediterranean culture over their own. In
the wake of the legions came peace, good roads, commerce,
arts, luxury.

Then, Rome's policy was a masterpiece of sane, cautious,
opportunistic liberalism. Roman citizenship was not imposed
as a yoke or suddenly thrown open to half-barbaric tribesmen.
Each Gallic city, whether subject or free, retained its own

municipal laws. But neither did Rome proclaim that between conqueror and conquered the gulf must remain impassable. Full Roman citizenship was held out to individuals as a privilege and as a reward. It was of their own free will, and not without due probation, that the natives sought to exchange their status for one that admitted them among the rulers of the world.

The transformation wrought by this moral conquest was impressive. Fair cities, in the modern sense, arose everywhere: Lyons, Toulouse, Bordeaux, Rheims, Autun, Cologne. They possessed abundant water supply, public baths, temples, basilicas or civic halls, triumphal monuments, theaters, stadia. Even a remote country town like Lutetia (Paris) had its share in that development. The villas of the Gallo-Roman aristocracy, centers of vast rural estates, were models of intelligent luxury. Nor was this a purely material veneer; the very spirit of the Gauls had been won over.

It is striking that two of the very last poets of Latin antiquity should be Gauls, and perfect models of Roman citizenship. Ausonius (ca. 310–394), professor, courtier, administrator, was one of the great personages of his time. As a poet, he is an all-too-skillful versifier and a master mosaist of classical quotations. But he had an amiable vein of his own; in his poem on the river Moselle, he reveals a quiet descriptive talent; and there are happy touches in his sketches of family and academic life. In the tragic twilight of the Roman world, he seemed unaware of the travail and portents about him. He was a Christian, although his religion does not seem to have vitally affected his art and his thought.

Rutilius Namatianus (early fifth century), on the other hand, was a pagan of the pagans. He embraced in the same burning faith the crumbling religion and the threatened city. The Goths were near the walls of the capital; his own estates in Gaul had been ravaged; but still the poet hailed Rome as the eternal mistress of the world:

She alone has received the conquered into her bosom,
She alone has tended all mankind under a common name;
A mother rather than a queen, she has turned her subjects into
    citizens;
She binds together the remotest lands by ties of pious reverence.
Thanks to her yoke of peace, the stranger believes himself in his
    own country;
We have all become a single people.

Never did the civilizing mission of Rome inspire a more
ardent tribute of reverence and love. After four centuries,
Vergil's great call: "Thy fate it is to rule nations . . ." found
a noble echo.

This is the obverse of the Roman medal and we are justly
impressed with its magnificence. There is a reverse side, which
is far from pleasing. Rome, praised without stint, has also
been attacked without measure. Some blame her for destroying the independence of promising nationalities; others ar-
raign the intrinsic faults of the Roman world.

No doubt the conquest itself was hideously cruel. Caesar
ravaged the land with almost Teutonic thoroughness. He
massacred or sold into slavery, by the hundred thousand, men
whose sole crime was defending their hearths. Caesar was a
man of exquisite refinement: the ferocity of the civilized may
reach a higher pitch than that of the barbarians. Still, it
might be argued that the result was worth the price. The
Gallic tribes had been constantly at war; after those eight years
of torment, they were to know for generations the majesty of
Roman peace.

Did the Roman conquest stifle the Gallic spirit? Here also,
we must not judge hastily. The alleged victim is a shadow.
There is no evidence that the confused mass of barbarians
living and fighting in Gaul had achieved a creative unity of
its own. It seems much more probable that, in the first century
B.C., the Gauls were groping for exactly what Rome had to
offer. Their association with Mediterranean culture was a ful-

fillment, not an abdication. I find it hard to mourn over an alleged Celtic golden age which, in spite of advocates as eloquent as d'Arbois de Jubainville, Camille Jullian, and Funck-Brentano, seems to me the merest ghost of a might-have-been.

If we attempt to strike a balance, it seems safe to affirm that Roman civilization was superior to that of Celtic Gaul. But Rome herself had irremediable faults. At its very best, her culture was derivative; and immediately after the Augustan Age, it began to decline. No wonder that, in four centuries, Roman Gaul, imitator of imitators, did not produce a single new thought, or a single original work of art.

Rome pursued in Gaul what might be called a Tory policy. She stood for law and order—as represented by the rich and the well born. She did not impose the aristocratic system upon the Gallic cities; but she favored, strengthened, hardened it. In the second century of the Christian era, the masters of the Gallo-Roman villas led a life of luxurious refinement; but it was the flower of a regime rooted in slavery. It was not the vast domains, the *latifundia,* that destroyed Italy or Gaul; the *latifundia* were "collectives" probably more efficient than individual holdings. It was the fact that the *latifundia* were run for the exclusive benefit of the few.

The key word of the Roman system was exploitation. It was not directly the exhaustion of natural and human resources that caused the ruin of Rome; it was the unmitigated profit motive. Luxury was the reward of graft, usury or slave-driving. Officials treated their charge as a mine. The *Herrenvolk,* the imperial rabble of the capital, expected bread and games as a tribute from the conquered world. The Praetorians and then the Legions followed the universal trend. Since conquest and administration had become a holdup, the soldiers, who wielded the ultimate power, preyed upon the conquerors. They started the profitable business of murdering and creating emperors. After the Revolt of the Gracchi (133–123 B.C.) there was no serious attempt at reform. A government of the world by the rich and for the rich pursued its inexorable rake's course. It ended in the destruction of the very wealth which had been its only goal.

4. DOWNFALL OF THE ROMAN WORLD

The Roman world has been portrayed as a beleaguered fortress which, after a siege of four hundred years, finally had to capitulate to the barbarians. This is a misleading view. The contest between settled civilization and wandering barbarism was as old as Rome herself. Civilization won, as long as it remained true to its own principles. Rome never lacked men, for the barbarians were eager to enter the empire peacefully, as colonists or auxiliaries. To the very end, an army under Roman discipline was more than a match for countless hordes. Just as Marius had destroyed the Cimbri and the Teutones in 101 B.C., Julian, in 356 A.D., with thirteen thousand soldiers, defeated an enormous horde of Alamans. Stilicho, with thirty thousand, routed the two hundred thousand of Radagaisus. For twenty-five years, in the fifth century, Aëtius in Gaul was victorious wherever he turned. The barbarians had no sense of unity among themselves, and felt no reluctance in serving the empire. A well-organized government could have held the Germans at bay with the help of German troops.

But how could Rome protect her immense borders when every general was heading Romeward in order to secure the purple; when the Praetorians massacred their newly elected chief simply because they wanted another bonus, a *donativum;* when the emperors, out of jealous dread, had their best generals assassinated, men like Aëtius and Stilicho?

The ancient world, reaching the summit of order and peace under the Antonine emperors, ended not in the fifth century but in the third. In 257, the Franks and the Alamans harried Gaul from the Rhine to the Alps and the Pyrenees. Treasures were hastily buried; the sanctuary of the Arvernian Mercury, the pride of Gaul, was plundered and burned down. Rome, distracted by civil war, could barely defend herself; Gaul had to work out her own salvation. For sixteen years (257–273), there was a separate Gallic Empire. An energetic leader, Postumus, drove back the barbarians, restored regular government, repaired the roads. But the evils of the Gallic Empire were the same as those of Rome. Four Gallic emperors were murdered in two years. Finally, Tetricus made his peace with the restorer of Roman unity, Aurelian (273). Two years later, Aurelian himself was assassinated; a new invasion of the Franks and the Alamans flooded Gaul, worse than that of 257. The barbarians roamed at will, pillaging every city.

The recuperative power of the Roman world was not yet exhausted. The administrative reforms of Diocletian (284–305) served their purpose: the barbarians were held in check. Constantine (306–337), Theodosius (379–395), were to receive the name of "Great." Thus the Roman historians and their innumerable followers showed themselves curiously indifferent to the cataclysm of the third century. It was not a mere crisis; it was the end of an era. When the cities of Gaul were rebuilt, they were smaller than the old; and they were surrounded by high walls of defense into which the fire-scarred fragments of ancient splendor had been hastily thrown. The Roman world was precariously pieced together again, but it never recovered its organic unity. The social and political regime that prevailed thereafter was feudal rather than imperial. At the same period, we first hear of the *Bagaudae,* bands of peasants goaded into rebellion and brigandage, an evil that could never be completely suppressed, until it merged into the universal chaos of the fifth century. The Dark Ages had begun indeed.

By 400, the collapse of the Roman system seemed manifest. In 410, Rome herself was desecrated by the Goths of Alaric; in 455, by the Vandals of Genseric; in 476, the Western Empire came to an end with the deposition of Romulus Augustulus; in 481, with Clovis, the new Frankish monarchy began.

Yet it was not the end. Theodoric the Great, the Ostrogothic ruler of Italy (489–526) showed the possibility of a co-ordination between the military rule of the barbarians and the survival of Latin culture. Under him, Cassiodorus, Boethius, Symmachus continued classical antiquity without a break. Clovis himself was ready to receive investiture from Rome; and Justinian nearly restored the unity of the Mediterranean basin. The great Belgian historian Henri Pirenne offers the striking hypothesis that the ancient world disappeared only with the rise of Mohammedanism. When control of the inland sea was lost, the culture of which that sea had been the main highway was shattered; it perished in the west and sickened in the east. Theodoric had inserted himself into the Greco-Roman tradition; Charlemagne (768–814), in spite of his high-sounding title, represented a new departure. The twilight of the west, which began in 257, may have lasted until the seventh century.

One thing is certain: by the end of the sixth century, in Gaul at any rate, darkness was absolute. The triumph of the barbarians was the result, not the cause, of anarchy; but it only made confusion worse confounded. The romantic view that the invaders brought with them new blood, new virtues, simplicity, courage, candor, loyalty, chivalry, is sheer nonsense. The barbarians were fully as corrupt as the worst Romans; but in addition, they were barbarians, brutal and deceitful. It took the world five hundred years to recuperate from that orgy of senseless violence. The recovery, when it came, was due to no merits in the Barbarians themselves. Greco-Latin civilization resumed its course, preserved and purified by the Christian church.

5. CHRISTIANITY AND THE FRANKS

In the protracted crisis that lasted from the middle of the third century to the sixth, three great factors were at work.

The first was the inner decay of the Roman Empire, an empire politically, socially, economically bankrupt. The second was the wild surging of the barbarians, which a well-governed Rome could have curbed. The third was the growth of the Christian church.

The earliest names in French religious history are those of St. Pothinus, a venerable bishop, and St. Blandina, a slave girl, who were martyred in Lyons under Marcus Aurelius. At an uncertain date, probably under Decius, St. Denis, bishop of Paris, was beheaded. St. Martin, bishop of Tours, is known as the apostle of Gaul. The pagan reaction attempted by Julian the Apostate was futile. By that time, the church had far more vitality than the empire; and no ruler could breathe life into gods that had fallen into dust.

The victory of Christianity was that of the spirit over soulless superstition. The teeming Pantheon of Rome answered no question and afforded no comfort. The worship of the state had become a mockery, when the worst emperors were hailed as divine. Noble as was the philosophy of a Marcus Aurelius, it could not bring hope to a darkening world. Christianity, and Christianity alone, stood clearly against the moral evils of Roman life, cruelty, greed and lust. It stood no less boldly against the essential faults of the economic regime. In a society ruled by the rich and based on the profit motive, it preached the gospel of poverty, and dared to ask: "What shall it profit a man if he shall gain the whole world?" It transcended, although it could not abolish, slavery. Without an open, direct fight, the Christians undermined the eternal verities of greed and pride, simply by ignoring them. Their spiritual revelation was also a social revolution within.

With this social revolution, this challenge to established values, went a political revolution. Not on the conscious plane: the forms of the Roman state remained unaltered; they merely lost their reality. The central government could no longer make its power felt. The rich had frankly assumed authority, and senator was practically synonymous with landowner. But in the growing anarchy, wealth shrank and disappeared; public office, once a privilege, became a crushing burden. The paradoxical situation arose of magistrates chained to their hereditary and ruinous honors. Those who wanted to preserve some riches fled from power. The masses were left untended, with the barbarians prowling by.

The local population, abandoned by their masters, sought other leaders. The bishops had unrivaled prestige, and they became the chief personages in the cities. And at that time, the bishops were elected by the faithful. This is one of the most elusive moments in history. We can discern, in the murk of barbarian chaos and imperial impotence, the faint outline of a Christian and democratic commonwealth.

It did not materialize. The brutal fact had to be faced that power was in the hands of the barbarians. The church needed a secular sword. Had the Gallo-Romans and the barbarians been of the same faith, it is conceivable that the war lords might have been guided, or at least restrained, by the bishops. But one of those coincidences occurred, which prove that history cannot be demonstrated with the rigor of a theorem. It happened that many of the barbarians entered the eastern empire at the time when the heresy of Arius was in the ascendant. Untrained in theological subtleties, they accepted blindfolded the wrong doctrine, and denied that the Son was coequal with the Father. When they reached the west, their Arianism created a gulf between themselves and the Catholic, or Trinitarian, population. Even Theodoric, tolerant and just, could not reconcile his subjects to the rule of a heretic.

In Gaul, the Visigoths and the Burgunds, who were occupying the center and the south of the country, were Arians. The Franks, a lesser tribe, ruling the Lower Rhine, the Meuse and the Scheldt, were still pagans. When their leader Clovis was converted to orthodox Christianity, he became, not another conqueror merely, but the champion of the Catholic Gallo-

Romans against their heretical masters. The saintly chronicler Gregory of Tours was to call him, in spite of his unabated ferocity, "a man of God." Although one of the least numerous and one of the least civilized among the Germanic tribes, the Franks were thus able to dominate the greater part of Gaul, and to impose their name upon the land.

The whole career of Clovis, which French schoolboys used to learn as though it were sober history, is bathed in an atmosphere of legend. But that legend is one of the most potent facts in the long evolution of the country. At Rheims, St. Remi baptized the proud Frank, bidding him burn what he had adored, and adore what he had burned. A dove came from Heaven, bearing a vial of holy chrism, with which the king was anointed. Henceforth the church and the monarchy were, not one, but inseparably linked. The king's coronation amounted to a sacrament. He was a sacred character, and possessed the healing touch. Before it could harden into a reality, the hope of a Christian democracy had disappeared. In its stead, we find a conception which was to endure for thirteen hundred years: the close, if not invariably harmonious, association between the church and the crown.

The alliance achieved its main purposes. The Arian heresy was stamped out. In exchange, the Frankish kings were promoted from mere adventurers to at least rudimentary sovereigns. Paris became their capital as the reward of their conversion. St. Genevieve, the spiritual leader of the city who had averted Attila, the "scourge of God," would not let Clovis enter until he had been baptized. Most important of all, the distinction between conquerors and conquered began at once to wane; there were Gallo-Roman commanders in the Catholic army of Clovis. Territorially and spiritually, the future unity of France was made possible.

Not all the results were so fortunate. The church, as a consequence, became barbarized. The Frankish chieftains grabbed for themselves the richest prizes in the impoverished land—abbeys and bishoprics. So there were bishops and abbots who could not speak Latin or write any language. They killed their enemies with Odinic gusto and mutilated their servants for trifling faults. For the Franks, while receiving baptism, did not become civilized overnight. The story of the Merovingian dynasty has little to chronicle except a confused and dreary series of monstrous crimes.

That dynasty of tough warriors and lusty murderers trailed off into lazy incompetence. The last Merovingians were known as the do-nothing kings. Power passed into the hands of their chief servant, the mayor of the palace; and that manager of the royal estate became practically an omnipotent prime minister. Finally, the Merovingian shadow was removed; and Pippin the Short, with the approval of the Pope, made himself king.

This second, or Carolingian, dynasty does not strictly belong to French history. It represents a resurgence of Germanism. Neustria, the western part of the Frankish kingdom, was slowly assimilating the Roman tradition; the rougher eastern Franks, or Austrasians, prevailed.

Charles, son of Pippin, and grandson of Charles the Hammer who had saved Christendom at Poitiers, revived the shadowy Roman Empire (800) and thus deserved to be known as Charlemagne or Charles the Great. But although he fought Lombards and Saxons, he was a Teuton himself. It was only three centuries later that he was turned into a French hero by the epic poets of the Crusade era. He is one of the most impressive figures in history; Charles V and Napoleon considered him their model. Yet the renaissance he sponsored was a false dawn. Charles himself could not curb the growing independence of the local lords nor stop the raids of the Norse pirates. The ninth and tenth centuries were the darkest of all.

In the course of the quarrels for territory and prestige among the three grandsons of Charlemagne—Lothair, Louis and Charles—two events took place which technically mark the beginning of French national history. We have already mentioned (see p. 45) the Oaths of Strasbourg (842) which acknowledged the division of the Frankish realm into areas of Romance and Teutonic speech. In 843, by the treaty of Verdun, the two lands, France and Germany, were separated; and between the two was created for the eldest brother, Lothair, an invertebrate dominion called by his name Lotharingia, Lothringen, Lorraine. As late as 1945, the French and the Germans were still fighting over Lothair's heritage.

The Carolingian Empire was reunited for two brief seasons: from 875 to 877, under Charles the Bald; from 884 to 887, under Charles the Fat; and it revived once again when Napoleon, emperor of the French (1804–1814), made himself king of Italy and protector of the Rhine confederacy. In 887, Charles the Fat was deposed by the western nobles for having failed to help the count of Paris, Odo (Eudes), against the Northmen. For a full century, the dynasty of Charles and that of Odo strove for the crown. At times, the descendants of Odo ruled as dukes of the French under the name of a do-nothing Carolingian, just as the Carolingian mayors of the palace had wielded power under the last Merovingians. In 987, Hugh Capet was elected king. He was supported by the bishop of Rheims, and by that Gerbert of Aurillac who was to become the great Pope Sylvester II. The alliance between church and state was still effective. The new king of France, whose descendant claims the throne today, was the bishops' candidate.

Now the history of France as a separate entity may at last begin. What elements have we found so far? From the point of view of race, a mysterious pre-Gallic substratum, a Celtic strain which cannot be defined or measured, with an uncertain, but undoubtedly large admixture of Germanic blood. From the point of view of speech, a Romance dialect, but extremely different from classical Latin. In the domain of culture, a full share in the splendor of Rome but also a decadence which, in the ninth century, seemed irretrievable. In the realm of institutions, an equivocal kingship, both elective and hereditary, both of Frankish and of Latin origin. That monarchy had two great assets, the possession of strategic Paris, and a close alliance with the church. Far more important than the secular power was the church, which had preserved the vestments, the language, the political divisions of the Roman Empire. Finally, in social structure, we find that stage of dissolution, just short of complete chaos, which was to be rationalized into the feudal regime. The France of 987 seems very poor, very crude, very remote; yet she was, unmistakably, France. And the eleventh century was to be an age of glorious awakening.

CHRONOLOGICAL SUMMARY, PREHISTORY–987

PREHISTORY

Cro-Magnon (Upper Paleolithic)

PROTOHISTORY

	B.C.
Ligurians, Iberians (Basques)	
Rome founded (traditional)	753
Massalia (Marseilles) founded by Phocaeans	ca. 600
Celtic invasions: La Tène culture, Iron Age	ca. 500
Gauls sack Rome	390
Cisalpine Gaul conquered by Rome	190
Gallia Braccata (Narbonensis) created	121
Marius defeats Cimbri and Teutones	102–101
at Aquae Sextiae, 102	
and Vercellae, 101	

ROMAN GAUL

Conquest of Gaul by Caesar	58–51
Vercingetorix surrenders at Alesia	52
	A.D.
St. Denis, martyr, patron saint of France	?
Invasions of Franks and Alamans	257
Separate Gallic Empire (Postumus, etc.)	257–273
Unity restored by Aurelian 273	d. 275
New invasions, Franks and Alamans	277
Roman emperors	284–395
Diocletian, 284–305; Constantine, 306–337;	
Julian, 361–363; Theodosius, 379–395	
Ausonius, poet and official	310–394

THE FRANKISH MONARCHY: MEROVINGIANS
AND CAROLINGIANS

Robertian (later Capetian) lines   887–987
Charles the Simple (Carolingian) grants Rollo
  (Hrolf, later Robert) duchy of Normandy   911
Hugh Capet elected king   987

PART TWO

Old France

CHAPTER IV

France in the Middle Ages

1. OUT OF FEUDAL CHAOS

FOR GENERATIONS, the term Middle Ages was used to cover the ten centuries between the downfall of Rome in 476 and that of Constantinople in 1453. The whole period was thought of as one of unrelieved barbarism and gloom—what Rabelais, the great humanist of the Renaissance, was to describe as "Gothic night." It seems hardly necessary now to correct this misconception. The civilization which flowered in magnificent churches, in great universities, in cities teeming with joyous work and turbulent freedom could not be called either primitive or decadent. The words Dark Ages, as we have seen, apply literally in France to the rule of the Merovingians and Carolingians (481–987); even the mighty hand of Charlemagne was unable to establish permanent order. But with the beginning of the eleventh century, a strange revival of confidence and energy could be felt. This new surge of activity in every domain has no name in history; yet hardly any time better deserves the hackneyed title of "Renaissance." In the famous phrase of the Burgundian monk Raoul Glaber, "it seemed as though the earth were shaking off the rags of its antiquity, to clothe itself anew with a white mantle of churches."

History should be the resurrection of the past. But it suffers from an incurable political bias. It insists upon giving us, not the life of the people, but the chronicles of the kings; and

in our democratic age, since the state has said, "I am the king,"
history loves to dwell on the annals of national governments.
But governments are a small part of life. The chief end of man
never was to support or resist a distant ruler, whether personal
or collective. In the Middle Ages in particular, the first allegiance of man was to his church, not to his country. The
vague entity which was to harden into France was barely in
those days the French section of the Catholic international,
a province of Christendom. Not only had the church the words
of eternal life; she also ruled every moment of man's earthly
existence—private thoughts, family relations, hours of labor.
Next in importance to the church stood the local lord, mild or
brutal. The city dweller was engrossed in municipal affairs.
Economic conditions were molding the substance of daily
life: in the country, serfhood, tenancy or freehold; in the city,
membership in a guild or craft. The king, for remote villager
and even for country squire, was a faintly luminous character
in fairyland, less vivid, less immediate than angels or saints.
When—once perhaps in a lifetime—the sovereign was seen in
his glory, he was the chief figure in a pageant; when he un-
leashed the hounds of war, he was a scourge, like famine or the
Black Death. There is no doubt that Gothic art, scholastic
theology, the Crusades are more real to us than the deeds of
Robert the Pious or Louis X the Quarrelsome. The *Song of
Roland,* that stark epic of a fighting faith, is far more alive
than Philip I, the fat but energetic ruler under whom it was
presumably composed. The frail merry notes of *Aucassin and
Nicolette* reach us, miraculously lovely and clear, across the
centuries; and the ballads of François Villon still haunt us
with their wild and poignant beauty. The only history worthy
of the name is the history of civilization.

But we must remember that our main purpose is to trace
the increasing consciousness of modern France. Now "France"
in the tenth century was not even an intelligible geographical
expression like "Italy" before 1859. It was not nature, race,

the clearly defined desires or the manifest interests of the people that made a single nation out of Bretons, Gascons, Provençaux, Flemings, Lorrainers: it was history, and we must add royal history. If the Capetian dynasty did not create France, it provided the indispensable center of crystallization. The royal domain, monarchical power, national consciousness grew together and became welded. In so far as it is possible to write a connected history of France in the Middle Ages, one must note the steps of that threefold evolution.

The task will not be an easy one. It takes an effort to realize how weak the Capetian monarchy was in 987. The royal power in England after 1066 offers a totally different picture. There the conquest created a definite regime; the authority of the king was felt throughout the land; the greatest nobles, even when they proved fractious, were his subjects, in no sense his equals. In France, the early Capetians just managed to exist in their little duchy between Seine and Loire. That they survived at all is due to a fortunate accident: for generations, they had male heirs who could be elected to, and associated with, the crown in their father's lifetime. With the centuries, the elective system, which proved such a source of weakness to Germany and Poland, was lost to memory. When the direct line of the Capetians failed at last in 1328, the hereditary principle had become firmly established and the next of kin, from a junior branch, the Valois, came to the throne. There lives a prince today who can legitimately claim the crown of France as the descendant of Hugh Capet.

In theory, the king was "first among his peers," and his title was acknowledged, in shadowy fashion, as far as Catalonia on the southern side of the Pyrenees. In actual fact, he could be defied by any minor baron whose castle happened to command the high road between two royal cities. So, when William of Normandy was conquering England (1066) and Godfrey of Bouillon was liberating Jerusalem (1099), Philip I, a vigorous ruler (1060–1108), had to confine his activities within a narrow circle. Even Louis VI (1108–1137), likewise fat and able and much better known to fame, was absorbed most of the time in petty struggles within fifty miles of Paris. The sire of Montlhéry, some twelve miles from the capital, was one of the thorns in his all-too-solid flesh.

In theory again, the king was the keystone of the feudal edifice. In fact, he was immersed in feudal chaos. There never was a feudal *system:* it is a retrospective utopia.[1] There was an enormous and confused mass of customs; when these were at last written down, it was because other forces were growing that were seeking not to confirm but to limit traditional privileges. The charters are not in their essence *laws*, that is to say codified reason; they are *treaties*, registering the balance of power at a particular stage of a contest. These innumerable documents were later rationalized to some degree; and later still, they were tinged with an idealism which did not properly belong to them. Feudalism turned chivalrous when it ceased to be real; the armor of the knights became a work of art just when artillery had made it obsolete. Already at the time of the chronicler Froissart (1337–1404), feudalism was enjoyed as pageantry. And it was as conscious make-believe that it delighted the Romantic age, early in the nineteenth century.

There is one stark element of reality about the so-called feudal regime: the sharp division of society between the dominant class and the commoners. The term *feudal* properly applies only to the relations among the members of the ruling caste. The rest of the people were by no means all serfs and the serfs themselves were not slaves; but in the Dark Ages (before 1000) and in the early Middle Ages, they had no clearly stated rights.

The power of the ruling caste or nobility was based frankly on force. The lord was the strong man with sword and steed,

---

1 It was rightly said: "The feudal system was introduced into England, not by William the Conqueror in the eleventh century, but by Sir Henry Spelman in the seventeenth."

FEUDAL FRANCE

armor and castle. Over a definite area, he had authority because he could enforce it; the central government could not,
and thus became a shadow. Scholars still debate whether
feudalism was of Roman or German origin; as a matter of
fact, it is a condition that arises whenever a large organized
state falls into dissolution. In our own century, we saw
"feudal" conditions prevail in Morocco and at certain stages
of the Chinese and Mexican revolutions. When the state re-
covers, feudalism recedes.

From this realistic definition, two consequences appear. In
the first place, feudalism implies personal loyalty. If you join
a band, the essential condition is to obey the leader. It is only
in a high degree of civilization that it is possible to have "a
government of laws and not of men." The essential feudal
act is to do homage to the chief, who in return pledges his
protection.

The second consequence is that when force is the final
argument, property is not recognized as an abstract and absolute principle. Under feudal conditions, no man owns any-
thing outright. He holds his position, "with the privileges
thereunto appertaining," only because he can fill it. An estate
is thus conferred in exchange for service; if the duties are not
performed, the estate is forfeited. Vassals and suzerains are
thus bound together by obligations which are personal and
functional.

But this scheme—if the word is not too definite—arising out
of anarchy, never succeeded in extricating itself from anarchy.
The lord is the strong man who sells security because he finds
it more profitable to keep order than to loot; but if looting
turns out to be the better business, the lord will not hesitate.
From the robber barons of medieval Germany to the dissent-
ing caids of Morocco or the tycoons of China, the line has always been hard to draw between gang leader and feudal chief-
tain. Throughout French history, and until the reign of Louis
XIV, the "nobility of the sword" easily relapsed into thoughts

of plunder. The situation was even worse in Germany. In England, we must repeat, the Norman conquest had been a revolution; sweeping ancient confusion away, it had created an order capable of indefinite progress.

In spite of its fundamental roughness, there is something appealing about the feudal connection; personal and functional, it had blood and sinews. But it could not be rationalized and at the same time preserve this realistic and human character. It was affected by two factors, which were alien to its original principle.

The first was *heredity*, the natural desire of a man to transmit his wealth and power to his son. But then the estate might fall into the hands of a child or of a weakling; and when it did so, its functional nature was lost. The church, in the Dark Ages, was exposed to that danger; infants fell heirs to abbeys and bishoprics. The peril was averted by enforcing the celibacy of the clergy.

The second was the substitution of *territorial* for *personal* allegiance. In Capetian times, the bond was no longer between man and man but between estate and estate. Now, as the same man could acquire many lands, he could have many suzerains. The Count of Champagne, Henry the Liberal (ca. 1152), for instance, had to swear fealty to the following overlords: the emperor, the king of France, the duke of Burgundy, the archbishops of Rheims and Sens, the bishops of Autun, Auxerre and Châlons-sur-Marne, the abbot of St. Denis. The sense of individual loyalty thus became lost. Feudalism had been a rudimentary but vigorous organization of warriors; it turned into an inextricable maze of hereditary claims.

With the revival of vigor and confidence that marked the eleventh century, a struggle began, barely conscious yet unremitting and determined, against feudal anarchy. This struggle took many forms. The church tried to subject the fighting caste to a law nobler than the sword. The evils of private warfare were mitigated by a series of rules known as the Peace of

God and the Truce of God (first mention, 1027). Many individual lords were made to feel the curb of religious discipline. The cities, as they grew in wealth, turned themselves into sturdy little commonwealths, defying feudal tyranny, wrenching from their masters the recognition of definite rights. But, in France, the antifeudal movement was not primarily ecclesiastical or municipal. The one great instrument for the creation of order was the monarchy. As compared with the church, it could meet feudalism on its own earthly ground, and oppose force to force. As compared with the cities, it offered a much greater concentration of power, for in France the cities were never able to form effective leagues. When they acted in concert, it was through the king, and in support of the king: municipal militias helped Philip Augustus win the battle of Bouvines (1214).

The interminable fight of the monarchy, the church and the cities against feudalism lasted as long as the Ancient Regime; formally, it did not end until August 4, 1789, when all feudal privileges were at last abolished. It seldom was a clear-cut battle. The antifeudal forces were themselves tinged with feudalism. Bishops and abbots were feudal lords. A city strove first of all to turn itself into a sort of collective baron. Its battlemented walls made it a castle; the towering belfry was the equivalent of the proud baronial keep. The city had its men-at-arms, its banner and pennon, its crest and armorial bearings, its defiant device. In like fashion, the kings fought the feudal regime without challenging it; they were quarreling with individual lords not with a principle. It is only in the writings of modern royalist historians that the Capetians, Valois or Bourbons were infallibly true to the destiny of their race. Medieval kings were so little aware of the evils of feudalism per se that they created new and dangerous feudal states almost as fast as they destroyed them. The formidable Burgundy which for nearly a century balanced the power of France

had been given away by John the Good, in 1363, to his son
Philip the Bold.[2]

2. RISE OF THE CAPETIANS, THE FIRST HUNDRED YEARS' WAR

If the Capetians, from very modest beginnings, managed to
extend their domain and their power, it was because they possessed three incomparable assets.

The first was their royal title. Almost shorn of real significance at the time of Hugh Capet's election, it remained the
symbol of vague but potent memories. The king was the heir
of Clovis; France, in the narrower sense, might be a mere
duchy, not larger than Burgundy, Brittany, Normandy or
Aquitaine; but the name evoked also the ancient realm of the
Franks, from Flanders to the Pyrenees.

The second asset of the Capetians was their possession of
Paris. In Chapter II, we have attempted to indicate the commanding importance of the capital.

[2] Note: It is difficult to trace the stages of such a prolonged and confused
process. Here are a few important dates as indications:

1214 Communal militias help Philip Augustus win the battle of Bouvines.

1274 (?) Philip III grants first patent of nobility to commoner. The king, instead of being the first of the nobles, becomes the fountainhead of power
and privilege. By the time of the Revolution, most of the noble families
were so by royal creation.

1315 Louis X proclaims "all Frenchmen free, for such is their right by the
law of nature." Equality, five hundred years later, was to be the corollary
of liberty.

1346 First use of artillery, which was to destroy the privilege of the heavily
armed feudal fighter.

1445 Organization of standing royal army: the "fighting caste" ceases to have
any justification.

1624–1642 Richelieu. He orders dismantling of feudal castles; puts down duel-
ing, last trace of private warfare among members of the fighting caste; gives
greater powers to *Intendants*, direct representatives of the king in the provinces.

1661 *seq.* Louis XIV turns feudal nobles into courtiers.

1789 August 4. The nobles, of their own accord, renounce their feudal privileges.

As a third asset, the new dynasty preserved the traditional alliance between the monarchy and the church. The abbey of St. Denis, for instance, was a constant supporter of the royal house, and Abbot Suger was the able adviser of Louis VI and Louis VII. The Papacy and the great monastic orders were of course international; but the local clergy considered the king their natural protector and their "secular arm." From this close association arose the persistent trend known as "Gallicanism": in matters of administration and finances, the French or Gallican clergy insisted on a large measure of home rule. The king defended these national claims; a defender easily turns into a master. The vague word "trend" is more accurate than "doctrine"; Gallicanism never disputed the Pope's authority in questions of faith or spiritual discipline; it never grew into a heresy or a schism. It simply emphasized the Catholic character of the French crown as well as the *national* character of the French clergy.

The Capetian dynasty gathered strength and prestige through a contest which might have caused its destruction. The conquest of England by the Normans in 1066 created an abnormal situation: the duke of Normandy remained the vassal of France but, as the ruler of England, he was actually more powerful than his sovereign. The scales were further tipped against France when in 1154 Henry of Anjou (Plantagenet) succeeded to the English throne as Henry II. His own domains were extensive enough: Anjou, Maine, and Touraine. In 1152, he had married Eleanor of Aquitaine (or Guyenne), whose union with Louis VII of France had been annulled; her portion was the whole southwest of France—Poitou, Guyenne, Gascony, Toulouse. Finally, Henry claimed suzerainty over Brittany, Wales, Scotland and part of Ireland. The Angevin Empire greatly overshadowed the lands directly controlled by the Capetians.

There resulted a protracted conflict (1152–1259) which has sometimes been called the First Hundred Years' War. In spite of the apparent disparity of forces, the Capetians emerged victorious. The Angevin Empire was a loose and hasty accumulation of territories; the Capetians, as we have seen, had a superior title and a definite strategic center. But the factor in their favor was found in the personalities of the rulers. Philip II of France (1180–1223) was more than a match for his opponents, the two sons of Henry II Plantagenet: Richard Coeur de Lion (1189–1199), choleric and unsteady and John Lackland (1199–1216), craven even in crime and clumsy even in craftiness. Philip II was lacking neither in physical courage nor in wile; and he added to both a remarkable sense of statesmanship. Using in turn arms, deceit and the law, Philip managed to snatch from John Lackland the bulk of his continental possessions. The growth of the Capetian dynasty is well shown by the formidable coalition formed against Philip; it banded together King John of England, the count of Flanders, and Otto IV the German emperor. These Philip signally defeated at Bouvines in 1214. Although the support of the communal militias may have been overrated, in the rejoicing caused by that victory there was a first anticipatory tinge of national sentiment.

The greatness of Philip's reign was not exclusively diplomatic and military. It was in his time that the University of Paris was organized. The cathedral, Notre Dame, was under construction; the great royal palace, the Louvre, was rebuilt; new fortifications girdled the city; the two main streets were paved. The sagacious and vigorous king so greatly impressed his contemporaries that he was called Philip Augustus.

Early in the eleventh century, there had arisen in the south a sect of heretics known as the Cathars or Albigenses. Its tenets remain something of a mystery. *Albigenses* is patently a misnomer, for their center was Toulouse rather than Albi. *Cathar*, a word of Greek origin meaning *pure*, is ambiguous. The heretics were called "the good men," and it seems that they led ascetic lives; but—like all persecuted minorities—

they were also accused of abominable vices. Of their essential
doctrines little is known. Missions, crusades, and the Inquisition were used against them. As they enjoyed the protection of
the nobles and the sympathy of the masses, it was necessary, in
order to suppress them, to conquer the whole south. The war
was long and implacable. The king of France appeared again
in the same role as Clovis: the secular arm of the church.
Finally, the lands of the counts of Toulouse, which hitherto
had boasted political independence and a culture more refined
than that of the north, passed under the sway of King
Louis VIII (1223–1226). — *after P was him, short reig*
marked by considerable vigo

At his death (1226) the barons, conscious of the growth of
a power which was overshadowing theirs, took advantage of
the minority of his son to rebel: a pattern repeated many times
in French history, and as late as 1648. But the regent, the
Queen Mother Blanche of Castile, was able to hold her own,
and to transmit the royal power unimpaired to her son
Louis IX (1226–1270).

Louis IX was a valiant warrior and a good administrator
but his chief service to his line and to his country was his renown for Christian virtue. Just as he enriched Paris with the
perfect jewel of Gothic art, the Sainte Chapelle, Saint Louis
gave his dynasty the inestimable prestige of holiness. He settled the age-long conflict with England, not merely by the victories of Taillebourg and Saintes (1242) but by the generous
and statesmanlike treaty of Paris (1259). The customs and
coinage of good King Louis remained standards for ages to
come.

There is an image that has remained dear to the French
people: the king dealing paternal justice even to the humblest
of his subjects under an oak tree in the forest of Vincennes.
Thanks to him, his royal successors, however unworthy, incarnated in the eyes of the masses an ideal of Christian equity.
Up to 1789, the oppressed would sigh: "Ah! if the king only

knew!" It is appropriate that the great court of justice, the Parlement of Paris, should have been organized by St. Louis in 1258. In the growth of the monarchy, military power was but the instrument, glory the eternal temptation; what the people really wanted of their king was that he should protect them from feudal confusion by extending the rule of justice.

The middle of the thirteenth century is the glorious summit of medieval culture; and at its apex stood the perfect king. In the long eclipse of the Holy Roman Empire, it was the saintliness rather than the power of Louis IX that made him the first secular character in Christendom. His prestige enhanced, although it did not create, the supremacy enjoyed by French culture at that time; never again was it so complete, not even under Louis XIV. French was already, in the words of Brunetto Latini (1265), "the most delectable language and the most widely spread among all people." The University of Paris was the greatest center of theological studies. The new art, French art, *Opus Francigenum,* which the Italian Renaissance in derision was to call *Gothic,* spread from the cities of the royal domain to all parts of Europe.

But if Louis IX was the most perfect flower of royal chivalry, he was also the last. His crusades, which did not meet with the approval of his more worldly counselors, were not popular movements but personal undertakings. Both ended in failure. (Egypt, 1248–1254 and Tunis, where he died, 1270.) The holy king was already an anachronism. His friend Joinville gave us a garrulous, naïve and delightful account of a sovereign who could fight and who could pray, but who was also capable of gentle mirth. — succ. was Phil. 3 1270 – 1285

No contrast could be more striking than that between Saint Louis and his second successor, Philip IV the Fair (1285–1314). Instead of candor and scrupulous honesty, touched with Christian mansuetude, we find craft and violence, the iniquious mockery of the prosecution he launched against the

Knights Templars, the constant tampering with and debasement of the royal currency. Instead of a sovereign who was a firm and self-respecting, but respectful, son of the church, France had a king whose envoy slapped an aged Pope in the face and who, forcing the election of a French bishop to the Holy See, made him almost a chaplain of the French crown.

But this reign of financial embarrassment, unscrupulous makeshifts, and fitful violence was also strangely modern in a less disreputable sense. The personality of the handsome and taciturn king remains an enigma; but under him, the Roman concept of the sovereign as the source and the embodiment of the law was revived and expounded by his jurists. For three centuries, the king's power had grown *against*, but *within*, the feudal order. Now for the first time the issue was clearly drawn. The nobles stood for nothing but force and custom; the king's authority represented, at times unworthily, the majesty of the law. From that time on and until its formal abolition in 1789, feudalism was clearly a waning survival.

It was under Philip the Fair that the States-General came into definite existence. The kings had repeatedly convened, for counsel and especially for financial support, the clergy and the nobles of their various provinces, and also the representatives of the cities. In 1302, the three estates or classes of the whole kingdom met by royal summons in the cathedral of Paris. Under its sacred vaults, the assembly supported the king's policy against the Pope. The States-General might have been the embryo of a parliament; but they were destined to remain a might-have-been. The nobility could never unite with the commoners to organize a truly national government; their sole purpose was to defend their privileges. The States-General were called only in critical hours, as a desperate remedy; the sovereigns generally managed to play one class against another, and thus to preserve or even to extend their own supremacy.

3. TWO TORMENTED CENTURIES, THE VALOIS KINGS AND THE SECOND HUNDRED YEARS' WAR

Medieval civilization reached its peak about 1270. By 1300 it had already lost much of its vitality. Yet in France it lingered through the chiaroscuro of two equivocal centuries, until the light we call the Renaissance was manifest to every eye.

The three sons of Philip the Fair—Louis X the Quarrelsome, Philip V the Tall, Charles IV the Handsome—reigned in succession; all three died without male issue. Their sister Isabella had married Edward II of England; and in 1328, Edward III, her son, claimed the French throne as the next of kin.

His claim was set aside; it was ruled that no woman could inherit the French crown. This principle is known in history as the Salic Law. The French kings had forgotten for many centuries that they were "Salian Franks." The jurists conveniently remembered: the legal mind was learned and ingenious even in those days. Thanks to this antiquarian legerdemain, Philip of Valois, nephew of Philip IV, was proclaimed king. This clash, not between two nations but between two branches of the same royal house, caused the most disastrous struggle in French history, the (second) Hundred Years' War (1337–1453). But at the end of the conflict, France was more firmly knit, more conscious of her identity, than a century before.

The first two Valois kings, Philip VI (1328–1350) and John the Good (1350–1364) had neither the feudal and Christian virtues of the great exemplar of their race, Louis IX, nor the groping sense of the modern state which partly redeemed Philip the Fair. They were medieval knights but in externals only. They displayed the personal bravery, the prodigality, the childish ignorance that might be expected of common men-at-arms. Their opponent, Edward III, was an able sovereign, making daring use of his sturdy yeomen and of their skill with the long bow. After inconclusive warfare about side issues—Flanders and Brittany—England and France grappled directly at last. Philip's array of undisciplined knights was defeated by a much smaller force at Cressy (Crécy) in 1346; and in the next year Calais was lost. John the Good was even more ignominiously beaten at Poitiers in 1356 and made a prisoner.

The dauphin (heir apparent) Prince Charles was regent during the captivity of his father John the Good. It seemed as though France would relapse into the horror of the Dark Ages. Bands of pillaging soldiers of doubtful nationality and shifting allegiance were roaming throughout the land. The Black Death or plague swept away one-third of the French population. The *Jacques* or peasants rose in wild revolt, as the Bagaudae had done a thousand years before. They burned castles and murdered nobles, as they had so often seen their own huts destroyed and their brothers slain.

In this great need, the dauphin summoned the States-General. The king and the nobility had revealed their ineptitude; now the bourgeoisie or urban middle class attempted to seize control. Led by the provost of Parisian merchants, Etienne Marcel, the States-General imposed upon the dauphin a veritable constitution or Great Ordinance (1357). Marcel, however, was but indifferently supported by the more substantial of his townsmen. He was driven to an understanding with the rebellious peasants or Jacques, and with Charles the Bad, king of Navarre, a sinister figure flitting adventurously between the French and the English parties. The great provost was denounced as a traitor, and slain by the supporters of the dauphin (1358). The revolt of the Jacques was ferociously put down, the States-General proved abortive, and by the peace of Bretigny (1360), one-third of France was signed away. King John was released from captivity; but, unable to fulfill all the obligations of the treaty, he gave himself up to the English again and died in London.

Charles V (1364–1380), a weak-bodied, scholarly, shrewd

ADDITIONS TO THE FRENCH MONARCHY, 1273-1494

ENGLAND

London

English Channel

Bay of Biscay

Biscay

Rhine R.

Rhône R.

Moselle R.

Bruges · Antwerp
Ghent · Brussels
ARTOIS 1477 · Tournai
Lille · Cambrai

Calais

Aymouth
PONTHIEU 1477

Harfleur
Le Havre

Mt. St. Michel

NORMANDY

ISLE OF FRANCE

Caen

Nancy

Rouen

Rennes

BRITTANY 1491-1515

MAINE
LeMans

ANJOU 1481
Tours

Loire R.

Angers

Orléans

BLOIS

Blois

BERRY

Bourges

NIVERNAIS

Nevers

BOURBONNAIS

Dijon

Besançon

BURGUNDY 1477

POITOU 1371

Poitiers

la Rochelle

Saintes

MARCHE 1309

MARCHE

Lyons

LYONNAIS 1312

Vienne

Grenoble

AUVERGNE

DAUPHINÉ 1349

Bordeaux

GUYENNE 1453

Bergerac

LANGUEDOC

Rhône R.

Avignon

PROVENCE 1481

Aix · Nice

Marseilles

Bayonne

GASCONY

Toulouse

Carcassonne

Narbonne

Dates indicate when the regions came under control of the French Monarchy

Miles
0   50   100
Kilometres
0   50   100

Possessions of the English Kings in France upon the Accession of Henry VI, 1422 and kindly prince, aided by the military talent of his Breton constable, Bertrand du Guesclin, tired the British out and, without any brilliant victories, freed the whole land with the exception of five cities.[3] When he died, his son Charles VI (1380–1422) was a child of twelve. The uncles of the young king governed in his name and played ducks and drakes with the wise policies of Charles V. They dismissed his able but low-born advisers, whom in derision they dubbed the "marmosets." They squandered his hoard and oppressed the people. Paris and Flanders rose against their misrule, but in vain. As soon as he came of age, Charles VI attempted to renew the good traditions of his father; but he was struck with madness and his uncles resumed the course of their maladministration.

An insane king, a corrupt queen (Isabella of Bavaria), and factions fighting for the spoils: such was the story of the next generation. The duke of Burgundy, John the Fearless, had his rival the duke of Orléans assassinated in 1407. The count of Armagnac took the lead of the Orléans faction. Paris and the king's person passed by turns under the control of Armagnacs and Bourguignons. Massacre was retaliated with massacre.

Under these circumstances Henry V of England, eager to give the usurping house of Lancaster the prestige of foreign victories, renewed the French war. The crass inefficiency of the Armagnac nobility gave him a brilliant victory at Agincourt (1415). The disastrous plight of France did not allay the strife between Armagnacs and Bourguignons. John the Fearless, duke of Burgundy, was assassinated in 1419. His son immediately struck an alliance with the English. The queen, Isabella of Bavaria, sacrificed her own son, who was declared illegitimate; by the treaty of Troyes (1420), Henry V of England was made the heir to the French throne.

Both the mad French king and the youthful English conqueror died in 1422. Henry VI of England, ten months old, was acknowledged king of France by all the official powers in

---

[3] Bordeaux, Bayonne, Brest, Calais and Cherbourg.

Paris—the bourgeoisie, the university, the court of justice or *Parlement*. The French claimant Dauphin Charles, lethargic and bewildered, served as a rallying point for the anti-English elements south of the Loire, and was tauntingly called "the king of Bourges." He lived in indolence, squandering gaily what little was left of his estate. It looked as though France, still nominally the suzerain, would be held in vassalage by the English crown.

But "deals" such as the treaty of Troyes have a way of being annulled by the wrath of the common people. There arose out of the borders of Lorraine at Domrémy, a daughter of the peasantry, a miracle of inspiration and shrewdness, of gentleness and valor, Joan of Arc. "Angel voices" called her to save the kingdom. The local lord gave her an escort and she made her way to Chinon where she was received by Charles, the still uncrowned king. The pleasure-loving prince and his court were at first tempted to scoff. But they were carried away by the faith of the Maid. She gave them the "signs" they had asked for and she was entrusted with a small army.

With marvelous insight, Joan had set for herself two essential objectives, the one military, the other spiritual. In a few days, she liberated Orléans, the key to southern France, which the English had been besieging for a whole year. Then she led Charles in triumph to Rheims, where he received the crown of his ancestors. This meant a new consecration not for the prince alone but for the dynasty. From this ceremony, the religious and national character of the monarchy emerged with perfect definiteness. The mediocre sovereign was now hallowed by a double investiture; he was king by the grace of God and the will of the people.

This victory in the realm of the ideal still had to be translated into material terms. Paris and the richest parts of the land were still in the hands of the English or of their ally the duke of Burgundy. But there are few cases in history in which the primacy of principles was more clearly manifested. Because Joan of Arc placed essentials first, she proved to be the supreme realist.

Her miraculous mission was at an end and she wished to retire. Urged to remain in the king's service, she was betrayed to the Bourguignons at Compiègne, sold to the English, condemned by a church court as a witch and a heretic, and burned at the stake at Rouen (1431). Charles made no effort to save the heroic Maid who lived and died for the king of France and the Catholic faith.

There was no dramatic change; yet the tide had manifestly turned. France was rallying. The treaty of Arras (1435) effected a reconciliation between the king of France and the duke of Burgundy. It was England's turn to be distracted by civil wars. Charles VII the Well-served reorganized his army and finances. Jacques Cœur was a new portent: a merchant and banker who, as *argentier* or treasurer, was also a good servant of the state. By the battle of Formigny (1450), Normandy was reconquered. By the battle of Castillon (1453), Guyenne was recovered after two hundred and fifty years of English rule. Calais was now the only French city that remained in the hands of the English.

After a century of ubiquitous warfare, of forays by royal troops or by nondescript armed bands, of peasant rebellions followed by massacres, of feuds between noble factions, of devastating pestilence, the country was physically ruined. But its spirit, although stunted and warped in many ways, was in the main more vigorous than ever. France recovered with startling rapidity.

Louis XI (1461–1483) continued the work of reconstruction undertaken by his father. But the fighting caste, the feudal lords, dreaded royal order. The nobles united against the king in a League of the Public Weal—a bold misnomer for selfish greed. It must be said that they were only following the example that Louis, a rebellious son, had given them under Charles VII. Louis XI escaped defeat through cunning, pertinacity, and luck rather than through the force of arms or through political genius.

Only one rival remained formidable, the House of Burgundy. For a hundred years, it had been attempting to establish a new Austrasia, a new Lotharingia, independent of either France or Germany. This vague gigantic dream did not disappear without a trace; ultimately it was to be realized in shrunken form as the kingdom of Belgium. In this contest with an ambitious and powerful vassal, Louis XI was more than once betrayed by his haste and his overweening craftiness; the "universal spider," as he was called, managed to entangle himself in his own web. He was saved from disaster less by his own skill than by the blundering fury of his rival, Charles the Reckless.[4] The "mad bull of Burgundy" defeated by the Swiss, was slain under the walls of Nancy, and Louis secured a part, but only a part, of his heritage.

Great romancers, Sir Walter Scott and Victor Hugo, have given dramatic and damaging pictures of Louis XI. Crafty, suspicious, cruel with a slow and cold relish, he is one of the most unattractive characters in French history. In his old age, haunted with an insane and craven fear of death, he sought refuge in superstition. As a statesman, he has been overrated, in particular by his adviser and historian, Philippe de Commines. Nevertheless, in his contempt for the trappings (as well as for the virtues) of chivalry, in his love for absolute authority and political intrigue, in his reliance upon middle-class officials and counselors, in his genuine capacity for organization, the mean-looking old man at Plessis-lèz-Tours was no longer a medieval king.

Just as the traditions of the early Middle Ages cling most fondly to the personality of Louis IX, the perfect knight and gentle saint, so the fifteenth century, a time of lurid contrasts,

---

[4] The French make a useful distinction between Philip the Bold (*Hardi*), John the Fearless (*Jean-sans-peur*), and Charles the Rash or the Reckless (*le Téméraire*).

is most fittingly symbolized by Louis XI. The classic serenity of thirteenth-century culture was gone; the age was romantic like a stormy evening sky. It was the time of flamboyant architecture, rich and tormented, in which stone was made to writhe like a flame. Amid the appalling distress of the peasant masses, it was a time of lavish luxury. The great nobles, Burgundy, Orléans, Berry, were vying with one another in riotous display. It was the time when true chivalry was at its lowest ebb and when its externals became more elaborate and more consciously picturesque than ever before. It was an age of mysticism, superstition, and free thought. Morbid, decadent, macabre with Gilles de Rais, the black baron, an artist in lust and murder, it was also the age that brought forth *The Imitation of Christ*. Its great theme is the dance of death, and its supreme poet is Villon. It has the phosphorescence of corruption, with the promise of splendid rebirth. By the time Louis XI died (1483), the Turks had already been thirty years in Constantinople, the printing press was in operation, and all eyes were turning toward the great light in Italy.

4. THE MEDIEVAL HERITAGE

What survives of the Middle Ages in the France of today? First of all, religion. The cradle of Christianity is the Holy Land, and its field is the world. But Catholicism in France has a French, not a Syrian, Greek or Italian, coloring; and, in the best sense of the term, it is still medieval. The fierceness and the magnificent Oriental imagery of the Old Testament remains somewhat alien to the reasonable temper of the French. They have little taste and little aptitude for the mystical subtleties of Neo-Platonism. They leave heresies to the Byzantine mind. The great dispute of the Schoolmen about the nature of general ideas was philosophical rather than theological. The University of Paris gave form to medieval thought, but took no flight into the unknown. Although the

French as a people did not sever their bonds with the Holy See, they always asserted their autonomy within the Roman fold. To the very end of the Ancient Regime, kings, magistrates, bourgeois, and many members of the secular clergy insisted upon the liberties of the French or Gallican church.

The favorite French saints are rooted in French earth, from St. Denis, St. Martin, St. Genevieve, down to the heavenly patron of the humblest village. Even the Virgin is revered, not only as the Divine Mother, but as attached to this particular sanctuary, to this or that bit of French soil, a kindly neighbor who can understand the home dialect. Under the austere simplicity of trinitarian dogma, there were in medieval France hosts of angels, saints and demons, some of them older than Rome or Judaea, in immediate contact with every moment of life. Even unbelievers among the French have never quite lost the sense of intimacy with their spiritual past.

Of that past, the French have magnificent remains in their great Gothic churches. Gothic art, it must be remembered, had nothing whatever to do with the Goths; it arose within the royal domain, in Ile-de-France. It is in or near Paris, at St. Germain-des-Prés, St. Julien-le-Pauvre, St. Martin-des-Champs, St. Denis, Notre Dame, that we see the first unmistakable examples of that noble style. The elaborate Gothic structure grew, as it were, within the heavy mass of the Romanesque. We can see, from church to church, the arch rise to a point, the pillars soar to slender shafts, and glorious windows take the place of massive walls. Gothic style spread over western Christendom, especially in the north. In spite of revolutions and wars, no other land has preserved such a wealth of Gothic churches as France; not only the supreme quartet, Chartres, Amiens, Rheims and Paris, but others scarcely inferior in majesty and charm, Rouen, Tours, Le Mans, Metz, Bourges, Laon, Beauvais; and a multitude less known to fame, like those delicate masterpieces that had to be pounded into rubble in the Normandy campaign of 1944. To the French, the elegant Jesuit churches of the seventeenth century are mundane, the stiff uninspired pastiches built in the nineteenth century are frigid. To feel the warmth of a truly communal religion, one must kneel in a medieval church.

That feeling is so deep, because the church embodied the many-sided life of the whole people. The faith of the Middle Ages was as varied as it was ardent. There was crude superstition no doubt, and not exclusively among the ignorant masses; but medieval also was the great soul of St. Bernard. And faith did not preclude a surprising amount of free thought in every sense of the term. There were irreverent quips and anticlerical jibes in the popular tales; Aucassin spurns a heaven "fit for sniveling monks"; Jehan de Meung filled the second part of the *Romance of the Rose* with pungent, earthy, satirical common sense; and what could be freer than the passionate logic, the fearless quest for truth of Peter Abélard? The house of God was indeed the house of the people. Under the guidance of the bishop, artists, artisans and common laborers united in building the cathedral, a Bible in chiseled stone and radiant glass, a hall for political meetings, a monument of civic pride.

The cathedrals have suffered much from heretics and revolutionists; perhaps they have suffered most of all from classical architects, who have ruthlessly altered them to suit their own "enlightened" taste. But they have grown with the nation, and age is now the substance of their splendor. Not one of them is complete as envisioned by its builders. Indeed, we shudder at the thought that Rheims, for instance, might have had seven spires. If we could see them in their novelty, with the dazzling white of their stonework, the rich polychromy of their statues, the star-studded azure of their lofty vaults, they might strike us as gaudy. They are the old companions of an old nation; but like the people itself, they are vigorously alive.

In France, it is these popular Bibles of stone almost alone that have preserved for us the medieval spirit, for religious literature of the period is disappointing. It has produced nothing that even remotely compares with the *Divine Comedy*. The greatest writers of Catholic inspiration, like St. Bernard, wrote in Latin. There is crusading zeal in the *Song of Roland*, but even that stark masterpiece is feudal rather than Christian, and the other epics of the fighting caste are gray steel without a spiritual gleam. The Grail stories belong to the age of courtly romance, and the curse of make-believe is upon them. Chrétien de Troyes is a clever society novelist, not a mystic. A few miracles of the Virgin still have some vitality.[5] The enormous Passion plays (Arnoul Gréban and Jean Michel) were elaborate failures. Perhaps they developed too late, in the tormented and unsteady fifteenth century. The wind that bloweth where it listeth did not stir them into life; and their revivals on the parvis [6] Notre Dame in our own days were honorably antiquarian rather than profoundly religious.

Historically, the universities are a legacy of the Christian Middle Ages: they sprang from the cathedral schools. The multitude of students who flocked to Paris to follow such masters as Abélard was gradually organized into "nations," (provinces or languages), *facultés* or schools, and residential halls or *collèges*. The first charters were granted by Philip Augustus about 1200. It was then that the slopes of Montagne-Sainte-Geneviève became known as the Latin Quarter, still alive as it was in those days with passionate disputations, quarrels and laughter. But these medieval universities had withered before the end of the Middle Ages. They survived, gray and surly, until the Revolution; but for three centuries, French philosophy, scholarship, science had been forced to find other chan-

[5] In our own time, there were distant echoes of these Miracle plays in *The Tumbler of Notre Dame* by Anatole France and *Sister Béatrice*, by Maurice Maeterlinck. A purer note was struck by Charles Péguy and Paul Claudel.

[6] Cathedral square.

nels.[7] No protest was raised when the Revolution finally ex-
orcized those scholastic ghosts.

The nobility also constitutes a tenuous, indeed a purely
nominal link between modern France and the Middle Ages.
Today there are princes, dukes, marquises, counts, viscounts,
barons in France. Readers of Marcel Proust must have noted
with what gusto he listed the many titles of Baron de Charlus.
But the privileges the nobles once enjoyed were abolished in
1789. Very few aristocratic families can trace their origin to
the feudal fighting caste; they owe their rank to royal favor
—and frequently to actual purchase. The French nobility
never was an elite; born out of barbaric chaos, it strove to
perpetuate chaos. In the Middle Ages, the kings, supported by
the bourgeoisie and the greater part of the clergy, kept up a
fitful yet unremitting fight against that unruly element. When
these petty sovereigns waging perpetual war among themselves were curbed at last by the national monarchy, they
turned from turbulent fighters into greedy courtiers; they
were a little less dangerous to the state, but not a whit more
useful. They never acquired the sense of responsibility, both
local and national, which long justified the existence of the
British peerage; or the stern, almost monklike devotion to
the state which gave the Prussian Junker of the last three centuries a sinister but undeniable impressiveness.

The third estate, on the contrary, the urban middle class or
bourgeoisie, which came to consciousness in the Middle Ages,
was to increase steadily in power until, in 1789, it openly
captured the state. Some of the most interesting forms of its
activity, however, proved abortive: the communes and the
guilds. Yet they were spontaneous creations, vigorous at first,
born in strife, asserting the rights of the common man against
the privileged orders. The commune or chartered city could
have developed into a municipal democracy; the craft or

[7] E.g. the Collège de France, the Observatory, the King's Garden (natural
history), the academies, etc.

guild, which prescribed fair practices, protecting customers and producers alike, has an appeal, even for the modern mind. Yet both communes and crafts had lost their vitality even before the sixteenth century. Like the universities, they lingered through the classical age as mere vestiges, incapable of further growth, retaining only enough energy to squabble and to snarl.

The key to this decay, in all cases, is found in the single word *custom*. Medieval society was original and intensely alive; yet it did not trust itself. It was hopelessly retrospective, haunted with thoughts of decadence:

> *Bons fut li siecles al tems ancienour* . . .
> *Toz est mudez, perdude at sa colour* . . .
>
> Good was the world in days of yore . . .
> All is changed now and has lost its color . . .[8]

The vague memory of Roman splendor and of early Christian virtue made the present seem corrupt, feeble and dark. So the whole duty of man was to cling to the wisdom and strength of the past; an eternal tendency, which the English mind still nurses with consciousness and pride. Such a tendency is useful as a check to rashness; but if it prevails too long, the result is paralysis and death. Reverence for custom too often means the worship of privilege, and privilege is but the hallowing of injustice. So it was with the communes and the guilds. Their only concern was, not to meet the future, but to protect their vested interests. To brush away their last traces, in 1789, was to restore freedom.

But if communes and guilds proved to be ever narrowing blind alleys, the bourgeoisie had discovered other paths to self-realization and power. The king found among his bourgeois his financiers, his magistrates, his administrators. They rose above mere custom by appealing to a principle: they made the king the living symbol, the source and origin of the law.

---

[8] *Life of St. Alexis*, ca. 1050.

Thus through him they magnified themselves, their office, and their class against feudal anarchy and priestly encroachments. Roman law in northern France was not an unconscious heritage; it had to be rediscovered and it was deliberately used to combat definite evils. With Philip the Fair, with Charles V, with Louis XI, we see the first lineaments of classical France, and of nineteenth century France as well: a bourgeois bureaucracy serving the king, because the king was the state; ultimately removing the king, when his interests and theirs came to the parting point. The France of Thiers, Guizot, Waldeck-Rousseau and Raymond Poincaré had its origins in the twelfth century. That bourgeoisie reigned, humble or arrogant, almost without a challenge, until the critical years between the two world wars.

The spirit of that bourgeoisie has survived, not in government only, but in literature. The epithets "naïve," "romantic," "feudal," "Christian," are sometimes glibly applied to the whole of the Middle Ages. They do not adequately describe the bourgeoisie. That class was shrewd, realistic, inclined to mockery, with no slight admixture of the cynical. The places of pilgrimage, where relics were worshiped, where legends of heroism and holiness were told, were markets and fairs as well; between religious services, the merchants struck their bargains and swapped spicy stories. Parody closely followed the epic. *The Voyage of Charlemagne to Constantinople and Jerusalem*, probably as early as *The Song of Roland,* is broadly ironical in tone. To the chivalrous exaltation of woman, the bourgeois opposed woman's frailty. In Chaucer, so close to the French bourgeois spirit, the sentimental tale of patient Grisilde is followed by a rollicking satirical *Envoy*. In this sharp and conscious contrast, Chaucer was following the great classic of the time, *The Romance of the Rose*. The first part, by Guillaume de Lorris, is a delicate allegory of courtly love; but the second, by Jehan de Meung, is a robust, realistic, free-thinking encyclopaedia of the bourgeois world.

The Romance of Reynard the Fox, a vast cycle of folk tales popular in northern France, reverses all the values of the feudal epic: success belongs by right not to the heavy sword but to the nimble wit. The same cult of sharpness is found even in religious themes. The saints play tricks on Satan, who is buffoon and dupe as well as villain in the cosmic drama. A peasant with the wiles of a lawyer wins his way into Paradise, defeating St. Peter in legal argument. It is a peasant again who outsmarts shyster Pathelin, the fox in a lawyer's gown.

As a rule, however, the peasant does not appear in such a favorable light. Folk literature, in the Middle Ages, is of the town not of the farm. The hind, the boor, the clown are despised and dreaded. From *villanus,* the villager, derives our word *villein;* it became, in English, the *villain,* wicked and depraved, in French *vilain,* ugly and mean. Not until La Bruyère, at the end of the seventeenth century, was it discovered that these "human-faced animals" were men indeed.[9]

The themes, the very forms of the *fabliaux* or tales and of their dramatic equivalents the farces, have survived throughout the ages. Rabelais the great Renaissance scholar, Molière the classical dramatist, La Fontaine the delicate poet, Voltaire, the philosopher of the Enlightenment kept alive, in some aspects of their work, the broad mocking realism of the medieval bourgeois. So did Balzac, Guy de Maupassant, Anatole France. This is not the highest level that the French genius can reach; but, of all forms of art, it is the most universal and the most permanent. There are many ways of losing one's self into the land of Faëry; but it is to the same earth that, after our most daring flights, we must inexorably return.

Periods and cultures are not objective realities. They are symbols or, literally, myths. So they constantly alter in the

---

[9] This bias, strange in a predominantly agricultural country, survived in Guy de Maupassant, Emile Zola, Roger Martin du Gard.

folk mind that creates them. We cannot speak of the Middle Ages as solid fact, but of the successive images that these words evoked.

The Renaissance, the Neo-Classic period, the Enlightenment, the Revolution were one in spurning the "barbarism" of those five great centuries (1000–1500). As we have seen, "Gothic" was meant to be a term of contempt, and to this day the French language does not fully recognize the difference between the Dark Ages and the true Middle Ages; the whole millennium from the fall of Rome to the Revival of Learning was long supposed to have been engulfed in the same night of ignorance and fear. This adverse view lingered among nineteenth century republicans. Even Michelet and Victor Hugo denounced, as freethinkers and democrats, what they once had loved as artists and poets. What struck them most in the age of faith and chivalry was the stifling of thought and the degradation of the poor. There is a lurid legend of the Middle Ages, a "Gothic" tale of terror; the fires of the Inquisition, the crypt in which a man is left to rot alive, the dreadful ingenuity of the torture chamber are accepted as valid symbols.

There is a counterpart, the Golden Legend of the Middle Ages. The period became a vanished utopia. The thirteenth was proclaimed "greatest of centuries." Of this idealization, there are three principal forms. First, there was mere picturesque enjoyment, the Froissart–Walter Scott tradition, all adventure and gay romance, love, faith, and heroism happily blending in the resplendent knight, Crusades, quests and tournaments, "the shield, the pennon and the plume." When this Gothic revival had spent itself, there came the esthetic socialism of Ruskin and William Morris. This was a dream world not of steel-clad warriors, but of artisans practicing their craft with loving scrupulous care, their humblest task illumined with a religious glow—a paradise for pious house decorators. Deepest and most enduring, there was—there is —the conception of the medieval period as an age of faith so absolute, so all-embracing, so organic, that the political, social, economic institutions, the art and thought of the time, all bore the mark of the same sovereign unity. This is the view of Paul Claudel and Jacques Maritain, best expressed in our language by Henry Adams in his *Mont-Saint-Michel and Chartres.*

It is a truly noble conception. Unfortunately, it is a dream. The historian who does not soar on the wings of faith sees in the Middle Ages an epoch, not of flawless unity, but of complexity, bewilderment and inner strife.[10] In the fourth and fifth centuries, three elements were violently thrown together: the tradition of pagan and imperial Rome, Christianity, and a flood of barbarians. The result was chaos. Out of this chaos, the medieval world, like Milton's lion, "now half appeared, pawing to get free his hinder parts." The Renaissance introduced no new principle. Through the irresistible agency of time, the three elements have become more intimately blended. The old contradictions in our culture still exist, but they are not so glaring as seven hundred years ago.

It was Christianity that cemented together the ruins of the ancient world and the rough-hewn block of Teutonic barbarism. Christianity is embodied in the church, and the constant dream of the church, her prime *raison d'être,* has been to establish and maintain unity. All attempts at material unity proved abortive in the Middle Ages; the theocratic ideal of Gregory VII failed almost as lamentably as the imperial ideal of the Hohenstaufen; the wrath and despair of Dante are the witnesses of that failure. What about spiritual unity, the only unity that fully deserves the name? Christianity was supreme, no doubt; but medieval Christianity was not one. The Carthusian ascetic, the mendicant in the market place, the political abbot like Suger, the feudal bishop, the school-

---

[10] With the perspective of half a millennium, a civilization easily appears simple and harmonious enough compared with the tangle and darkness through which we are groping today. Such is the virtue of remoteness that, five hundred years hence, some future Henry Adams may write a book on *Chungking, Washington and Moscow: A Study in Twentieth Century Unity.*

man, the Templar present a picturesque and varied gallery. But this brilliant diversity is not what chiefly concerns us. The essential point is that the many forms of medieval Christianity were not the manifestation of the same soul.

By the side of the most exalted mysticism, we find in the Middle Ages an ecclesiasticism which had donned the garments and been infected with the spirit of imperial Rome; a rationalism which attempted to co-ordinate Aristotle and Holy Writ; among the masses, a teeming polytheism, a rank fetishism, an unblushing worship of images and relics. By the time it reached the west, Christianity had become a mass of contradictions. A universal faith, it trailed with it the Hebrew Bible, the embodiment of fierce tribal pride. An Oriental religion, charged with the subtlety of the Alexandrian intellect, the fruit of an ancient, overrefined culture, it was suddenly turned over to eager but rough children. A religion of other-worldliness and superhuman perfection, it had to be adjusted to the habits of life of very solid and choleric barbarians. The very essence of the Christian spirit, meekness and love, negated the foundations of the feudal world, force and pride.

Because of these unreconciled contradictions, we are still disconcerted by the unaccountable flight of medieval thought. The men of that time pass from the secular to the spiritual plane, from sober fact to allegory, from reason to custom, from charity to ferocity, from childishness to decadent subtlety, with what appears to us capricious abruptness. The most tempting explanation is that the Middle Ages were simply immature. There is hardly a puzzling trait of medieval psychology that is not found in the children of today. Trust and effusive affection, with streaks of cruelty, selfishness, violence; vagueness in essentials coupled with painful literalness and formalism; implicit faith in authority with outbursts of fierce rebellion; and, above all, no capacity, no desire, to draw a sharp line between sober fact and make-believe: all these elements existed in castle and cloister, *as they exist in the modern nursery.* Self-control and the critical sense were not fully developed. Individuals were not deficient in reasoning power, strength of purpose or ripe experience; there were magnificent, fully adult personalities in the Middle Ages. But the spirit of the times had barely reached adolescence.

CHRONOLOGICAL SUMMARY, 987–1499

I. CAPETIAN DYNASTY, DIRECT LINE

HUGH CAPET	987–996
ROBERT THE PIOUS	996–1031
HENRY I	1031–1060
PHILIP I	1060–1108
Norman conquest of England	1066
Song of Roland	ca. 1080
First Crusade	1095–1099
LOUIS VI THE FAT (Abbot Suger, adviser)	1108–1137
War with England	1119
Abélard condemned	1122
LOUIS VII THE YOUNG	1137–1180
Second Crusade	1147–1149
Henry of Anjou (Plantagenet)	1152–1154
marries Eleanor of Aquitaine, 1152	
becomes king of England, 1154	
Chrétien de Troyes, *Perceval* etc.	ca. 1170–1180
PHILIP II AUGUSTUS	1180–1223
Third Crusade	1191
University of Paris chartered	ca. 1200
Conflict with England	1194–1214
Richard Coeur-de-Lion and John Lackland	
Victory of Bouvines, 1214	
LOUIS VIII	1223–1226
Albigensian Crusade	1179–1226
LOUIS IX, SAINT LOUIS	1226–1270
Guillaume de Lorris, *Romance of the Rose,* Part I	ca. 1237
Victories of Taillebourg and Saintes	1242
Crusade in Egypt led by Louis IX	1248–1254
Parliament of Paris established	1258

Treaty of Paris   1259
Crusade, and death of Louis IX before Tunis   1270

PHILIP III THE BOLD   1270–1285
Commoner granted patent of nobility   1274
Jehan de Meung: *Romance of the Rose*, Part II   1277

PHILIP IV THE FAIR   1285–1314
Quarrel with Boniface VIII   1294–1302
Defeated at Courtrai   1302
States-General, Paris   1302
Joinville, *Life of Saint Louis*   1309
Templars prosecuted   1307–1313

LOUIS X THE QUARRELSOME   1314–1316
All Frenchmen declared "free according to law of
  nature"   1315

PHILIP V THE TALL   1316–1322

JOHN I dies at birth   1322

CHARLES IV THE FAIR   1322–1328

II. CAPETIAN DYNASTY: VALOIS BRANCH

PHILIP VI OF VALOIS   1328–1350
Second Hundred Years' War begins   1337
Defeat of Crécy (Cressy), first use of gunpowder   1346
Loss of Calais   1347
Dauphiné acquired   1349

JOHN II THE GOOD   1350–1364
Defeat of Poitiers, King John prisoner of the English   1356
States-General, Etienne Marcel leads reformers   1357
"Jacquerie," rebellion of peasants, crushed   1358
Treaty of Bretigny   1360

CHARLES V THE WISE   1364–1380
Bertrand du Guesclin, constable, in command

CHARLES VI   1380–1422
Froissart, *Chronicles*   1373–1404 (?)

Feud between Armagnacs and Bourguignons   1410 seq
Defeat of Azincourt (Agincourt)   1415
Treaty of Troyes   1420

CHARLES VII THE WELL-SERVED   1422–1461
Joan of Arc   1429–1431
  raises siege of Orléans, 1429
  has Charles crowned at Rheims, 1429
  condemned and burned at Rouen, 1431
Treaty of Arras with Burgundy   1435
Permanent army organized   1445
Battle of Formigny, Normandy reconquered   1450
Battle of Castillon, Guyenne reconquered   1453

LOUIS XI   1461–1483
François Villon, *Grand Testament*   1461
Leagues of the Public Weal
  (Nobles vs. king)   1465–1472
Conflict with Charles the Reckless of Burgundy 1467–1477

CHARLES VIII
Commines, *Reign of Louis XI*   1483–1498
Brittany united with France, 1491, not final until 1547
Expedition to Naples   1494

LOUIS XII FATHER OF THE PEOPLE   1498–1515
Conquers Milan   1499

CHAPTER V

The Classical Age

1. THE RENAISSANCE AND THE ITALIAN WARS

"For that time was darksome, obscured with clouds of ignorance, and savoring a little of the infelicity and calamity of
the Goths who had, wherever they set footing, destroyed all
good literature; which, in my age, hath by divine goodness
been restored into its former light and dignity." [1] These words,
addressed by Gargantua to his son Pantagruel, express with
all possible definiteness the very spirit of the sixteenth
century Renaissance. It was a deliberate condemnation of
"Gothic" barbarism, an eager return to the light of antiquity.
Such it was felt to be at the time; such it remained in the
minds of generation after generation for three centuries.

Yet if the word Renaissance, a *rebirth*, has any meaning,
it applies more literally to the eleventh century than to the
sixteenth. At that time, we find the evidences of restored confidence and restless energy in every field: in the great movement
of the first Crusade; in the rapid progress of Romanesque
architecture from a debased pastiche of the Byzantine to an
art singularly robust and original; in the transformation of
that art into early Gothic; in the growth of definite vernacular
literatures; in the first faint adumbrations of a national or-
ganism and of a national feeling. The very dynasties that
ruled in the eleventh century are still represented today; and

[1] Rabelais, *Gargantua and Pantagruel*, Book II, Chapter VIII, Urquhart's
translation.

our culture has never known again such an eclipse as that of the Dark Ages. Then indeed was *our* world born.

This great revival, full of conflict and power, culminated in the thirteenth century. The medieval period closed appropriately with the vision of Dante, a *Summa Poetica* to be placed by the side of the *Summa Theologica* of St. Thomas Aquinas, by the side also of those supreme poems and treatises in stone, the cathedrals of Chartres and Paris, of Rheims and Amiens. And after that? Not the dark again; but, in France at any rate, a strange sickly twilight in which both faith and reason nearly lost their way. The true Middle Ages ended with the direct line of the Capetians (1328), and perhaps even before.

Why this arrested growth? First of all because the medieval mind allowed itself to be clogged with custom, a defeatist clinging to the past, right or wrong. And chiefly because the "light of the world," Christian thought, had lost much of its pure effulgence. The Papacy suffered greatly in prestige from the "Babylonian" captivity at Avignon (1309–1376) and from the Great Schism. The University of Paris was stifled by the overgrowth of formal scholasticism. St. Thomas had arrayed the data of revelation according to the form of Aristotelian logic; but he had performed his task almost too well. His successors, incapable of transcending him, lost themselves in the intricate maze of their own subtle absurdity. The beacon set on Mount Saint Genevieve [2] now diffused palpable darkness.

So Rabelais (1494?–1553) was not wholly wrong in referring to the period from which France was just emerging as "darksome, obscured with clouds of ignorance." But the darkness was not absolute, only a darkening. In its recovery of vigor and daring, the sixteenth century was continuing the thirteenth, not the third.

The spirit of the Renaissance was not a return, but an onward surge. It was manifested in the vital inventions—

[2] The hill in the Latin Quarter or university district of Paris.

gunpowder, compass, printing press—and in the world-wide
explorations fully as much as in classical scholarship. The influence of a few Greek manuscripts peddled by refugee gram-
marians after 1453 has been grossly overemphasized. The
West had never lost touch with Constantinople; but it had
failed to understand its veritable treasure. The rediscovery
of antiquity was in fact self-discovery. The light was within,
not twenty centuries back. The age of Rabelais found with
delight that it had at last grown equal to Greek art and
thought. The keynote of the Renaissance was not imitation
but energy, which is freedom and hope. Rabelais was incidentally a pedant; but he stands above all for an enormous
joy of living. He reveled in generous wines and copious fare
but it was for knowledge and experience that his gluttony was
truly unappeasable. The men of that age did not shatter their
medieval cell to crawl into a classic dungeon. The motto on
the gate of Rabelais' dream university, the Abbey of Thélème,
is not, "Follow ancient wisdom," but, "Do as you list," *Fais
que vouldras.*

Italy had not suffered spiritually to the same extent as the
north from the depression and confusion of the fourteenth
and fifteenth centuries. Dante, the epitome of the Middle
Ages, was already a mature and conscious artist; and he was
immediately followed by Petrarch and Boccaccio. Italy at
that time was manifestly the torch bearer. The men of the
French Renaissance imagined that they were attempting to
recapture antiquity: in fact, their obvious but unconfessed
goal was to catch up with Italy. For generations, French art
was a blend of local tradition with Italianate ornaments. The
châteaux of the Loire region and in particular Chambord,
in Paris the City Hall, the delightful churches of St. Etienne-
du-Mont and St. Eustache still offer a bold and picturesque
medieval silhouette; the details only come from beyond the
Alps; and the direct influence of Greece is surprisingly small.
The same thing holds true for literature. Aristotle became

the autocrat of poetics, as he had been the supreme master of logic; but it was Aristotle interpreted and at times twisted by Italian scholars. The French poets of The Pléiade, Ronsard, du Bellay, Baïf pastiched elaborate odes from the Greek, and these were still-born; but they made magnificent use of the sonnet, which they had borrowed from the Petrarchan school.

For half a century (1494–1544) and under three kings, the French indulged in the costly diversion known as the Italian Wars. It is often said that they brought back the Renaissance from these expeditions, as though it were a chance infection. As a matter of fact, they went over the Alps in quest of that glorious booty, still unnamed. It was the prestige of Italy that drew them southward. If the kings had had a clear sense of the country's natural line of expansion, they should have turned their eyes toward the north. But they ignored Lille, Brussels, Antwerp, in their eagerness to clutch at Naples or Milan. Charles VIII (1483–1498) a fantastic youth, Louis XII (1498–1515) a sane and kindly king, Francis I (1515–1547) haunted with dreams of pleasure and magnificence, all rushed to Italy as though under a spell. There was not an atom of realistic sense in these triumphant and disastrous cavalcades: kings and nobles, instinctively, obeyed the fascination of Italy the "Mother of Arts as once of Arms."

The reign of Francis I (1515–1547) was at first the jocund day of the French Renaissance. The king was young, handsome, chivalrous, artistic. For his *début,* he had won a brilliant victory at Marignano (1515) over the Swiss, then the most expert fighters in Europe; and—a charming gesture—he wanted to be made a knight by Bayard, "the knight without fear and without reproach." He appeared then as the friend of Leonardo da Vinci, as the builder of the new Louvre and of Fontainebleau, as the founder of the great humanistic school, the Royal College, which still exists as the Collège de France. The country knew internal peace, and thanks to the economic trans-

formation throughout Europe, it enjoyed a substantial measure of prosperity. The period like the king, had undeniable
glamor. It still remains in the memory of the French as a
vision of learning and luxury, of elegance and valor.

But the morning glow soon turned to gray. Francis I, the
refulgent young knight, under the curse of dissolute living,
fell into early decay. The bitterness of religious strife, without
as yet breaking into open war, was increasing beyond control.
And the Italian wars, which at first had been gay adventures,
widened into a bitter and perilous conflict between the House
of France and the House of Austria.

For the French were not the only foreigners who had
swooped down upon Italy attracted by the prestige of the land
and the dissensions among the Italian states. Germans and
Spaniards were there also, and in Emperor Charles V, Francis I encountered a formidable rival. Charles had inherited
many lands: the Austrian domains of his grandfather Maximilian I; the Netherlands and Franche-Comté which had belonged to the Duke of Burgundy; Aragon and Castile, with
their Italian dependencies Naples, Sicily, and Sardinia. He
was the lord of the fabulous newly discovered Indies; and in
1519, he was elected emperor. France felt dwarfed and en-
circled. To resist the overlordship of Charles V seemed a
matter of national life or death.

Charles V was not merely the more powerful of the two;
he was also the shrewder. With uneasy lulls, the war between
Valois and Hapsburg raged for over thirty years (1522–1559);
and France was repeatedly on the brink of disaster. In 1525
King Francis was defeated and captured at Pavia; taken as a
prisoner to Madrid, he had to sign away some of his richest
provinces. But, although he had taken Bayard as his model,
Francis could be as "realistic" as any modern diplomat. Released from captivity, he repudiated the treaty of Madrid, as
a pact signed under duress. And, although he bore the title of

His Most Christian Majesty and was repeatedly the ally of the Pope, he also sought the assistance of the Grand Turk and of the German Protestants.

Charles V, in spite of his vast resources and of his political skill, found it difficult to keep his unwieldy empire together. The Lutheran Revolt in Germany, which had turned into actual warfare, proved a constant source of weakness to him. So he had to be satisfied with a compromise peace with Francis at Crespy-en-Valois in 1544; and in weariness he retired to a cloister in 1555–1556. The long and ruinous struggle for preserving the balance of power flared up again between the sons of the original contestants and was closed at last by the treaty of Cateau-Cambresis in 1559. The Italian dream of the Valois kings had faded. Yet, in spite of many defeats, French national pride and French national consciousness had grown. The Italian Wars opened the first diplomatic and military contest that had the whole of Europe for its theater. In 1526, when Burgundy was ceded to Charles V, the deputies of that province asserted their right and their will to remain French. Under the son of Francis I, Henry II (1547–1559), France resumed the course of her natural expansion; she recovered Calais and acquired stepping stones in Lorraine, the three bishoprics of Metz, Toul, and Verdun.

2. THE REFORMATION

The Reformation was at first a renaissance. It also was a manifestation of energy, confidence, and hope. Man had so grown in mental stature that he could reject mere custom, hoary as it might be, and brand it as abuse and superstition. The same robust joy is notable in the early reformers as in the Renaissance scholars. Luther's table talks reveal much the same lust for life as Rabelais' enormous fantasies. It was Ulrich von Hutten, a reformer, who best expressed the exultant feeling of the awakening: "The wind of freedom blows!" "O time! It is a joy to be alive!"

We are apt to think of *the* Reformation as a unique event in European history: Luther's bold defiance, and the birth of Protestantism. This interpretation is too narrow. There were many reformations in the long existence of the Christian church; and that of the sixteenth century assumed many forms. The church has a divine mission but it has to be carried out by earthly means; she spurns power and riches but they cling to her in spite of her yearning for humility; she transcends reason yet must express herself through the language of human reason. These inevitable antinomies create eternal tensions and the need for constant readjustment. The church had repeatedly to be saved from barbarism or worldly corruption: by the Benedictine discipline in the sixth century, by energetic popes and the Cluniac order in the eleventh, by the passionate zeal and democratic methods of the Friars in the thirteenth. The reformer had his place under the new dispensation, as the prophet under the old. It was universally felt in the fifteenth century that a new cleansing of the church was due. There had been reforming movements in England, in Bohemia, in Italy, as well as in Germany and France. All this indicated a crisis; it need not have meant a schism.

In France, the reforming spirit in the course of the sixteenth and seventeenth centuries assumed not one but at least four different forms: Gallicanism, Humanism, Calvinism, and the Tridentine Counter-Reformation.

We have already defined Gallicanism. It insisted on the autonomy of the French church. The sacred character of the French monarchy, since the baptism of Clovis, had conferred upon the king a quasi-ecclesiastical authority. This long tradition had been strengthened by the prestige of Saint Louis. It was finally hardened into the Pragmatic Sanction of Bourges issued by Charles VII in 1438; the king, at a time when the power of Rome was at its lowest ebb, openly claimed the right to supervise, if not to dictate, the discipline of the French church. Louis XI receded from this extreme position. Francis I, in 1515–1516, concluded with the Pope a concordat which recognized the partnership between the temporal and the spiritual. That instrument remained in force for nearly three hundred years; but the original ambiguities of the compromise were never dispelled. As a matter of doctrine, the claims of the Pope remained absolute; but the kings never abandoned their prerogative as protectors of the French, or Gallican, church. This position was reasserted in 1682 by the Declaration of the Four Articles drawn up by Bossuet, bishop of Meaux, voted by the Assembly of the French clergy, and solemnly adopted as the law of the state. The Gallican idea broke down at the time of the French Revolution just because the Assembly, without a particle of "divine right," attempted to push it to its logical extreme. It was reintroduced by Napoleon in his new concordat (1801–1802), almost surreptitiously, in the form of unilateral additional articles. It remained an issue until the final separation of church and state in 1905.

Now the desire for exactly this kind of autonomy—a national church closely associated with the national sovereign—played a great part in the Lutheran Reformation as well as in the Anglican. There were no doubt theological problems involved. But Henry VIII and a number of German princes welcomed first of all a vast increase in their power and in their wealth. This worldly incentive did not exist for the French kings. They were the associates rather than the subjects of Rome. A rebellion against the hierarchy, far from increasing the royal power, would have threatened it.

The second aspect of the reforming spirit we have called the humanistic. It was the rejection of ecclesiastical abuses and superstitions, the assertion that every man has the right to be guided by his own conscience and his own reason, in other words complete freedom of thought in religious matters. This was the spirit of the early Humanists, and of Erasmus in particular; its greatest exponent in France was Rabelais. This spirit never turned into a sect, for that would have been the denial of its own principle; and, because it has neither name nor organization, it has been ignored by many students of French religious history. Yet it represents one of the essential elements in the French soul. The men in that tradition showed no desire to destroy the national church, because they knew what spiritual treasures were associated with it. Rabelais and Montaigne in the sixteenth century, Descartes and Molière in the seventeenth did not abjure Catholicism. Voltaire in the eighteenth insisted on remaining within the fold: he was, like Satan in the Book of Job, the assayer fulfilling the purpose of the Lord. In the nineteenth century, Lamennais, Lamartine, Michelet, Victor Hugo were the heirs of that free religious thought. It is by no means extinct today.

These two factors, the Gallicanism of the kings and the complete emancipation of the Humanists explain the comparative failure of the third aspect of the Reformation in France: of Protestantism in the formal sense of the term and particularly of Calvinism. Yet the Protestant movement was by no means negligible. Lefebvre d'Etaples before Calvin won a number of earnest souls. Among them was Marguerite of Angoulême, queen of Navarre, a gifted Renaissance princess and the beloved sister of Francis I. John Calvin was French of the French, although he failed to conquer France. Born at Noyon in Picardy (1509), he was active as a very young man in the University of Paris (1533). But it was as the theocratic ruler of Geneva (1541–1564) that he won his world-wide fame. To the French, Calvin did not offer freedom, but a sterner, heavier yoke. To the pure souls who wanted to flee the corruption of the Valois court, Calvin's asceticism was not the only possible refuge, for the church had many austere monastic orders. There was probably in France a time when the reform-

ing spirit balanced the conservative; Francis I himself was
finely poised between the two tendencies. But that was before
Calvin had sharpened the issue to the point of creating a
schism. France as a whole did not want to break with her past.
Genuine Huguenots in France were a vigorous, indeed an
admirable body of men; but they remained a very small minority.

What we have called the fourth aspect of the Reformation
is known in history as the Counter-Reformation. It began
with the Council of Trent (1545–1563) and was formulated
in the Tridentine Decrees. Its effects were not fully felt in
France until the end of the religious wars, that is to say until
the seventeenth century. But they were profound and they
are too often passed over in silence by Protestant historians.
This development is part of the great spiritual drama that we
call the Reformation. There was in the French church under
Henry IV, Louis XIII, and Louis XIV a remarkable revival of
discipline, piety, and learning. The abbey of Port-Royal, for
instance, was transformed by a young abbess from a pleasant
country house into a center of stern, well-regulated religious
life. The Oratorians founded by Cardinal de Bérulle, the
St. Sulpice Seminary under M. Olier, the Trappist Cistercians,
reborn under Abbot de Rancé and many other contemplative
or charitable orders show the extraordinary vitality of the
French church in that period. A faith represented by St.
François de Sales, St. Vincent de Paul, Arnauld, Pascal,
Bourdaloue, Bossuet, Fénelon shows no sign of diminishing
vigor. This spiritual harvest was reaped in the seventeenth
century, but the seeds had been sown in the sixteenth. This
must be remembered: if the majority of the French turned a
deaf ear to the preaching of Calvin, it is not because they were
lacking in religious earnestness and not because they failed
to recognize the need for a thorough reform. But they wanted
to reform themselves within their own tradition; and above

all, they wanted a freedom not arbitrarily limited, a freedom of their own choice.

In 1560, the religious wars, looming for a quarter of a century, broke out at last with incredible fury. It was a protracted, confused, deadly squabble, tragic without grandeur. Martyrs and heroes were not lacking; yet what remains clear in our memory is the acrimonious pedantry of the theologians, shrill amid the brutalities of hired or fanatical cutthroats. Atrocities repaid atrocities; the Huguenot, Captain des Adrets, vied in ruthlessness with the Catholic, Blaise de Montluc.

The word "religious" applied to these wars is a misnomer, and indeed a sacrilege. Religion merely added a touch of intensity to another surge of feudal anarchy. As in the darkest days of the Hundred Years' War, princely families, oblivious of king and country, were fighting for the spoils. Guises (or Lorraine) and Bourbons-Condés, worse than Armagnacs and Bourguignons, were using their creed as a cloak.

This explosion of disorder had one essential cause: the weakening of the royal power. Henry II (1547–1559), who was not a remarkable prince, had yet managed to curb actual hostilities. But at his death, power fell into the hands of his widow, Catherine de Médicis. Between Huguenots and Catholic *Guisards*, the Queen Mother could only steer a panic-stricken course, punctuating deceit with assassination. She was the actual ruler under the reigns of her three degenerate sons, Francis II (1559–1560), Charles IX (1560–1574) and Henry III (1574–1589).

Low cunning is the straightest path to crime. The climax was reached in 1572. A marriage was arranged between Henry of Bourbon, king of Navarre, a Protestant leader, and Margaret of Valois, a Catholic princess, the sister of Charles IX. Prominent Huguenots and among them one of the greatest figures of the time, Admiral de Coligny, were attracted to

Paris for the ceremony; and on the night of St. Bartholomew (August 23–24th), thousands of them were massacred by fanatical ruffians.

This senseless fury failed to restore peace. There had been three wars between 1560 and 1572; there were five between 1572 and 1589. The king ceased to be a ruler, or even an arbiter; his party became merely a third faction, in addition to Huguenots and Catholic Guisards. From 1585 to 1588, it happened that the leaders of all three factions were called Henry. Henry, duke of Guise, head of the Catholic League, the ally of Spain, ruled the capital without a formal title and was called "the king of Paris." He was murdered at Blois in 1588. Henry III, the Valois king, was assassinated in his turn in 1589. The third Henry, Henry of Bourbon, king of Navarre, was ultimately to share the same fate in 1610.

3: THE HEALER: HENRY IV

Lovers of dramatic romance still relish the *haut goût* of that age, its Baudelairian blend of depravity and religious bigotry, of morbid refinement and frantic violence; Voltaire called that nightmare "a silken robe smeared with blood." Chancellor de l'Hôpital preached tolerance in vain. Yet sanity, which unfortunately is seldom dynamic, asserted itself at last. A Gascon gentleman, Michel Eyquem de Montaigne (1533–1592) by name, exposed in his *Essays* the cruel vanity of all fanaticism. What certainty does man possess that he should be ready, for the sake of hazardous convictions, to "roast his fellow-man alive"? Our nature is unstable as water; and a survey of opinions once held to be sacrosanct reveals only a tangled mass of superstitions. The very title of the work is a lesson in modesty; for the meaning of *essays* is *attempts*. The book, by turns familiar, profound and quaintly pedantic, is not words on paper, but a man—a man who with smiling unassuming courage dares to challenge our most cherished self-delusions. He is not a cynic and not even a skeptic in the purely negative sense of the term. He is a true humanist, who despises pretenses, abhors cruelty, and does not run away from the humble truth. Without Montaigne, neither Descartes the rationalist nor even Pascal the mystic would have been possible. Every philosopher, before he expounds the secrets of the universe; every statesman, before he sends men to slaughter, should ponder the *Essays* of Montaigne.

Montaigne played no part in politics; but the fundamental sanity which had found a voice in him finally assured the triumph of Henry IV. The triumph was arduous and slow; for the situation at the death of Henry III was a curious one. The legitimate heir to the throne was Henry of Bourbon, king of Navarre, a Protestant, and the leader in the field of a small virulent minority. But it happened that this Huguenot king was the least Calvinistic of men. He shared neither the asceticism of the Genevan master, nor his implacable logic, nor his ruthless autocratic temperament. Henry had lived at the Valois court and was stained by its corruption; he had fought at the head of partisan bands and the brutality of camp life had coarsened him. Yet he was at heart humane, shrewd, temperate. His ideal was not a new Jerusalem, but the good life and the good living of Rabelais, toned down by adversity and by the healthy skepticism of Montaigne. But he was a Montaigne on horseback, his white plume waving with gay defiance. He was, according to the folksong, a triple-threat man: he could drink, he could fight, and he could make love. Vivid, lusty, swearing and rollicking, he had been taught patience and cunning. With the same dramatic sense as Benjamin Franklin, he knew how to cultivate his own legend, to play his own part with conscious perfection.

The blend of kindly humor and soldierly energy in Henry IV proved irresistible. He alone could have effected the necessary compromises without a disastrous loss of prestige. He called his conversion, dictated by political motives, "turning somersault," too picturesque a phrase for an ardent believer; and he averred with a wink that "Paris was well worth a Mass" (1593). Yet, miraculously, his Gascon smile on this solemn occasion detracted nothing from his dignity. He could appease his enemies and buy them off, yet remain unquestionably the master. With a merry twinkle that softened the threat, he would allude to the "big stick" he had in reserve, the force that could impose peace if persuasion should fail, "*bâton qui porte paix.*"

His opportunism, cheerful and wary, firm and supple, won the day. A party had arisen, *les Politiques*, which said to Leaguers and Huguenots: "A plague on both your houses!" In the name of the Parisian bourgeoisie, six authors joined in bringing forth the *Satire Ménippée.* The mocking common sense of that inspired lampoon against fanaticism proved irresistible: in France, it is fatal to be ridiculous. Henry was crowned at Chartres in 1594. Paris surrendered to him; and in 1598, he issued the Edict of Nantes which he hoped would end the politico-religious conflict. The settlement was a truce made acceptable through weariness rather than through genuine tolerance and it contained at least one factor of further strife: the Protestants, given fortified cities of refuge, remained an armed self-governing minority within the state. But the intentions were generous and wise and the immediate results were good. Reasonableness did not have an easy victory; Henry had to use gentle but persistent pressure on his courts of justice (*parlements*) before they would register the great edict.

With peace restored, prosperity returned. Henry's constant companion and friend, Sully, proved an uninspired but very able administrator. New industries were created—and Sully, like Jefferson an inveterate agrarian, grumbled. Great public works were undertaken, the first model of far-sighted city planning: the Place Dauphiné and the New Bridge (*Pont*

EXTENSION OF THE FRENCH FRONTIERS
16th to 18th centuries

ENGLAND

English Channel

THE EMPIRE, 1648

Rhine R.

LILLE, 1668
MAUBEUGE, 1678
CALAIS, 1559
MARIENBOURG, 1659
AIRE, 1678
PHILIPPEVILLE, 1659
ARTOIS, 1659
CHARLEMONT, 1678
BOUILLON, 1678
MONTMEDY, 1659
LONGWY, 1679
SAARLOUIS, 1680
CAMBRAY, 1678
AVESNES, 1659
SEDAN, 1642
STENAY, 1641
CLERMONT, 1632
DUCHY OF BAR
DUCHY OF LORRAINE, 1766

Arras
Dieppe
Havre de Grace
Rouen
PARIS
Versailles
Chartres
Orleans
Strasbourg
Brest
Rennes
Angers
Nantes
Dijon
Besancon
Nevers
Chalon
SUNDGAU, 1648
FRANCHE COMTE, 1674-1678
GEX
BRESSE - BUGEY, 1601

F R A N C E

Miles
0   50   100
Kilometres
0   80   160

La Rochelle
Jarnan
Clermont
Macon
Lyons
Vienne

Bay of Biscay

Bordeaux
Garonne R.
Valence

SAVOY

DUCHY OF ALBRET, 1607
COUNTY OF ARMAGNAC, 1607

Avignon
Aix
Arles
Marseilles

Bayonne
Pau
Toulouse
Montpellier
Narbonne

KINGDOM OF NAVARRE, 1620
COUNTY OF FOIX, 1607
COUNTY OF BIGORRE, 1607
CERDAGNE

COUNTY OF ROUSSILLON, 1659

S P A I N

Mediterranean Sea

Neuf) in Paris combine, like the king himself, dignity with a smiling charm.

Henry's chief service to his race, however, was to renew and to strengthen the bond between dynasty and people. The Valois kings almost to a man had been aristocrats, contemptuous of the herd. Henry's genuine goodness of heart and keen political sense impelled him to covet and to deserve *popularity*. Nothing will serve but the cliché: "He made his name a household word." He could be humorous and familiar; but even his jesting had a practical side. His homely formula, "A chicken in the pot for every peasant on Sunday," is the perfection of a political slogan. He and Saint Louis form an oddly assorted pair; they were the two sovereigns who felt sympathy for their humblest subjects. Louis IX had striven to bring them justice; Henry wished them a modicum of luxury. These two, the saint and the sinner, were the great assets of the dynasty because they lived in the people's memory as "do-gooders." The throne preserved, until 1789, that hoard of democratic good will. The harshness of Richelieu, the extravagance of Louis XIV, the frivolousness of Louis XV, could not completely exhaust it. In the dawn of the Revolution, the people said of Louis XVI: "Henry IV has been restored to us"; and Louis almost responded to this call of a people's love.

Henry IV was murdered by a fanatic in 1610, in time perhaps to be saved from disastrous folly. He was ready to embark, for no clear cause and without adequate preparation, on an ambitious foreign policy which might have jeopardized the still precarious revival of French prosperity. His Huguenot friend and chief adviser, Sully, ascribed to him a "grand design" for the reconstruction and peaceful governance of Europe. Such a thought may have flitted through the king's active and generous mind; the definite plan was probably Sully's.

4. CLASSICAL DISCIPLINE: RICHELIEU

France had seen anarchy, and recoiled; in the seventeenth century she was to extol, in reaction, the ideal of discipline and to submit with eagerness to its very excesses. The first half of the century marked in every field a conscious effort toward order. Manners, language, literature, religion were tamed and purified, even though originality had to be mutilated. Malherbe, "tyrant of words and syllables," a stiff vigorous poet and a surly pedant, won the day against the freer fantasy of Mathurin Régnier and Théophile de Viau. In government, the same progress was achieved but not without cruel jerks: too much depended upon a few all-powerful individuals. Henry IV had been a miracle of tactful firmness; his widow, Marie de Médicis, who became regent, was weak and muddle-headed. Under her favorites, the store of gold, authority and good will left by the wise king was frittered away. It took the ruthless hand of Richelieu (1624–1642) to check the mad course toward renewed chaos.

Richelieu's portrait, by Philippe de Champaigne, shows him in his resolute, well-knit complexity—of the priest, only the vestments; the energetic features of a soldier accented by the defiant moustache and pointed beard of a musketeer; and the steady, searching, distant gaze of the statesman. A scion of the lesser nobility, he had won his way at the court of Louis XIII through the favor of the Queen Mother, Marie de Médicis. When he reached power, he discarded her as a worth-less instrument. He fought his battle alone: a nod from Louis, and the pack of enraged courtiers would have been upon him. But in his taciturn way, the king upheld his minister and Richelieu, long ailing, died in harness.

Richelieu claimed to have had three principal aims: to check the power of the Protestants, that of the feudal nobility, and that of the House of Austria. He conquered the last strong-hold of the Protestants, La Rochelle, and reduced them to the common law; but he respected their religious freedom and he had Huguenots among his most trusted commanders. He struck hard at the last remnants of the feudal spirit: some of the highest in the land because they had defied the king's power were beheaded. Castles that could be used as private fortresses were dismantled: the great cardinal-duke was a more ruthless destroyer than were the Jacobins. Finally, he fought over again, but with greater success, the battle of Francis I against the Hapsburg hegemony. He, a prince of the church, hired German and Swedish Protestants against His Catholic majesty, the emperor. France took part, indirectly at first, in the Thirty Years' War. After Richelieu's death, but thanks to his policy, the treaties of Westphalia (1648) and of the Pyrenees (1659) made the supremacy of France apparently absolute.

Power was the sole passion of Richelieu's somber, warped, frustrated nature. He clutched at it with iron claws just because it was so precarious. His conscience as a churchman and as a subject was at ease: he was serving the anointed king. Richelieu made sharper a dangerous, distorted ideal of absolute dominion and prestige. Louis XIV only continued his work; Napoleon at his worst only carried it to its logical extreme. Richelieu infected the national mind with his own virus. He never was beloved; but, even in our own days, there are men who are still haunted with his dream; and it is not orthodox in republican France to consider Richelieu as an evil genius.

Evil perhaps, but the man and the work were nonetheless somberly impressive. Richelieu is a hero of the will, not an apostle of gentle light. In this he was typical of a whole generation. The dramatist Corneille is the poet, not of duty, but of will power; his heroes, who may be fanatics like young Horatius or criminals like Medea, are as determined, as inflexible, as Richelieu himself. And this holds true of the great scientist and philosopher René Descartes. Today, it is not his excessive rationalism, his reconstruction of the world on the sole basis of conscious thought that most impress us: it is his unflinching courage. He dared to reject all outward and traditional authority and to explore alone the depths of his own doubt, until he could doubt no more. A royalist and a Catholic, he is one of the forefathers of democracy; for he believed that the common man had in him the power to judge rightly. Jacques Maritain, the great Neo-Thomist philosopher, calls Cartesianism "France's national sin." He may have added in the secret of his heart: *Felix Culpa!* Happy transgression! For Descartes made it possible for the passionate Blaise Pascal to say: "The whole dignity of man consists in thought."

About the year 1636, it may be said that the new synthesis— classical in art, rationalistic in philosophy, absolute in government—had reached its perfect focus. By that time, Richelieu had thwarted the worst intrigues against his rule; the queen-mother had been exiled, the king's brother humiliated, the proudest of the nobles, Montmorency, executed. In 1635, the academy was formally founded, with the intention of imposing discipline upon literature. In 1636 appeared *Le Cid* by Corneille, the first unmistakable masterpiece of French classical tragedy. In 1637, Descartes brought out his *Discourse on Method*. The age was fearless, proud of order as a condition of strength; but there was stiffness and gloom in its very grandeur. Surely history is a kaleidoscope. The face of France no longer wore the smile of Henry IV and Montaigne, aware of human frailty, modest and indulgent in its shrewd irony. Yet Richelieu, Corneille, Descartes cannot be expunged from the French tradition; it was their spirit that preserved France in 1940.

Richelieu did his work cruelly, wastefully, but thoroughly; so thoroughly that the foreign origin, the cowardice, the corruption of his successor, Cardinal Mazarin, could endanger but not ruin it. Louis XIII had died in 1643. With a five-year-old king, the regent a foolish queen, her favorite as actual ruler, no wonder the forces of aristocratic anarchy, repressed but not wholly destroyed by Richelieu, surged up again. This uprising became a capricious little war called *la Fronde*, the sling, as though it were a child's game; a fantastic war in furbelows with noble ladies deliberately playing romantic parts, with great soldiers like Condé and Turenne shifting their allegiance, accepting Spanish support at the bidding of headstrong beauties. A colorful comic opera; but the state and the people paid the cost, and it was crushing.

The pattern is familiar enough; it had recurred a dozen times in French history. One element was exceptional: the Fronde started as a rebellion of magistrates. The *parlements* —the one in Paris enjoying unquestioned pre-eminence— were not deliberative bodies; they were courts of justice. But they had long claimed political power. They asserted that they had their origin in the *Curia Regis*, the omnipotent king's council of Frankish times; they chose to consider themselves as co-ordinate with the monarchy; they assumed the name of "Sovereign Courts." It was one of their functions to register the king's edicts; and they "remonstrated" with the crown when a new law seemed to them contrary to the French tradition. Thus they came to assume a position somewhat akin to that of the American Supreme Court since the days of John Marshall. The king could enforce his will and personally appear in *parlement* to order registration; but the courts were permanent and pertinacious and the struggle often ended in a compromise.

A manifest abuse had vastly increased the independence of the *parlements*. It had become customary for judges and other officials openly to purchase their positions; under Henry IV, this evil practice had actually been sanctioned by law. The bench thus became the property of a caste, *la noblesse de robe*, the nobility of the gown. This was no doubt a check on absolutism; the courts were an organ of the state, not the passive tools of the kings. But they used their power to defend privileges, not to establish general principles of law, or to foster needed reform. They struck defiant attitudes as though they were the champions of liberty and on rare occasions the people were with them; but, as a rule, they were frankly reactionary. The royal power was actually far more democratic, i.e. far more concerned with the common welfare. The *parlements* remained a nuisance throughout the eighteenth century. They vanished unregretted in 1789.

Magistrates and noblemen wearied themselves out. Mazarin, supple and smiling, endured amid the hoots and jeers (*Mazarinades*). He was in full enjoyment of the queen's favor, in possession of the king's person; so the incredible Italian adventurer could pose as "France." Through civil war and European strife, he managed to lead young Louis XIV to safety, and left him a position of unquestioned power at home, of unrivaled prestige abroad. Incidentally, the wily cardinal amassed an enormous fortune; the profit motive was held to be legitimate in those days.

5. THE GRAND MONARCH: LOUIS XIV

In 1661, Mazarin died and Louis XIV, twenty-three years old, took into his hands the full direction of affairs. If he did not say, "I am the state," it is only because it went without saying. His early experience had inspired him with a profound horror of disorder, a deep-rooted distrust of the aristocracy and, above all, an almost morbid dread of falling again under the tutelage of a prime minister. The Fronde and Mazarin account to a large extent for the autocratic temper of the sovereign.

He stepped on the stage at exactly the right moment. The Classical Age had reached its summit. The young king, eager for pleasure, magnificence and glory, was the proud symbol of a pacified, orderly, self-confident France. For twenty-five years, the emblematic sun of the Grand Monarch shone with uninterrupted splendor. It shone on victories and conquests. In three wars—how remote and futile they now seem—Louvois the organizer, Turenne and Condé the great captains, Vauban the engineer who could build and capture fortresses staged for him splendid pageants; and Louis himself would appear at the climax, like the gorgeous central figure in a ballet. It shone on elaborate court functions, for which Versailles provided a fitting stage: galleries of marble, heavy gilding and mirrors, avenues of noble trees disciplined by the master hand of Le Nôtre, fountains rising harmoniously like a hymn of praise. It shone on literary masterpieces: it was the age of Molière, Racine, Boileau, La Fontaine, Bossuet. The portraits of that generation breathe robust health and invincible calm; the whole reign, at that time, was not an adventure but a consummation. No revolt, no opposition; at least none audible enough to mar the majesty of that peace.

No wonder Europe was impressed by that unique combination of strength, repose, and charm. Spain had to yield precedence; the Pope was reminded that, in the temporal sphere, the supremacy of the great king was not to be challenged, the doge of Venice was brought to Versailles to abase himself. But these triumphs of brutal pride were actually flaws in the glorious regime: its true victory was to be genuinely admired, and sedulously aped. German princelings copied the splendor and the etiquette of Versailles. They imitated even the most questionable attributes of Jovelike majesty. Because Louis XIV carried off adultery in Olympian style, flaunted and glorified his favorites—elegiac La Vallière, haughty Montespan —the elector of Brandenburg felt in duty bound to have an official mistress. To us, the pomp of the Louis XIV epoch, the ritual of its pleasures may seem stiff and heavy like the monumental wigs and the brocaded robes; to contemporaries, they meant sheer enchantment.

We have mentioned before the classical *synthesis*. Paradoxically, under Louis XIV, the right word would be the classical *compromise*. Unity was achieved not so much through inner harmony as through miraculous balance. The age has been defined as cultural bimetallism; there were at least two sets of values but, for a quarter of a century, they were kept in a fixed ratio. The chief element was neither rationalism nor tradition, neither individual liberty nor absolutism, neither pagan art nor Christian thought, but equilibrium, measure, sanity, reasonableness.

Louis XIV himself, in his best years, was a curiously moderate man. He curbed but he did not destroy the privileges of nobility, *parlements*, provinces; he respected the self-government of the French church, as he wanted it to be respected by Rome. He took away from the feudal aristocrats the substance of their power; but he showered favors upon them. His court was their gilded cage; he felt safer when he had them under his masterful glance; but he appeared among them as a gracious host. It took the spiteful genius of Saint-Simon—a great nobleman whose *Memoirs* have an intensity of life rivaled only by Shakespeare and Balzac—to discover that, under its aristocratic social life, the reign was that of "a vile bourgeoisie." Louis XIV would have raised his eyebrows, not even amused, if he had been openly called, like Louis Philippe, the king of the bourgeois. Yet the great administrator and financier who made the splendor of the reign possible, Colbert, was a bourgeois, a tradesman's son. Louvois, who drilled and equipped the armies (and was only too eager to have them put to use), was the son of Le Tellier, a bourgeois. Vauban, who girdled the realm with fortresses which are classical masterpieces, was a country squire, the descendant of a provincial lawyer. Bossuet, favorite preacher, tutor of the king's son, theorist of monarchy by divine right, mouthpiece of the Gallican clergy, was a bourgeois. Boileau, the lawgiver of Parnassus, to whom the king himself gracefully bowed in matters of literary taste, was the quintessence of the bourgeois spirit. Louis treated the bourgeois Racine as a friend. He upheld the

bourgeois Molière even in his pitiless satires against vapid
courtiers, and in his attacks on religious hypocrites. The aristocratic writers of the time, La Rochefoucauld, Madame de
Lafayette, Madame de Sévigné did not stand high in his favor;
and young Saint-Simon, last champion of the feudal tradition,
was left to seethe with rage.

6. DECLINE OF THE CLASSICAL ORDER

Michelet divided the reign of Louis XIV in medical terms:
"before the fistula, after the fistula." More conventional historians place the turn of the tide in 1685, when the Edict of
Nantes was revoked and every trace of religious freedom disappeared. This was the logical consequence of absolutism and
its first irretrievable mistake. Arrogance and prodigality, long
admired as tokens of greatness, bore their fruit at last. Before
the end of the century, the great servants of the monarchy
were succeeded by mere courtiers, the great classical writers
had died. In the chorus of praise, grown stale and thin, dis
cordant murmurs could be heard. As late as 1697, Louis XIV
was still holding his own, *non pluribus impar;* but during the
war of the Spanish Succession (1701–1713) famine, bankruptcy
and utter defeat faced the aging monarch. Under the weigh
of infirmities, sorrows and repentance, Louis, never irreligious
grew more narrowly devout. The reign of resplendent mis
tresses was over; Madame de Maintenon, whom he secretl
married, aspired to be a mother of the church. The genuin
conversion of the master was hypocritically followed by th
court. The closing years of that interminable reign were son
ber; they were not ignoble. Under the bludgeoning of fate, th
monarchy preserved its indomitable dignity.

The rabble feasted riotously on the route of Louis XIV
funeral train. All the restraints of the last thirty years wen

thrown to the wind. Of this reaction, the regent, Philip, duke of Orléans, took the lead and remains the symbol.[s] The Regency still stands for elegant and corrupt cynicism. It stamped the whole eighteenth century indelibly; there were nobles after the pattern of Philip of Orléans down to the very end of the Ancient Regime, including his descendant *Philippe Egalité*. At any rate, that spirit prevailed almost without a check until the middle of the century. Young Voltaire was filled with it; and in old age, as the patriarch of Ferney, he had not abjured it altogether. The Regency showed it in an exaggerated form; its more subdued aspect was better exemplified by Madame de Pompadour (1745–1764), and her name is frequently attached to the whole period. The priestess of pleasure is far better remembered than the honest, kindly, tranquillity-loving minister, Cardinal Fleury (1726–1743).

The life of France in the eighteenth century is not adequately mirrored in politics, either domestic or foreign. Public affairs moved sluggishly and jerkily, carried by the momentum of the previous age. As on the tragic stage, this was a generation of epigoni or followers. There were court intrigues, favorites, squabbles with the *parlements*, as tedious as a twice-told tale. The long war of the Austrian Succession, for instance, was but a senseless shadow of earlier contests. For France, it had no meaning and reached no conclusion. After seven years (1741–1748), Louis XV made peace "like a king, not like a merchant." These proud words might be taken to mean that futility is the distinctive sign of crowned heads.

But it would be unfair to see in the Regency and the Pompadour era nothing but delightful sophistication and light-hearted immorality. No doubt it was a time of ethical chaos. The old order, with Louis XIV, had ended in moral bankruptcy, no new creed had been evolved, and scoffing skepticism

---

[s] Louis XIV's great-grandson, Louis XV, was only five years old in 1715. Louis XIV had attempted to curtail in advance the power of the regent, whom he did not trust; but his testament was annulled by the Parlement of Paris.

was the keynote. Wit and taste, however, were not the only redeeming features of the time. The breaking down of stiff artificial standards had released not libertinism merely but also a gentler spirit, smiling and humane. "In this world," says a father in Marivaux's play, *The Game of Love and Chance*, "one has to be too kind in order to be kind enough." The regent himself, with his glaring faults, had a generous heart and a liberal mind. Even the Marquise de Pompadour was singularly refined and keen-minded. Science and philosophy were in vogue in the best *salons*. Voltaire and Montesquieu knew how to turn a madrigal, an epigram, and even a daintily risqué tale; but they could also devote years to *The Spirit of Laws* or the *Essay on Manners*.

Long before the reign of Louis XIV had ended in ruin, bigotry and defeat, a new spirit had been growing, most clearly among his declared enemies—the English, the Dutch, the scattered Huguenot exiles—but at home also and in many forms. That spirit, if the word were not so trite, we might call a third renaissance; when it assumed consciousness, it was named the Enlightenment. Like the earlier renaissances, it was accompanied by an economic transformation—in this case the birth of modern credit, the rise of the financiers, the solid progress of the trading middle class, the definite beginnings of the factory system, well ahead of the industrial revolution. With it also, as in the eleventh century and in the sixteenth, went a thirst for discovery and adventure; it was an age of great navigators, of colonial expansion and contest, with an ardent curiosity for the exotic. Not order alone, but progress became the keynote.

It seemed as though the new world, the bourgeois world capitalistic and liberal, would have a full chance to grow whilst the absolute monarchy was falling into fairly innocuous desuetude. Such was the fortunate experience of England. On the continent however, and particularly in France the "liberal" tendency assumed many antagonistic aspects

The Ancient Regime was too decrepit either to check or to direct the liberal trend; infirm of will, it grew not more mellow but more arbitrary. Thus began, about 1750, a crisis of which the Revolution is only the most glaring episode; and that crisis was to continue, fitfully, for a hundred years.

CHRONOLOGICAL SUMMARY, 1515–1748

FRANCIS I   1515–1547
    Victory of Marignano   1515
    Concordat of Bologna   1516
    Conflict with Austria and Spain   1520–1559
    Defeat of Pavia   1525
    Treaty of Madrid   1526
    Rabelais, *Gargantua* and *Pantagruel*   1532–1562
    John Calvin, 1509–1564,
       Christian Institutes   1536–1541
    Treaty of Crespy (end of Italian wars)   1544
    Council of Trent (Counter-Reformation)   1545–1564

HENRY II   1547–1559
    Calais recaptured   1558
    Treaty of Cateau-Cambresis   1559

THE THREE SONS OF HENRY II

Predominance of Queen Mother Catherine de
    Médicis   1559–1589
    Religious (and factional) wars   1560–1598

FRANCIS II
    married Mary Stuart of Scotland   1559–1560
    Conspiracy of Amboise, 1560

CHARLES IX (10 years old at accession)   1560–1574
    Massacre of Huguenots St. Bartholomew's Night   1572

HENRY III   1574–1589
    Guise partisans (Catholic League) vs. Bourbon-
       Condé partisans (Huguenots)
    Guise in control of Paris ("King of Paris")   1588
    Guise assassinated at Blois   1588
    Henry III assassinated at St. Cloud   1589

HOUSE OF BOURBON, 1589–1792

HENRY IV (Henry of Navarre) 1589–1610
  Montaigne's *Essays* 1580–1595
  Victories
    Arques (1589) and Ivry (1590) 1589–1590
  Henry IV abjures Protestantism 1593
  Henry IV crowned at Chartres 1594
    aided in reconstruction of France by Sully
  Edict of Nantes (religious settlement) 1598
  Treaty of Vervins with Spain (liberation) 1598
  Henry IV assassinated 1610

LOUIS XIII (9 years old at accession) 1610–1643
  Regency of Marie de Médicis
  Richelieu in control 1624–1642
  Siege of La Rochelle, Huguenot stronghold 1627–1628
  French Academy founded 1635
  Corneille's *Le Cid,* first great French classical
    tragedy 1636
  Descartes's *Discourse on Method* 1637

LOUIS XIV (5 years old at accession) 1643–1715
  Anne of Austria, regent; Mazarin, minister 1643–1661
  Treaties of Westphalia 1648
  Fronde, rebellion of *parlements* and nobles 1648–1653
  Treaty of the Pyrenees with Spain 1659

PERSONAL RULE OF LOUIS XIV 1661–1715
  Colbert, superintendent of finances 1662–1683
  Heyday of Classical Age: Boileau, Racine, Molière, La
    Fontaine, Bossuet; Mansart; Lulli; Lebrun; Le Nôtre
  First war (War of Devolution), treaty of Aix-la-
    Chapelle 1667–1668
  Second war (with Holland),
    treaty of Nimwegen 1672–1678
  Revocation of the Edict of Nantes 1685
  Growth of critical spirit: La Bruyère, Bayle, Fénelon
  Third war (War of the League of Augsburg) treaty of
    Ryswick 1688–1697

Fourth war (War of the Spanish Succession)   1701–1714
Treaties of Utrecht (1713) and Rastadt   1714

Louis XV (5 years old at accession)   1715–1774
Philip, duke of Orléans, regent   1715–1723
John Law's bank and Mississippi scheme   1718–1720
Montesquieu, *Persian Letters*   1721
Cardinal Fleury (ministry)   1726–1743
Voltaire: *English (Philosophical) Letters*   1734
War of the Austrian Succession, treaty of Aix-la-
    Chapelle   1740–1748
Madame de Pompadour   1745–1764
Montesquieu, *Spirit of Laws*   1748

CHAPTER VI

The Bourgeois Liberal Revolution:
1750 - 1848

1. RISE OF THE BOURGEOISIE

ROYAL absolutism had grown within feudal chaos; bourgeois
liberalism, with the same confused gradualness, grew within
the monarchy by divine right. Autocratic in principle, aristocratic in form, the rule of Louis XIV was in fact, as we have
seen, a solid bureaucracy through which the middle class, the
third estate, actually controlled the government. The nobles
were but cumbrous and costly ornaments; the king at his best
was not an hereditary despot but the living symbol of national
unity, order, and law.

The bourgeois, on the whole, had every reason to be satisfied with this arrangement. They were amassing wealth; the
first half of the eighteenth century was for them a period of
great prosperity. The more ambitious among them, the *Bourgeois Gentilshommes* as Molière would have dubbed them,
had access to honors as well. In Great Britain, the peerage has
been constantly refreshed by admitting into its ranks the most
prominent—at any rate the wealthiest—among the commoners. That excellent system prevailed, although in looser
form, under the Ancient Regime. The best servants of the
state won or bought titles; the draper's son, Colbert, became
the founder of an aristocratic house. There was a "nobility of
the gown," composed of magistrates, no less proud of its pre-

rogatives than the "nobility of the sword." The financiers—a rising class before whom Louis XIV himself, in his decline, had to bow—acquired noble rank not only for their daughters but for themselves. Privileges that are within conceivable reach do not seem intolerable. Indeed they will be defended by those whose chance of winning them is small. They are the splendid prizes in the lottery of life and the humble do not want to be robbed of that dream. In the Napoleonic armies, a private carried a marshal's baton in his knapsack; in America, the barefoot boy may become a president or a millionnaire; under Louis XIV, a tradesman might have a vision of his son as another Colbert.

There was a nobler aspect to this healthy social fluidity: the aristocracy of wit enjoyed almost unlimited privileges. Even in the first half of the seventeenth century, Vincent Voiture, the son of a provincial merchant, became "the little king" of the Hôtel de Rambouillet salon, a charmed circle to which the highest born were proud to belong. The French Academy was a club of gentlemen interested in good language: princes, prelates, and commoners met there on terms of social equality. Louis XIV scrupulously observed as well as enforced etiquette; he could mark with the utmost nicety the slightest difference in rank; but apart from that punctilious and purely formal courtesy, there were few noblemen whom he treated with as much consideration as the bourgeois Boileau and Racine. Voltaire, a Parisian bourgeois, was early admitted into the brilliant and naughty society gathered at the Temple by a great nobleman, Philip de Vendôme, grand prior of France; there wits and princes met as boon companions, all restraint forgotten, including that of rank. It looked as though the social structure of France could alter by imperceptible degrees without a cataclysm.

But it was not to be. The rise of the bourgeoisie in the eighteenth century was extremely rapid. Sieyès was not far wrong when in 1789, in an epoch-making pamphlet, he

(would become !!!)

claimed that the third estate had become "everything." On the other hand, the privileged orders did not resign themselves gracefully to the role of ornamental fossils. As their usefulness, long waning, finally vanished altogether, their pretensions increased. The bourgeoisie was most cruelly snubbed at the time when it should have been more fully recognized. Under Louis XVI, it would have been almost impossible for Bossuet to become a bishop, or for Vauban to become a marshal of France.

Let us cite a few episodes in that sharpened conflict. At the Temple, young Voltaire was insulted by a Rohan—a minor member of the proudest family in France. The commoner discovered that, for his aristocratic friends, courtesy was but condescension and social equality a thin veil covering the brutality of feudal prejudice. Voltaire could get no sympathy and no redress. Cudgeled by the valets of Rohan, he challenged the high-born and cautious bully; for this, he was sent to the Bastille, and finally into exile. In London, he found his utopia. There, the merchants of the city had nothing to fear from feudal arrogance. A "wit," Addison, could marry into the aristocracy and be entrusted with important functions in the state. Voltaire, and Montesquieu soon afterward, realized the difference between an organic regime such as England's and one that had grown stiff and brittle with senile decrepitude. With this realization came the first premonition of a possible upheaval. Sieyès's revolutionary pamphlet: *What is the Third Estate?* is a belated retort to the drubbing that Rohan's valets gave young Voltaire.

A generation later, Madame Geoffrin, who held a salon famed throughout Europe, could not herself be received at court because, although kings called her *maman*, she was but a bourgeoise. Beaumarchais, the watchmaker's son, with his teeming brain—inventor, musician, unofficial diplomat, financier—was snubbed by those lords who had "merely taken the trouble of being born." Under the gay Spanish costume of Figaro, Beaumarchais took up the challenge. When his comedy, *The Wedding of Figaro*, was performed in 1784, the revolution was already complete in men's minds. The very aristocracy had laughed away its own privileges.[1]

The bourgeois revolution was therefore under way throughout the eighteenth century. If it finally broke out in 1789, it was only because the antiquated privileged orders had attempted to throw a feeble dam against the irresistible stream. The essential reality was the increasing force of the money-making class, not the obstacle and its spectacular removal. The violent struggle, from 1789 to 1794, seemed to hasten but actually retarded the process. Revolution, like war, means waste; but the men responsible for a revolution are those who seek forcibly to check a natural trend.

2. PHILOSOPHY OF THE BOURGEOIS REVOLUTION: THE ENLIGHTENMENT

The shift in the balance of power between the classes was associated with several movements in European thought; but it was not determined by any one of them. The nature of such an association is difficult to define. Manifestly ideas are the consciousness of experience; but they become a factor in accelerating evolution. Philosophies are not motive powers; they are sign posts and traffic rules. Without such aid, a social advance would be far slower and more uncertain.

The philosophy that guided the eighteenth century was founded upon reason. Thomas Paine called his time "the Age of Reason": the term might be applied to the whole period.

[1] By the side of this revolution through laughter (*castigat ridendo mores*), there was also on the stage, oddly enough, a "tearful" revolution. Classical tragedy dealt exclusively with the high born. A bourgeois could be the hero—or the butt—of comedy but he was beneath the notice of the loftier muse. In the eighteenth century, it was realized that a commoner might suffer too, without being ludicrous. The result was a hybrid called the lachrymose comedy or the middle class tragedy. The masterpiece of the new drama was *The Philosopher without Knowing It* by Sedaine, a play with a definite thesis, extolling the dignity of the merchant class.

This confidence in reason was the natural consequence of Descartes' daring attitude: "Doubt until you can doubt no more; accept nothing as a truth unless it appears to you clearly and evidently to be such; for man is endowed with the power of discriminating the false from the true." But this rationalism might as well be considered the result of Bacon's experimental method. The eighteenth century was not devoted to abstract thinking on a mathematical model; it was intensely interested in physics, chemistry, and natural science. Voltaire was much more of a Baconian than of a Cartesian.

But whether Descartes or Bacon be the acknowledged master, the classical compromise as we have called it, the bimetallism attaching co-ordinate values to tradition and to reason, came to be discarded. The majestic but superficial harmony that characterized the age of Louis XIV lasted barely twenty-five years. Glory rather than tyranny had suppressed the critical spirit; when the failure of the Grand Monarch became apparent, men realized how precarious the balance had been. But, even if Louis XIV had not failed, the rise of reason above tradition would have taken place *because of his success:* trends may be accelerated by contradictory causes. In 1687, Perrault read before the academy a poem, *The Century of Louis the Great.* "Under Louis, we the moderns have equaled the ancients: what is to prevent us from going beyond them?" As soon as a generation dares to trust its own judgment against "the wisdom of our ancestors," it has become radical. The Quarrel of the Ancients and the Moderns, tedious and abortive in the literary field, marked nonetheless a revolution in thought.

This fundamental change had two corollaries—one negative, the other positive. If the classical compromise is denounced, if reason becomes the sole standard, then tradition as such becomes wholly indefensible. Everything that was rational in the past is claimed and annexed by reason. It is not a tradition to speak the truth: it is a principle. The field of mere tradition is therefore restricted to whatever is unreasonable. Customs, precedents lose all authority. They are blemishes in the purity of our thought; their true names are superstitions, abuses, privileges. And the great iconoclastic fight of Voltaire is on. Voltaire did not want to efface history but to understand it; deceptions, myths, and legends should be exposed. He turned upon the past a pitiless light as his master Bayle had done before him. But he did not destroy in a spirit of levity or vengeance or cynicism. His task was to clear the path.

The positive consequence of rationalism is a belief in progress. This was already clear in the fathers of modern philosophy. Descartes saw no limit to "the advancement of learning": science would some day conquer disease and even death. He might have said, with Bacon and Saint-Simon the socialist: "The Golden Age is not behind us, but ahead of us." Pascal, certainly not a rationalist of the shallower sort, conceived of mankind as a single man, constantly growing and learning. We are the ancients; compared with us, the ancients were adolescents.

This faith in progress did not take the vulgar form it was to affect in the nineteenth century. It was not complacent. Progress is not automatic; it only challenges us to further efforts. It was not materialistic. No doubt the *philosophes* enjoyed intelligent luxury, and no age offered a more refined setting for social pleasure. But they rejoiced even more in the progress of *les lumières*, the Enlightenment; and most of all in the progress of *l'humanité*, kindliness, tolerance. Under the Reign of Terror, Condorcet, persecuted, in hiding, penned his *Essay on the Progress of the Human Mind* with serene luminous courage.

Such is the faith of the Enlightenment—with as many shades, of course, as there are powerful individuals. Montesquieu is not Voltaire; Buffon is not Diderot; the staff of the *Encyclopedia* is a motley crew; and each philosophical salon strikes a note of its own. No period that is intensely alive—the thirteenth century, the Renaissance, the Classical Age, the Enlightenment—can be reduced to a simple formula. Only mediocrity can achieve uniformity. Unequal, strangely mottled, marred by flippancy and indecency, the Enlightenment about 1750 is nonetheless one of the happy moments in the history of France and of mankind, a rare blend of refinement and strength. It adopted French manners, and gave an added charm to Parisian life but it was in truth European and perhaps England's best gift to the world. America should dwell upon the age of Voltaire with sympathy for it was in that spiritual atmosphere that the country was born. Washington and Franklin were men of the Enlightenment, and Jefferson perhaps its most perfect epitome.

There was another element in the Enlightenment that was to prove its undoing: the notion of a *return to nature*. In spite of their faith in indefinite progress, the best minds of the period were still haunted with the old ideal of fixity as the sole warrant of truth. Tradition is not to be trusted as the guardian of truth; for tradition changes and is not universal (every *philosophe* had Montaigne's *Essays* and Bayle's *Historical Dictionary* within reach). Where is permanent truth to be found? "In nature." Already the classicists Molière and Boileau had used *nature* and *reason* almost interchangeably. Through what Descartes calls common sense, man is able to reach under the illusions of time and tribe the essential, the *natural* verities. Hence a growing faith in natural law in the physical world: to the rationalist, a miracle is a scandal for it is caprice, not law. There is likewise a natural moral law, deeper than prejudice or custom; and as a warrant for that law, there must be a lawgiver, the god of natural religion.

These ideas were not new. As early as 1315, Louis the Quarrelsome had proclaimed that the French had a natural right to be free; and Rabelais two centuries later had sung a great hymn to *physis*, nature, the kindly, the beneficent, whose service is perfect freedom. But the return to nature became sharply defined about the middle of the eighteenth century. When, in 1753, the Academy of Dijon proposed as a subject for a prize essay: *On the Origin of Inequality among Men and whether it is justified in Natural Law*, the very title implied the whole philosophy which was to be known as Rousseauism. Rousseau was one of those geniuses who dare to express that which lurks obscurely in millions of minds.

There was therefore a Rousseauistic element in the Enlightenment. Voltaire and Rousseau were constantly associated in the public mind. Blake denounced them in the same breath; the Revolution carried their remains to the same pantheon; reaction later ascribed to them jointly all the evils France had suffered. But these alleged brothers-in-arms were enemies. Voltaire had too keen a mind not to realize the perils of Rousseauism. The mystic appeal to an undefined absolute called nature was the denial of the intellectual and scientific Enlightenment. Rousseauism trusted the dark, irrational forces—intuition, passion, instinct. It extolled the primitive; it scorned intelligence as shallow and civilization as sophisticated. Diderot and the Encyclopedists became Rousseau's declared adversaries. Thus, on the ideological plane, France and Europe were to witness a three-cornered fight: tradition, progress, primitivism, clashing and combining in disconcerting fashion. In like manner—but with no rigorous symmetry—there was on the social-political plane a contest among the aristocracy, the bourgeoisie, and the people.

It was necessary to indicate these vast if shadowy forces—the rise of the bourgeoisie, the Enlightenment, Rousseauism—if the story of the period were not to be a mere chronicle of caprice, greed, ambition and violence. Never was the life of a country more gloriously divorced from the dismal tale of deceit and incompetence which too often usurps the name of history. The important events of the eighteenth century are not the hollow victory at Fontenoy or the ludicrous fiasco at

Rossbach: they are Montesquieu's *Spirit of Laws*, Voltaire's *Essay on Manners, Candide, Philosophical Dictionary*, Diderot's *Encyclopedia*, Buffon's *Epochs of Nature*, Rousseau's *Discourses*, his *Emile*, his *Social Contract*.

3. BANKRUPTCY OF THE ANCIENT REGIME

In 1744, Louis XV on his way to war fell sick at Metz. At the news of his danger and of his recovery, the country was swept by a wave of passionate loyalty. The king was still "France." It was then that he was called "the Well-Beloved," a title that was to assume a bitterly ironical tinge, for no king was ever more thoroughly hated and despised. His private life was a scandal, his administration was chaos, his foreign policy was disaster. The defeats in the Seven Years' War against Prussia and England (1756–1763) did not have the somber dignity which gave a tragic depth to Louis XIV's sunset. The French laughed at their own generals, such as Soubise, but their laughter was mirthless.

Yet the Well-Beloved was by no means wholly despicable. A very bad husband, he was a very good father. Madame de Pompadour, his favorite for twenty years, was an extremely intelligent woman; she was genuinely appreciated by the writers of the time; directly and through the Marquis de Marigny, she had an excellent influence upon the arts. There was something healthy and ingenuous about the frank vulgarity of Madame du Barry. The king had wit; he could remember at unexpected moments, with a Voltairian chuckle, that he was "the Lord's Anointed." On public occasions, he displayed a majesty not unworthy of Louis XIV himself. His irremediable fault, which damned the regime, was the complete divorce between his personality and his function. As a king, he was purely a figurehead, impressive and impassive; as a man, he was immensely bored with the solemn show. His one desire was to escape. He viewed the grand monarchical

pageant with blasé indifference and, among his friends, with
a sardonic smile. He had, in his heart, abdicated. The state
was too unwieldy for him to steer; as for mending the creak-
ing mechanism, that was beyond his capacity or his ambition.
He shrugged his shoulders: "Bah! the old machine will last
my lifetime, at any rate!"— "After me, the deluge!"

So Louis was not qualified to be one of those "enlightened
despots" who were then the hope of the *philosophes*. In French
history whenever the king weakens, feudal anarchy breaks
loose again. At this time, it did not take the crude form of
civil war: the age was eminently civilized. The courtiers fought
for the spoils not sword in hand but with a whisper or an
epigram. Louis XIV had attracted the nobility to his court for
his own safety as well as to his own glory; Louis XV, brought
up in that court atmosphere, became the prisoner of his own
prisoners. They acted as a screen between him and his people.
The king became definitely the first of the nobles; his power,
which was meant to be a remedy against injustice, became the
fountainhead of privilege, the very shield and symbol of all
abuses. The great royal bureaucracy was still doing excellent
work; but the king was no longer the conscious center of its
activity. The unspoken abdication of Louis XV constitutes in
fact the true French Revolution.

The old monarchy, carried by the momentum of eight
hundred years, was to have not one but at least three more
chances: at the creation of the Maupeou *parlements,* at the
accession of Louis XVI, and in the early stage of the French
Revolution. The first, a puzzling, confused episode, occurred
in 1771. Louis XV suppressed the old *parlements* and established in their stead new courts of justice. On the face of it,
the act was tyrannical; the sovereign was breaking down the
last element of resistance to his autocracy. But it could be
argued that the *parlements* were hopelessly attached to antiquated tradition. The move might be interpreted as an effort
to modernize, to rationalize, the ramshackle edifice of royal

power. To the contemporaries, however, the Triumvirate entrusted with this reform, Maupeou, d'Aiguillon, Abbé Terray, appeared as the tools of a favorite from the gutter, Madame du Barry. At any rate, this equivocal attempt had no time to bear fruit; in 1774, Louis XV died of small pox, and his successor restored the old *parlements*.

Louis XVI was twenty. Heavy of body, sluggish of mind, timid of character, but by no means stupid, of a kindly disposition, and, for a wonder, thoroughly virtuous, he would have been a perfect constitutional sovereign. France felt his touching, his anguished desire to do right; the shameful experience of the Louis XV regime was forgotten and the monarchy popular again. There was a new freshness in the air, and a breath of Renaissance. Although England and France had fought and were to fight again, Anglomania ruled in Paris; liberty, simplicity, virtue, sentiment, reform were the order of the day. The blend of exquisite traditional refinement and renewed hope gives the reign of Louis XVI a unique pathetic charm. Talleyrand was to say: "A man who has not lived before 1789 has not tasted the sweetness of life." We might limit this statement: before 1789, but after 1774. The sweetness was that of promise, not that of decay.

Louis XVI called to power, as comptroller general of finances, the economist Turgot (1774–1776). The *philosophes* were quivering with joy. For Turgot was at the same time an able administrator—he had been very successful as *intendant* in Limoges—and a bold reformer. But the cabal of the privileged was too strong for him; public opinion was uncertain; and the king was weak. He dismissed Turgot with a sigh: "Only you and I, Monsieur Turgot, truly love the people." Another abdication of the monarchy.

Necker, a Genevese banker (1776–1781), was called in as a technician in the hope that he might restore financial order without embarking on radical reforms. A mere businesslike audit of the treasury, however, implied a denunciation of abuses. Then Necker's task was made more hopeless by France's participation in the war of American independence.

France launched upon that great adventure for two very different reasons; some wanted to get even with England for the humiliation of the Seven Years' War; many more—of whom young Lafayette was the symbol—were genuinely devoted to the ideal of liberty. Franklin, the sage of Passy, became the idol of Parisian society. Dying Voltaire blessed young America, in the person of Franklin's grandson, in the name of "God and liberty." But, revenge or crusade, the cost of the enterprise was crushing.

It was the moment that the nobles chose for a counter-offensive. Not only did they defend their privileges but they attempted to strengthen them. Never had the nobility been at the same time so prodigal and so grasping. The worst were the queen's personal favorites—Polignac, Lamballe. In the public mind, Marie Antoinette became the incarnation of frivolity and extravagance. In the tangled scandal of the Diamond Necklace, there is now little doubt that she was guiltless; but the French chose—avidly—to believe the worst of their queen. She probably never said: "Let them eat cake!" ("*Qu'ils mangent de la brioche!*"). But the silly legend had a sinister background of truth. Her very brilliancy, once admired, had become baleful. Burke was to consider her as the proud flower of ancient France and many are still taking the same romantic view; to the French, "the Austrian" as she was called, represented only the perfection of aristocratic futility. Unfortunately her lackluster husband, whom she despised, adored her. There are moments when uxoriousness is a deadly sin.

Calonne was called to save the finances of the state (1783–1787). He made a paradoxical attempt to spend his way out of the abyss. The method is not theoretically wrong: an expanding economy might have been France's salvation. The country had vast resources, and the industrial revolution was beginning to be felt. But Calonne had to fight against the same handicaps as Necker. The cost of the American war had been enormous, and those who were spending most freely the king's bounty considered it beneath their dignity to be taxed. Finally, the commercial treaty with England, well-meant and perhaps wise in the long run, had the immediate effect of hampering the growth of French industry. Calonne veiled the peril with smiles, loans upon loans, and doctored accounts: truly a rake's progress. At the end of his tricks, he had to advocate Turgot's thoroughgoing schemes and Necker's financial methods. With this last pirouette as a thwarted reformer, the amiable wizard vanished from the stage.

At last, the hopelessness of the situation was fully revealed. Loménie de Brienne tried two ultimate expedients: a consultative Assembly of Notables which, granted no real power, declined to accept any responsibility; and reform edicts, which the Parlement refused to register. Both Notables and Parlement pointed the same way out. The nation as a whole should be consulted by convening the States-General. The solution was at the same time radical and in harmony with tradition: Anglo-American ideas were to assume a historical French garb.

The immediate cause of the Revolution was therefore financial. The monarchy perished because it could not make ends meet. Revolution was an alternative—or a synonym—for bankruptcy. But the financial chaos was due primarily to social not to economic conditions. The old order had to pass away, because the privileged classes refused to correct abuses; and because the king, defender of the people, elected to stand with his ancient enemies, the feudal aristocracy.

4. THE CONSTITUTIONAL REVOLUTION: 1789–1792

Necker was called back to power. The States-General were convened for the first time since 1614. The franchise, although not universal, was far more liberal than in England; and the third estate was given as many deputies as the other two combined. France was seething with political controversy: clubs, papers, pamphlets, multiplied overnight. The winter was hard, adding a touch of irritation to the universal fever. Yet, when the States assembled at Versailles in May, 1789, the prevalent mood was one of confidence and loyalty. The dynasty still had a splendid chance.

The nobles, and particularly the court party, however, had not disarmed. They hoped that each order would vote as a unit: thus the third estate, in spite of its numerical superiority, would be outvoted by the privileged classes. The contest went on indecisively for several weeks. On June 17, the deputies of the third estate decided to form themselves into a national assembly, and invited the other two orders to join them. On the twentieth, locked out of their regular hall, they met in a covered tennis court (*Jeu de Paume*) and took an oath not to separate until they had given France a constitution. On the twenty-third, the king commanded the three orders to deliberate separately. The third estate refused to leave the hall. Mirabeau, a stormy petrel, a recreant noble representing the bourgeoisie of Provence, hurled at the master of ceremonies the famous words of defiance: "Tell your master that we are here by the will of the people and that we shall not leave unless driven by the force of bayonets." The king, in his sensible lethargic fashion, gave way.

But there were those about him who were not so easily resigned, and Louis XVI was swayed by them. By his order, troops were gathered near Paris, including German mercenaries. On July 11, Necker was dismissed. Paris took up the challenge. The threatened *coup d'état* of the court party was checkmated by an uprising of the people. On the fourteenth, the mob stormed the Bastille. It was an act of impulsive violence; but its symbolical value was unmistakable. Kant understood, although he was a philosopher. So did the courtier who reported the outbreak to Louis XVI: "You mean, it is a riot?" —"No, Your Majesty: it is a revolution."

Antifeudal violence spread throughout the land; and with it, a vague "Great Fear," because the earth had quaked. Some princes and nobles refused to read the lesson and fled the country, intending to return at the head of an army. But, at that time, they were very few. The Enlightenment had affected the privileged orders; Lafayette was not a unique exception. On the fourth of August, of their own accord, they abandoned their privileges. On the twenty-seventh, a Jeffersonian "Declaration of the Rights of Man" was adopted. The Revolution, it would seem, was accomplished and with a minimum of bloodshed and disruption.

Alas! the fine spirit of August fourth was not to remain unchallenged. It was known that the queen hated the liberal movement. Her frivolity had made her immune to the virus of modern ideas; she considered them a personal insult. She had shunned politics; now she entered that perilous field with the willfulness and the obstinacy of a pampered woman. Noble officers rallied to her: class interest and chivalry formed a powerful combination. It looked as though the abortive *coup d'état* of July 11 were to be attempted again. Once more the mob took action. The women of the Paris market marched to Versailles and brought back king, queen and dauphin with them. The grand palace of Louis XIV had been the curse of the Bourbons; now, returning to the Tuileries, Louis XVI was "restored" to his people. As on July 14, the gesture was symbolic and decisive. But the instruments were hideous or grotesque. From that moment, the royal family considered themselves prisoners (October 5–6).

Two men might have been able to save the monarchy: Mirabeau, Lafayette. Mirabeau had had a scandalous career; but he had a powerful mind and magnificent eloquence. He sincerely believed that, at this point, the king's power should not be further abridged. So if he was paid, it was to defend his own ideas. The court bought him and did not know how to use him. He died in 1791, universally admired and distrusted, a mottled soul and a wasted force. Lafayette would have been a godsend to a sincere constitutional monarch. He had youth, popularity, chivalry. On October 5, he had saved the queen by publicly kissing her hand: she never forgave him. In her eyes, the naïve idealist was a Cromwell.

All was not lost. France still wanted a king. Louis XVI, patient, almost humble, was resigned to lose all autocratic power. The hope of a peaceful transition from the old to the new was destroyed by the religious conflict.

There was at first no evil intention on either side; the age was one of tolerance and humanity. The state was bankrupt; the church was replete with riches, which, ill-distributed, had a corrupting influence. Let the state take over the property of the church, and pay to the clergy adequate stipends. Only those prelates and abbots would suffer who, like Cardinal de Rohan, lived in un-Christian luxury. The plan was plausible.

Unfortunately, the Assembly coupled with this plan a complete reorganization of the church on the same lines as the new constitutional state—the kind of ruthless standardization which Hitler was to call *Gleichschaltung*. Dioceses were made to coincide with the newly devised *départements,* and priests were to be elected by their parishioners. No question of faith was involved, the legislators argued; and in matters of administration and discipline, the Gallican church had always asserted its autonomy. True: but the Papacy had tolerated—with the greatest reluctance—the Gallican principle only because no radical reform was attempted, and because the head of the state, the king, was himself a sacred character. The Assembly, without a shred of divine right, was proposing to do what no king had ever dared. Private interests, partisanship and religious feeling united in resisting this ill-advised step. The Civil Constitution of the Clergy was accepted by many priests; but many also refused to take the required oath.

Now Louis XVI had at the same time the humility and the tenacity of a true believer. He would not have fought for his own rights; where the church was concerned, he was adamant. A gulf was created between the monarchy and the Revolution. Louis would command our unreserved admiration if he had openly taken his stand. But, considering himself as no longer free, he thought he had the right to dissemble. He remained on the throne, he swore fealty to the constitution, he appeared at the festival commemorating the fall of the Bastille and the rebirth of France; then, on June 20, 1791, his true feelings were revealed. He fled from his capital to join the counterrevolutionary troops of Bouillé. Caught at Varennes, he was suspended, but even then he was not deposed; France was still reluctant to discard the palladium of eight hundred years. So the recreant king was restored; he pretended to reign; his subjects pretended to trust him. Never have the "logical" French indulged in more desperate make-believe.

The king was not only the enemy of his own government; he had become a traitor to his own country. Austria and Prussia had threatened to intervene in his defense; he was compelled, as head of the state, to declare war upon them. But no one was deceived. When France suffered initial reverses, the king was made responsible; on June 20, 1792, the mob invaded the Tuileries. Louis, with his strange blend of lethargy and heroism, neither resisted nor yielded. Brunswick, commander of the allies, threatened Paris with destruction if the king were harmed. The people, incensed, stormed the Tuileries again; the king ordered his Swiss guard to cease firing, and took refuge in the Assembly (August 10, 1792). It was the end.

Lafayette, the last hope of the moderate Royalists, had to flee the country and was imprisoned by the Austrians. The rabble, in an orgy of fear, massacred thousands of prisoners suspected of counterrevolutionary activities. A new assembly, the National Convention, met on September 20 and proclaimed France a republic. In December and January, it sat in judgment of the king. On January 21, 1793, Louis XVI was guillotined.

5. THE FIRST REPUBLIC, 1792–1799

France, after half a century of Anglomania, had thus followed English precedent to the bitter end. Not without cause: the guilt of Louis XVI was more flagrant than that of Charles I. Many sovereigns had been murdered before; but this solemn regicide, in the name of the people's justice, caused Europe to shudder. England, Holland, Spain and the Empire joined Austria, Prussia and Sardinia in a coalition against the new republic.

There seemed to be no ray of hope. Enemies stood on every frontier. The army was disorganized: a majority of the officers of noble origin were either in exile or under suspicion. The drastic financial measures of the Revolution had created new depths of chaos. The west—Normandy, Brittany, Vendée— rose in arms against the Convention. Every parish had its pocket of resistance against the central government. And in Paris, the republicans were soon to send each other, in batches, to the guillotine. Yet France emerged, one, indivisible, and victorious. The mission of Joan of Arc was a miracle with a pure halo; this was a miracle with a sinister glare. But saint and terrorists spring from the same earth and are characters in the same epic drama.

In a crisis, a large inexperienced assembly like the Convention is unfit to wield executive power. The Plain and the Marsh, as the moderates were called, yielded to the more determined Mountain party; and the Montagnards themselves abdicated into the hands of a few energetic men. These ruled through the *Comité de Salut Public*. The usual translation, Committee of Public Safety, is wrong because it is too tame. *Salut Public* means Public Salvation; the country was in danger, and had to be rescued.[2]

[2] There was also a *Comité de Sûreté Générale* with police duties.

Anyone who hesitated was purged away; first the Girondists, liberal orators who had not realized the desperate character of the peril; then the extremists, Hébert and his ilk, because they placed their radical doctrines above the salvation of France; finally Danton and his friends. They had been among the prime movers of the Revolution, they were patriots and democrats, but with a suspicion of looseness; they were not indifferent to pleasure and profit; they were ready to compromise and show themselves "indulgent." The rabble-rouser Marat was stabbed in his bath. There remained in sole control of the Convention, through the Jacobin Club, the Commune of Paris and the *Comité de Salut Public,* a handful of fanatics, Robespierre and his acolytes, Saint-Just, Couthon, Lebas.

They were not demented by blood lust, like the killers of September, 1792, or like Marat. They were ruthless without a qualm, because they were incorruptible. Their terror was a psychological weapon; the actual number of victims was small, perhaps twenty-five hundred in Paris. In fourteen months, the terrorists of 1793–1794 made fewer victims than the moderates of Thiers and MacMahon after the Paris Commune in 1871; and compared with modern massacres in China, Russia or Germany, the French Reign of Terror is a mere incident. It has, however, deserved its name. It caused France to shudder, because it represented the tyranny of uncompromising virtue. An explosion of sheer violence is a catastrophe but it is brief; the puritanism of Robespierre threatened to make itself permanent. He was the Calvin of an enormous Geneva; and every dissenter was marked as a Servetus.

France had tolerated, nay applauded, the Terror, so long as it seemed the desperate but inevitable means of salvation. It was victory at the frontiers and, far beyond, that doomed the Terror in Paris. For, in 1793–1794, France was magnificently victorious on every front. Already at Valmy on September 20, 1792, the raw levies of Dumouriez and Kellermann had stood the cannonade of Prussian veterans. Early in 1793, France staggered under the combined attacks. By midsummer, the troops of the republic were on the offensive again. Within eighteen months, Belgium and the whole left bank of the Rhine had been conquered, Spaniards and Piedmontese driven back, and the fifth column crushed everywhere.

The causes of this dramatic reversal are extremely complex. According to the materialistic interpretation of history, the green grapes of Champagne played havoc with the Prussian army and forced it to retreat after Valmy: "On this day and at this place a new era begins in the history of the world," Goethe claims to have said. The French volunteers were filled with the spirit of the Marseillaise; but, unseasoned, they gave way at the first shock; it is only when the new levies were "amalgamated" with the stout veterans that discipline was restored. Aristocratic officers deserted; but far abler plebeians were promoted. In the technical arms and services, artillerists and engineers, the key men remained at their posts. In Belgium and the Rhineland, the local population offered no vigorous resistance; their patriotism was still uncertain and the ideas of the French Revolution had many supporters. The coalition against France was loose, incompetent, and profoundly selfish; when fighting in the west, Austria and Prussia were looking eastward, for fear Russia should gobble up too large a share of Poland.

So the debit and the credit sheets are both filled with confused items and it is hard to strike a balance. One thing is certain: France found a strategic and organizing genius in Lazare Carnot. Against the small and carefully trained armies of old Europe, he struck swift massive blows with his "nation in arms," twelve hundred thousand men. The republicans rushed ahead, ardent yet disciplined, with no regard for the learned chess game of classical tactics. Carnot was a modest man—he remained a captain all through the Revolution—and he hardly ever appeared on the battlefield. So even military historians fail to realize how completely he renovated the art of war, in which Frederick II and Napoleon were only accomplished virtuosi.

On June 26, 1794, the battle of Fleurus clinched the second conquest of Belgium and the victory of republican France. A month later, on July 27 (ninth of Thermidor in the new Revolutionary calendar), Robespierre fell. The rebellion against him was not that of humanity and liberalism; the men who overthrew him had been terrorists themselves. They were afraid not of Robespierre's tyranny but of his justice. The Incorruptible was taking "republican virtue" too literally. Moreover, the republic was growing dangerously democratic. A radical constitution had been voted; to be sure, it was to remain in abeyance until the war was over, but it was an ugly threat. The Maximum law, a rigid control of prices, was a curb on profiteering; and if gambling in the wildly inflated currency was an exciting game, the guillotine might stop it at any moment. It was high time to restore normalcy. So Robespierre was killed by a sorry pack. He haunts history as an enigmatic ghost; pure but not lovable; formidable yet precise, pedantic, almost old-maidish; the man of one book, Rousseau's *Social Contract,* made flesh.

With his death, the wild adventure into absolute democracy was over. The Revolution returned to its origins. Abstract principles and mob violence might both be used as instruments, but the one purpose was to establish the unquestioned rule of the bourgeoisie. The third estate was indeed "everything." It had turned definitely into a middle class: it had destroyed the privileges of the aristocracy, it had checked the rise of the proletariat. But it had to keep eternal vigilance against both the right and the left. The last year of the Convention (1794–1795) and the four years of the Directoire (1795–1799) were taken up with that fight on two fronts. At times the radical or Jacobin menace was uppermost, at times the royalist. Riots broke out, elections went the wrong way, and the balance had to be restored through a series of *coups d'état* and military interventions; until the regime perished in Brumaire (November 9, 1799) from an overdose of its own medicine.

The period has been vilified, and probably maligned. If there were occasional flurries of disorder in Paris, if the government was in constant financial straits, the country on the whole was recuperating. Lafayette, released at last by the Austrians, was impressed with the favorable change. The Directoire was "annoying, but not fatal." The immorality of the time cannot be denied. It was a reaction against somber bigotry, like the Restoration in England or the Regency in France. All the idealists were out of the way: ardent royalists or democrats in the grave or in exile, the purest patriots with the armies. To what is known as the Thermidorian reaction, the lingering shudder of the great crisis added a macabre touch; there were "balls of the victims," where merry widows like Joséphine de Beauharnais danced away their tragic memories.

6. NAPOLEON BONAPARTE

Thermidor cashed in on the victories of the Revolution. By the treaties of Basel (1795), the coalition against France was broken. Prussia and Spain withdrew, Prussia secretly agreeing that France might keep the whole left bank of the Rhine. England and Austria were still in the field. But the Directoire, incompetent as it might be in civil affairs, had a trained victorious army with able young commanders such as Hoche, Moreau, Bonaparte; and Carnot was still in control of military affairs. The war, however, was no longer a crusade; it had become an expedient. Bonaparte frankly told his barefoot troops that he was leading them to plunder the richest plains in Europe. This Italian campaign was to provide a marvelous demonstration of his resourcefulness, daring and skill. Austria had to make peace at Campo Formio (1797).

The victory, however, was precarious. Austria at once joined a new coalition with England, still irreconcilable, and with Russia, moving ponderously at last and for a time irresistibly. After seven years of fighting, the situation appeared as dark as in the worst days of 1793.

Bonaparte was in Egypt, seeking adventure and glory. At the news of France's plight, he returned, leaving his army to shift for itself and ultimately to capitulate. Before he had landed, however, Brune at Bergen, Masséna at Zurich, had already broken the back of the second coalition. Yet Bonaparte was hailed as a savior. The bourgeoisie had long desired "a sword" to make the new order secure: Bonaparte was a godsend. The *coup d'état* against the Directoire was engineered from within. Sieyès was to be the brains, Bonaparte the glorious instrument. But on the eighteenth of Brumaire (November 9, 1799), through Napoleon's fumbling, the plot nearly miscarried; the grenadiers had to be called in to retrieve the situation. Napoleon was the beneficiary of this swift turn of events. The sword alone had decided; Sieyès was relegated to second place, then dropped altogether. As first consul, the thirty-year old Corsican was the absolute master of France.

For a few years, he fulfilled every expectation. And the greatest of these was *peace:* peace with Austria at Lunéville (1801), peace with the church through a new concordat (1801–1802), peace with England at Amiens (1802). Peace, reconciliation, synthesis: the *émigrés* were allowed to return, and some of them worked side by side with revolutionists who had voted for the death of the king (*régicides*). The edicts of the Ancient Regime, the legislation of the revolutionary assemblies, the principles of Roman law were happily blended into a great Civil Code. With four assemblies (and no direct elections), with plebiscites conducted like military drills, with the tricolor preserved and regicides in high station, with the Bank of France established and the funds rising, it looked as though the bourgeois revolution had reached port at last.

Napoleon was a more efficient Louis XIV: the head of a vast bureaucracy devoted to the tranquillity and prosperity of the middle class.

Napoleon, although no philosopher, had a better head than Louis XIV. Yet he was not proof against the temptation of supreme power: personal glory. So he remained what he had called himself on the eighteenth of Brumaire, in his excited bombastic way, "the god of fortune and of war." The bourgeois who had picked him as the ideal policeman realized slowly that their guardian was not quite sane. For a decade, internal peace, prosperity and victory went together; but Madame Laetitia, Napoleon's mother, whispered: "If only it would last!" and Talleyrand knew for certain that it could not. But the bourgeois were the prisoners of their chosen protector. As soon as he could no longer silence them with the triumphal boom of guns, bells and *Te Deums,* the bourgeois raised their acrimonious little voices against him. When he was fighting his last desperate battles in 1814, every minor victory caused a drop in the Paris Bourse; and when he fell, the class that had chosen him heaved—as he had shrewdly prophesied—a sigh of immense relief.

Called to power to make peace, he was incapable of making peace. He always thought that a smashing victory was a final argument. He waged twelve wars and lost six—including the last. He left France smaller than he had found it. But he was not to blame for the original mistake, the treaty of Basel, the annexation of the whole left bank of the Rhine. The die was cast when he was a fledgling brigadier general out of a job. Europe could not accept this enormous extension of France: the rulers, because it destroyed the balance of power; the people, because it destroyed their self-determination and their self-respect. The Revolution had preached the rights of man: the first right of a German is to be a German and not a Frenchman. So dynasties and democracy were ultimately to unite against France, the conqueror. If the ruler had been Moreau instead of Bonaparte, the end might have come sooner but it would not have been different.

Paradoxical as it may sound, Napoleon achieved nothing. His famous sword acted as a catalyst; it precipitated reaction at home and conquest abroad but did not originate them. He has been called the creator of modern Germany; he hammered that amorphous confederacy into a military state; he turned the Germany of Kant, Beethoven, and Goethe into that of Fichte and Stein and ultimately of Bismarck and Hitler. But he does not bear the sole responsibility for that Frankenstein monster. German pride was reviving before 1800. Lessing had led the rebellion against the cultural hegemony of France. Herder had popularized the myth of the national soul. The Germans had already been thrilled with joy by the victories— and the treacheries—of Frederick the Great.

Napoleon left behind no permanent conquests; he left an architectural style and a legend. The style, a stiff Roman pastiche, had dignity and consistency; it was to be the last definite one for over a hundred years. The legend is multi-form. It is a grand epic of battle with the taut gray-coated figure, impassive, commanding, ever in the center. Even Napoleon's worst failures—Egypt, Russia—enriched his prestige through their exotic color or their tragic magnitude. The legend is also a perfect "success story"; the petty noble from an outlying, half-tamed province, who rises vertiginously, marries an archduchess, refers to Louis XVI as "my uncle," and gives crowns to his brothers. The legend, finally, is a romantic myth of the same period, with the same appeal as Faust, Don Juan, Prometheus. Napoleon was his own poet and his own hero; he consciously cultivated his prestige; he won the most lasting of his triumphs, a place in world folklore, by the side of Alexander, Caesar, Charlemagne; by the side also of King Arthur, Siegfried and William Tell.

7. CONSTITUTIONAL MONARCHY: 1814–1848

When Napoleon fell in 1814, the Bourbons were almost forgotten. But no other solution—Napoleon II, Bernadotte, Orléans, a republic—had a determined backing. As so frequently happens, it seemed realistic to slip back into the old groove; not because it was comfortable or efficient, but because it was well-worn. So the Bourbons returned, unwanted, unloved, having learned nothing and forgotten nothing. Talleyrand, who had already served and betrayed three or four regimes, was the chief and secret instrument of that restoration. He thought he could trump the allies' best card, *counterrevolution*, with the Bourbon claim of *legitimacy*. The trick served; but on the whole, it hurt the dynasty. Had Louis XVIII gained the throne frankly as a constitutional monarch, accepting the flag and the principles of 1789, he might have rallied the majority of the French to his cause. But, with the emphasis on legitimacy, with the white flag of the Ancient Regime, with the pretension to expunge twenty-five tremendous years out of French history, his position was absurd. In a few months, he had forfeited what tepid support the French had at first given him. Napoleon, caged at Elba, escaped almost alone (February 26, 1815). Before this one man who at any rate was real, the phantom called legitimate monarchy faded away.

The crazy gamble called the Hundred Days had its appointed end at Waterloo (June 18, 1815) and its long dismal epilogue at St. Helena (1815–1821). The Bourbons returned, more obviously than ever imposed by the Quadruple Alliance. Yet, thanks to the extreme lassitude of the French, thanks to a certain shrewdness on the part of Louis XVIII, the first ten years went smoothly enough. The White Terror was pale compared with the Red. The Romanticists reveled in a half-sincere revival of ancient loyalties. Chateaubriand, their model, did his best to throw a mantle of glamor over a very drab reality. The coronation of Charles X at Rheims in 1825 was a triumph of make-believe, a deliberate historical pageant. After this climax, the artificial prestige of the Restoration waned. The fame of Lord Byron, enthusiasm for Greek independence, liberalism, the Napoleonic legend were growing in unison. When Charles X put his divine right to the test by issuing autocratic ordinances, the bourgeoisie took up the challenge. Once more, the people of Paris was their spearhead. In July, 1830, Charles X was driven into exile and the tricolor of the bourgeois revolution was waving again over the Tuileries.

France had gone back to 1789 after having sampled Terror, Empire, and Ancient Regime restored. The third estate was to be "everything." A republic, even though moderate at first, might have fallen into democracy; the bourgeois, well versed in English precedents, sought to imitate the cautious revolution of 1688. A prince was in readiness, the duke of Orléans; of the royal house but of a junior branch; almost legitimate but needing popular assent. He was to be, not king of France but king of the French, their chosen head not their master. The constitution or charter was not to be granted by him out of his omnipotence; it was to be a contract, binding both parties. Lafayette, duped or weary, reluctant as ever to grab power for himself, urged the French to accept the "citizen king" as the one to make "the best of republics."

The July monarchy was for eighteen years (1830–1848) the very perfection of bourgeois rule. Legitimacy had been defeated, democracy was held in check. Worthy tradespeople went to court functions in their hackney coaches, and the king wielded, as a symbol, not a scepter or a sword but an umbrella. No more adventures abroad: *"Chacun chez soi, chacun pour soi,"* let everyone stay at home and attend to his own interests. Those who yearned for the blare of martial trumpets had to be satisfied with the Algerian campaigns—colorful, but an enterprise of limited liability—or with the revival of the Napoleonic legend. King Louis Philippe himself staged the return to Paris of Napoleon's remains (December, 1840). The thrifty, peace-at-any-price sovereign did homage to "the god of fortune and of war." The umbrella saluted the sword.

At home, only the rich had a vote, and used it unblushingly to bolster their privileges. To a demand for the extension of the franchise, Guizot answered, "If you want a vote, get rich!": plutocracy naked and unashamed.

Guizot, actual prime minister from 1840 to the end, was a philosophical historian who still commands our respect. He had studied the rise of the bourgeoisie throughout the centuries. He believed that this long evolution had reached its goal in 1830. As an interpreter of the past, he was justified. As a statesman, he failed to realize that historical development cannot be arrested at any particular date. The July revolution represented the triumph of an ideal which was already antiquated; it ought to have been realized half a century before.

There were at least three forces at work which the bourgeois monarchy did not understand and with which it was unable to cope. The first was *democracy*. The rights of man could not be limited to the highest taxpayers. The third estate was not "everything." Today, the reformers wanted a vote for the educated as well as for the rich; tomorrow, they would ask for manhood suffrage.

The second force was the *industrial revolution*. It had been retarded in France through half a century of political turmoil; but it was making headway and, in England, its results were already manifest. It led to the rise of a conscious proletariat and the social question. The bourgeoisie was still living in the age, not even of Adam Smith, but of Colbert; and Karl Marx was already at work.

The third force, not to be neglected by political historians, was *Romanticism*. Common sense was not enough. "Get rich" was not a soul-satisfying ideal. The regime was not incompetent but it was dull. Lamartine, a great lyric poet who was also the spiritual leader of the opposition, had pronounced the death warrant: "France is bored."

CHRONOLOGICAL SUMMARY, 1750–1848

Louis XV	1715–1774
Madame de Pompadour	1745–1764
Rousseau: *Discourse on Letters*	1749–1750
Diderot and d'Alembert: *Encyclopaedia*	1751–1780
Rousseau, *Discourse on Inequality*	1753–1755
Seven Years' War, treaty of Paris	1756–1763
Rousseau, *Social Contract, Emile*	1762
Voltaire, *Philosophical Dictionary*	1764
Lorraine united with France	1766
Corsica acquired, Napoleon Bonaparte born	1769
Maupeou *parlements*	1771–1774
Louis XVI	1774–1792
Turgot, minister of marine and finances	1774–1776
Necker	1777–1781
Alliance with America; treaty of Paris	1778–1783
Calonne, minister of finances	1783–1787
Loménie de Brienne (Assembly of Notables, conflict with Parlement)	1787–1788
Necker recalled to power	1788
The Constitutional Revolution	1789–1792
Meeting of States-General	May 5, 1789
States-General becomes National Assembly	June 17–23, 1789
(Oath of the Tennis Court)	June 20, 1789
Storming of the Bastille	July 14, 1789
Feudal rights and privileges renounced	August 4, 1789
Mob brings back royal family to Paris	Oct. 5–6, 1789
Death of Mirabeau	April 2, 1791
Flight of King to Varennes	June 20–25, 1791
Constituent Assembly dissolved	Sept. 30, 1791
Legislative Assembly	October, 1791–September, 1792
War against Austria	April 20, 1792

Mob invades Tuileries   June 20, 1792
New Insurrection; king a prisoner   August 10, 1792
Massacre of suspects in Paris prisons   Sept. 2–7, 1792
Victory of Valmy over Prussians   Sept. 20, 1792

THE FIRST REPUBLIC   1792–1799

National Convention   Sept. 21, 1792–Oct. 26, 1795
Monarchy abolished; Year One of the
    republic   Sept. 21, 1792
Louis XVI guillotined   January 21, 1793
War against England, Holland
    Spain, etc.   February 1, 1793
Insurrection in the west (Vendée)   March, 1793
Marat stabbed by Charlotte Corday   July 13, 1793
Reign of Terror: Royalists, Girondists,
    Hébertists, Dantonists executed   1793–1794
Victory of Fleurus   June 26, 1794
Robespierre overthrown and guillotined
    (9 Thermidor)   July 27, 1794
The Thermidorian reaction, Tallien,
    Fouché, etc.   1794–1795
Treaties of Basel (peace with Prussia and
    Spain)   March–June, 1795
Bonaparte helps suppress insurrection
    (Vendémiaire)   Oct. 5, 1795

DIRECTORY   1795–1799

Hoche pacifies the west (Vendée)   1796
Jourdan and Moreau invade Germany   1796
Bonaparte in Italy   1796–1797
Treaty of Campo Formio   1797
Bonaparte in Egypt and Syria   1798–1799
Second Coalition (Russia, Great Britain,
    Austria)   1798–1802
Brune defeats English at Bergen   Sept. 19, 1799

Masséna defeats Russians at Zürich	Sept. 26, 1799
Bonaparte lands in France	Oct. 8, 1799
Eighteenth of Brumaire; *coup d'état*	Nov. 9, 1799

NAPOLEON BONAPARTE   1799–1814–1815

THE CONSULATE	1799–1804
Victory of Marengo (Bonaparte & Desaix)	June 14, 1800
Victory of Hohenlinden (Moreau)	Dec. 3, 1800
Treaty of Lunéville with Austria	Feb. 9, 1801
Concordat with the Holy See	1801–1802
Chateaubriand: *Spirit of Christianity*	1802
Civil Code	1800–1804
Treaty of Amiens with England	March 27, 1802
Napoleon consul for life	Aug. 2, 1802

THE EMPIRE	1804–1814–1815
Third Coalition: Trafalgar (Nelson)	Oct. 21, 1805
Austerlitz (Napoleon)	Dec. 2, 1805
Treaty of Presbourg	Dec. 26, 1805
Prussia defeated at Auerstaedt (Davout) and	
Jena (Napoleon)	Oct. 14, 1806
Berlin Decree, continental blockade	Nov. 21, 1806
Indecisive battle of Eylau, victory of Friedland	
(June 14) Peace of Tilsit with Russia	July 7–9, 1807
Spanish War (England, Wellington)	1808–1814
War with Austria: Vienna, Aspern, Essling, Wagram	
(May–July, 1809) treaty of Schönbrunn	Oct. 14, 1809
Napoleon marries Marie Louise	1810
"King of Rome," *Eaglet,* Duke of Reichstadt born	1811
Russian Campaign: Borodino; Moscow	
burned	Sept. 15–19, 1812
Retreat: Beresina; Napoleon reaches Paris	Dec. 18, 1812
Campaign of Germany (War of Liberation)	
Prussia, Austria, Saxony, Bavaria join Russia	
Leipzig (Battle of the Nations)	Oct. 16–19, 1813
Campaign of France	1814
Allies enter Paris	March 31, 1814
Napoleon abdicates at Fontainebleau	April 11, 1814
Arrives in Elba	May 4, 1814

THE CONSTITUTIONAL MONARCHY   1814–1848

First Restoration   1814–1815
Louis XVIII   1814–1815–1824
Congress of Vienna   1814–1815
Napoleon returns
  the Hundred Days; Waterloo, June 18, 1815 1814–1815
  Abdicates, surrenders, exiled to St. Helena;
  dies   May 5, 1821
Allies re-enter Paris, restore Louis XVIII   July 7, 1815
Charles X   1824–1830
French land in Algiers   1830
Five autocratic ordinances; revolution   July 26–30, 1830

July monarchy, Louis Philippe I, King of
  the French   1830–1848
Heyday of Romantic literature   1830–1843
Louis Napoleon's attempt at Strasbourg; exiled   1836
Thiers: France on brink of war, Near-Eastern crisis   1840
Louis Napoleon's attempt at Boulogne; imprisoned   1840
Return of Napoleon's remains   Dec., 1840
Marshal Soult prime minister, Guizot chief
  influence   1840–1847
Guizot prime minister   1847–1848
Campaign for electoral reform. Revolution   Feb., 1848

PART THREE

Modern France

CHAPTER VII

Yesterday: 1848 - 1914

1. THE REVOLUTION OF 1848

THE GERMANS called 1848 "the crazy and holy year"; Arnold Toynbee defined it: a turning point where history failed to turn. Confused in the highest degree, ludicrous and tragic, it marked the beginning of our own era.

Europe as conceived by Metternich was antediluvian; dynastic and aristocratic, it was incapable of understanding either bourgeois liberalism or national sentiment. But the France of Guizot had become an ancient regime in its turn. In harmony with the Whig compromise of 1688, it had remained a government by the propertied classes for the defense of their vested interests, with King Log as a figurehead. It was unable to comprehend democracy or the social problem. Had Boileau returned to Paris in the eighteen forties, he would soon have felt at home. He had given Louis XIV the very counsels of peace that Louis Philippe was so sedulously following. Men like Dupin and Molé, or even like Thiers and Guizot, spoke a political idiom he could master with little effort. In spite of the "Gothic" invasion of the Romanticists, he would have found in the academy a solid majority attached to classical standards, and writers who were still composing *epistles* and *satires* in his own style. Even the material world had changed surprisingly little. It was less sharply contrasted under the citizen king than under the Grand Monarch; both splendor

and squalor had been toned down to a "reasonable" gray.
Agriculture was still the mainstay of national economy. In
most fields of industry, machinery had not yet supplanted the
handicrafts. The typical businessman was still the shopkeeper,
with his sharp-eyed wife at the cashier's desk. The horse still
provided the standard mode of locomotion. Few people as yet
had tried the new-fangled railways; fewer still had even heard
of the electric telegraph.

If on the contrary we take up the books, pamphlets, news-
papers of 1848, we find ourselves in the heart of our present
controversies. Universal (manhood) suffrage is taken for
granted. The dynastic state is superseded; wherever monarchy
is preserved, it is as the incarnation of national consciousness.
The redoubtable *Manifesto to the Communists* had just been
published. Within a few years, the industrial revolution, long
delayed, would cross the Channel and change the face of the
continent. With its railways, its vast public works, its credit
establishments on a national scale, its great expositions, its
widespread and tawdry luxury, the Second Empire is part of
our world. It seems old-fashioned just because it is not antique.

History does not flow evenly. It has pools and rapids; 1848
was a cataract. Nine months (February 24–December 10) were
crowded with more decisive events than the thirty-four years
of the Constitutional Monarchy (1814–1848) or the first forty
years of the Third Republic (1875–1914).

The collapse of the July monarchy in February, 1848, was
due to a mere accident. This fact reveals how precarious that
regime had been for eighteen years. The temper of the country was not revolutionary. There were hopes of a new heaven
and a new earth among a few intellectuals in Paris; but men
of sound sense could afford to smile at such dreams. There was
a network of "secret" democratic societies; but as a rule they
were well known to the police and without any real strength.
The Napoleonic legend, already past its zenith, had not
created a genuine Bonapartist movement. The general mood

was one of petty discontent and dull frustration rather than revolt. Business was poor; the government's policy was uninspired.

Among the more liberal bourgeois, there was a demand for a very moderate electoral reform. The least move in that direction would have dispelled the sense of stagnation. But the aged king was stubborn; Guizot, his right-hand man, was a haughty doctrinaire. A "reform" meeting in Paris was announced, forbidden, authorized, canceled again: nothing is so irritating as a fumbling autocrat. The Paris crowd demanded the resignation of Guizot; the king yielded—too late. A random shot was fired; the troops answered with a volley; the people carried their dead in tumbrels round the city; barricades sprang up everywhere in the narrow, crooked streets. Marshal Bugeaud, with his Algerian experience and prestige, offered to quell the rioting. Louis Philippe demurred. No coward, he was a man of peace. He was the sovereign of the bourgeois, and the bourgeois National Guard had shouted: "Reform! Reform!" He was king by the grace of the barricades: he yielded to the barricades. The marvelous feat of equilibrium was over. Louis Philippe, seventy-five years old, fled to England under the name of Mr. Smith.

Everyone knew who and what had been defeated: the middle-road July regime. No one knew who was the victor. The Paris bourgeoisie had refused to fight for the king; but all it wanted was a new team, not a new deal. Legitimists and Bonapartists were minorities. The one thing certain was that the decisive blows had been struck by the people of Paris, as in July and October, 1789, as in August, 1792, as in July, 1830. The people felt that in 1830 they had been robbed of their victory. They had fought in the name of democratic principles, and the result had been to bolster bourgeois privileges. This time, they meant not to be swindled again. On February 24, a "democratic and social" republic was proclaimed; on the twenty-fifth, the "right to a job" was formally recognized;

on the twenty-sixth, national workshops were established to cope with the economic crisis; on the twenty-eighth, a commission was set up to investigate the social problem, and Louis Blanc, a prominent socialist, by no means a utopian, was appointed as chairman.

These swift radical measures caused no immediate reaction. France was still bewildered. The head of the provisional government, the poet Lamartine, had good will, prestige, eloquence, moderation; and he was not devoid of political skill. He was the perfect antithesis of the Louis Philippe regime: he stood for generosity. For a time, France gave the Lamartinian republic the benefit of the doubt. The clergy solemnly blessed the newly planted "trees of liberty"—which, alas, refused to take root.

But there had been throughout the land a resentment, at the same time vague and deep against the dictatorship of the Paris mob, led by a handful of politicians, idealists and radicals. Provincial France was profoundly attached to peace and property; the Paris extremists threatened both. There had been everywhere in Europe national democratic uprisings. Paris wanted France to embark upon a new crusade: the French Revolution could not be safe except in a revolutionized Europe. Lamartine was aware that France, apart from a tumultuous element in the capital, would shrink from such a desperate venture. He did his best to reassure and appease the "legitimate" governments, and the revolutions were suppressed one by one.

The national workshops were, immediately, a relief measure. But their name, borrowed from Louis Blanc, seemed to indicate a trend toward socialism. Their management was entrusted to a conservative, whose secret desire was to demonstrate their absurdity. His *sabotage* was admirably successful. A hundred thousand men in Paris were set the task of digging out the sandy waste of the Champ de Mars and then filling it up again. Thus an army of discontent was mobilized right in the capital. The national workshops were suppressed with the same haste as they had been created, with the same clumsiness as they had been managed. They became a test; both sides had worked themselves up into the dangerous mood of the showdown. To suppress the national workshops was to proclaim the bankruptcy of the "democratic and social" republic promised in February. The Paris workers took up the challenge. On June 23, Paris was again bristling with barricades.

This time, the response of the country was unmistakable. Everywhere the provincial bourgeois and the peasant masses showed their determination to destroy the "Reds." Generosity was no longer the order of the day; Lamartine's government resigned. A general trained in Algerian warfare, Cavaignac, did what Bugeaud had offered to do; he crushed the insurrection, in three days of savage street fighting. He was a stanch republican; he had "saved society"; but he was to be branded as "the butcher of June." His tragic task accomplished, he was asked to remain in power as chief executive. The idealistic revolution of February was at an end.

On November 4, the new constitution was finally approved by the Constituent Assembly. It was of the American type: Tocqueville had had a hand in framing it. It provided a single Legislative Assembly, and a president elected by direct manhood suffrage. Not a few had misgivings: such a plebiscite might open the gate to Caesarism. It was Lamartine's eloquence that carried the vote.

On December 10, the presidential election was held. Out of over seven million votes, Lamartine, once the idol of the people, polled 17,000; Raspail, a radical with socialist backing, 36,000; Ledru-Rollin, candidate of the democratic left, 370,000; Cavaignac, the bourgeois Republican, 1,400,000; and Prince Louis Napoleon Bonaparte, 5,400,000. *Alea jacta est!* The die is cast! as Lamartine had said. The people had spoken, and with no ambiguous voice.

2. LOUIS NAPOLEON, 1848–1870

The man who thus stepped on the stage, and was to remain a protagonist for twenty-two years, was practically unknown. He was the son of Louis Bonaparte, that younger brother of Napoleon who, for a while, had been the very unhappy king of Holland. Louis Napoleon had been brought up in exile. After the death of Napoleon's son [1] and that of his elder brother, he had considered himself the active head of the Napoleonic dynasty; for his father and his uncles had no appetite for adventure. He had staged two attempts against the July monarchy: at Strasbourg in 1836, at Boulogne in 1840. Both had been blank failures. Pardoned and shipped out of the country after Strasbourg, he was formally condemned and imprisoned after Boulogne. He escaped in 1846. Gentle, dreamy, stubborn, he had an unquestioning faith in Caesarian democracy—the people's will incarnated in a providential leader. And he believed that the people's voice, if free, could utter but one name: Napoleon.

For many historians, Louis Napoleon is merely the rather pitiful embodiment of the Napoleonic legend. The truth is more complex. The legend was at its height in 1840, when Louis Philippe had the remains of the emperor brought back "to rest on the banks of the Seine, amid that French people He had so deeply loved." At the time of this glorious pageant, Louis Napoleon was a prisoner and forgotten. After June, 1848, his own confused personality happened to be, for a brief moment, in perfect harmony with the confusion of the national mind. The radicals had been sharply defeated; but if France wanted order, property, and peace, she did not want reaction. She craved a strong conservative power of revolutionary origin. The royalists, with Thiers at their head, knew that their own cause had no chance for the moment; so they

[1] The king of Rome, Napoleon II, the "Eaglet," the duke of Reichstadt (1810–1832).

thought it clever to vote for Louis Napoleon, "a dolt," who could be brushed aside at the proper time. But on the other hand, Caesarian democracy seemed direct, effective democracy as compared with the eternal squabbling of parliamentary politics. And the socialistic hopes of February, although repressed, had not been wholly destroyed. Cavaignac, the butcher of June, was hated by the workers; Louis Napoleon had socialist sympathies. He had written a pamphlet, inspired by Louis Blanc, on *The Extinction of Pauperism*, through a "reserve army of labor" organized into self-supporting communities. As in the case of Hitler, Louis Napoleon was backed by men of all parties, and for contradictory reasons. His name stood for order, for glory, for the principles of 1789, for curbing the Reds, for social progress—and above all, for the end of inane, selfish fumbling. He was indeed all things to all men.

He was no inert symbol. He remains an enigma to this day but there was extraordinary pertinacity and skill in his political conduct. As president, he was a national figure; above parties, he had no party. So the Legislative Assembly elected in 1849 was not Bonapartist. The idealistic and moderate republicans of the Lamartine type had been defeated; the Assembly was divided between a reactionary majority, and a radical minority. The president stood alone; and he alone stood for the country as a whole.

At first, he played his part correctly under a constitution which was both presidential and parliamentary. He gave the conservatives all the rope they wanted. He allowed them to disenfranchise three million workers. Then he appealed to public opinion, the direct source of his power. He toured the country, spoke surprisingly well, and was received with enthusiasm. In a land thirsting for tranquillity, both the right and the left were openly preparing a revolution. Louis Napoleon struck first. On the second of December, 1851, he declared the Assembly dissolved and universal suffrage restored. The final decision was left in the hands of the people.

The *coup d'état*, carefully prepared, went without a hitch. On the third of December, however, resistance was allowed, deliberately it would seem, to gather strength in Paris. It looked as though someone wanted the new regime to start with a display of force. Victor Hugo, who considered himself the soul of that resistance, conveys the impression that it was pathetically weak. As the workers of the Faubourg Saint Antoine told Representative Baudin, they did not want to die for a reactionary Assembly which they despised. But the moral victory of Louis Napoleon was not clear-cut. Both population and troops were uncertain, nervous; the days of June were not forgotten. On the fourth, a tragic accident occurred. The soldiers parading on the boulevards, believing themselves threatened, fired without command at innocent bystanders. Before that unaccountable panic could be checked, there were hundreds of dead.

In spite of this disastrous mishap, the country endorsed the president, three weeks later, by 7,440,000 votes against 646,-000. But, for the Parisians and for the republicans, the blood stain could not be washed away. Victor Hugo branded the *coup d'état* as a crime. And for nineteen years, Hugo in exile was a prophet of doom, cursing a regime founded on force and fraud.

The president, carrying out his mandate, drew up a constitution. It was a streamlined consulate: an all-powerful executive, elected by popular vote for ten years; an ornamental, appointed senate; a council of state, composed of technicians, and likewise appointed; finally, a very modest legislative body. The President toured the country again. He was hailed with cries of *"Vive l'Empereur!"* The Senate took the hint and consulted the people: by 7,824,000 votes against 253,000, the restoration of the empire was approved. On the second of December, 1852, Louis Napoleon formally became Napoleon III, by the grace of God and the will of the people, emperor of the French.

For eight years, there was political silence. The Assembly, although duly elected, was in reality handpicked. The emperor's power was unchecked. He used it to promote material prosperity; romantic dreams had faded and this was the age of realism. He succeeded magnificently. Of course, he was not responsible for the industrial revolution; but he understood it, as neither his predecessor nor his successors did. Paris was transformed under Haussmann, partly as a precaution against rioting, partly as a wiser substitute for the ill-fated national workshops, partly to enhance the glory of the reign. But, whatever the motive may have been, the plan was broadly, daringly conceived and executed with swift efficiency. Paris lived for seventy years on the impetus given by Napoleon III and his vigorous prefect. Ports, railroads, steamship lines were created. The *Crédit Foncier, Crédit Mobiliter, Crédit Lyonnais, Société Générale* gave new life to French finances. The pennies saved by peasant or shopkeeper were drained, gathered, used for large scale operations. The period had a curiously American quality—well ahead of America. The prosperity of the Second Empire, long remembered, was not a myth; if France recuperated so rapidly after 1871, it was because her economic structure was sound.

Yet the curse of ambiguity lies on this regime, in the economic as well as in the political field. Napoleon III proclaimed himself a socialist; Sainte-Beuve called him "Saint-Simon on horseback"; and indeed the emperor seemed to have adopted the Saint-Simonian principle: "The first duty of the state is to promote the material and moral welfare of the most numerous and poorest class." But he promoted welfare mostly through private capitalism; so that his reign appears at first as the paradise of profiteers—his half-brother Morny the most eminent among them. The emperor stood, too obviously, for material order and material welfare. He turned the spiritual welfare over to the Catholic church; and that was interpreted as clericalism, at a time when the Pope, Pius IX, had openly declared war on "liberalism, progress, and modern civilization."

Literature was not stifled. With the veterans Guizot, Michelet, Sainte-Beuve, Proudhon, with the new generation, Taine and Renan, the Second Empire was a brilliant and vigorous period in French thought. Toward the end of the regime, Offenbach, with his librettists Meilhac and Halévy, was to transmute frivolous pleasure into frail but undeniable beauty; this, however, is only one element, and a minor one, in the life and art of the time. The literature of the Second Empire is surprisingly earnest; indeed it is somber. The point to remember is not that *The Flowers of Evil* by Charles Baudelaire and that *Madame Bovary* by Gustave Flaubert were mildly prosecuted but that they were written, published, and appreciated.

Louis Napoleon had promised: "The empire stands for peace," and he meant it. Two years later came the first great war in four decades. England and France invaded the Crimea and, in spite of incredible blundering, finally reduced Sevastopol (1854–1856). Before the war actually began, the reasons assigned as its cause had been forgotten. Napoleon III wanted to humble tsarist Russia, so long a menace to western liberalism; and he desired above all to cement through an alliance an *entente cordiale* with England. France gained nothing from that costly adventure, except questionable prestige: at the Congress of Paris, the emperor appeared as the arbiter of the continent.

His second war, against Austria, had deeper meaning; but, for that very reason, it endangered a regime based upon ambiguity. Napoleon III and Cavour, the patriotic Piedmontese statesman, deliberately plotted war against Austria. Napoleon's faith in direct democracy had led him to the idea of self-determination, which was called at that time "the principle of nationalities." Let the will of the people be ascertained through plebiscites. If the Italians want to be united, no "legitimacy" should stand in the way. Austria was a foreign intruder in Lombardy and Venice, a reactionary influence in Parma, Modena, Tuscany. When war came, the emperor led an army into Italy and was victorious at Magenta and Solferino (1859).

It was a democratic, a revolutionary war, and never was Napoleon III so popular as when he returned, laurel-wreathed, to his capital. But the triumph filled his conservative supporters with misgivings. For the Papal state stood in the way of Italian unity. Napoleon III was one at heart with the republican hero, Garibaldi; but officially, he was the protector of the Pope, and his troops were defending Rome. To the very end, he was unable to extricate himself from that imbroglio.

By 1860, the superficial unanimity of the first eight years of his reign had dissolved. The opposition, still very small, was becoming vocal. Ailing, prematurely aged, the emperor attempted to make his regime less authoritarian. But the minister whom he chose as his delegate, a veritable vice-emperor, Eugène Rouher, had crude vigor and rudimentary skill rather than statesmanship. He could bully or quibble his way out of difficulties; he could not plan a long-range policy. The Mexican affair—which Rouher called "the deepest thought of the reign"— made matters worse. It was a protracted comedy of tragic errors. Napoleon may have erred in good faith; but the plain result was that France offended American sentiments, attempted to strangle a republic, lost men, money, and prestige. When the handsome nonentity Napoleon had placed on the crazy Mexican throne, Maximilian of Hapsburg, was shot at Querétaro (1867), it was accepted as an omen that Napoleon's miraculous luck had deserted him.

At Paris the opposition—royalist with Thiers, republican

with Jules Favre and later Henri Rochefort and Léon Gambetta—adopted an attitude which, for partisan purposes, was
shrewd and, from the national point of view, disastrous. It
consisted in urging upon the government a spirited foreign
policy, blaming it for its timidity, and yet refusing it the indispensable instrument, a modern army. The military reforms proposed by Marshal Niel were emasculated and made
inoperative by the Chamber which, with the waning of the
emperor's prestige, had recovered its independence. The
victory of Prussia over Austria at Königgrätz (Sadowa) in
1866 was gratuitously interpreted as a moral defeat for France.
The emperor was bidden to retrieve France's threatened hegemony. In 1867, he made half-hearted attempts to secure
"compensations"; the demands were irritating to the Germans, the refusal humiliating for the French.

Yet the decaying regime and the desperately sick sovereign
were to have a last spring of hope. Napoleon III determined
to turn the empire, frankly and openly, into a constitutional
monarchy (1869). He chose as his prime minister Emile Ollivier, long one of the leaders of the republican opposition, a
great orator and a genuine liberal. Moderate republicans and
monarchists rallied to the government. Caesarian democracy
was not quite forgotten; the emperor submitted the constitutional changes to the people through a plebiscite held on May
8, 1870. The rejuvenated empire was endorsed by 7,358,000
votes against 1,571,000. Gambetta had to confess: "The empire is stronger than ever." Ollivier could promise: "We shall
give the emperor a happy old age." And Napoleon III could
draw what seemed the obvious conclusion: "Between revolution and the empire, the country has been challenged to choose,
and has chosen. . . . My government shall not deviate from
the liberal line it has traced for itself. . . . More than ever,
we may envisage the future without fear." (May 21). This was
said a hundred and three days before Sedan.

3. *L'ANNÉE TERRIBLE*, 1870–1871

As with the Crimean War, the pretext of the Franco-Prussian War was forgotten before hostilities began. A Hohenzollern prince, a distant cousin of the king of Prussia, had been offered the vacant throne of Spain. France objected, and the candidacy was withdrawn. There the matter should have ended.

But the French had been taught that they must avenge "the humiliation of Sadowa." Now was the time to inflict upon Prussia a smarting diplomatic rebuff. This belligerent mood fitted in with Bismarck's plans. He had convinced himself that only a war against the "hereditary foe" could weld the German states into a nation; and he knew that his army was ready, while that of the French was in the preliminary throes of reorganization. Since the French chose to make the conflict an affair of honor, he would see to it that their pride be properly challenged. The king of Prussia, at Ems, had given the last request of the French ambassador a courteous but noncommittal answer; by slightly doctoring the report, Bismarck made it sound like an insult. Chamber, press, Paris mob fell at once into the trap. The partisans of an autocratic empire welcomed the opportunity; victory, renewing the prestige of the army, would enable them to sweep aside the foolish liberal experiment. The deep masses of rural and provincial France were averse to war; the emperor, tragically clear-sighted in his impotence, knew that his cause was not good and that his army was worse. Caesarian democracy might have saved the day, if the emperor had appealed to the whole people, against the tumult and shouting in Paris. But the emperor did not dare; he had lost faith in his mission. And so war was declared.

The issue was decided in the first four weeks. By August 18, MacMahon was in full retreat toward Rheims, Bazaine was blockaded in Metz. Even then, a wiser strategy might have mitigated the disaster; but the empress, left in Paris as regent, was moved by passionate pride and dynastic considerations.

MacMahon's weary and disorganized troops, instead of reforming so as to cover Paris, were ordered forward to relieve
Bazaine. They were deflected toward Sedan, and hopelessly
trapped. Napoleon III, a living corpse dragged about by the
army, did his best to be killed. Then, sacrificing prestige to
humanity, he resumed command only to capitulate (September 2). As soon as the news became known in Paris (September
4), the empire melted away. A republic was proclaimed, with
a government of national defense, headed by the commander
of the Paris garrison, General Trochu.

Legends die hard. In 1870, many Frenchmen believed, with
a despairing hope, in the magic virtue of mighty words and
lofty feelings: the republic, the spirit of the Marseillaise, the
holy wrath of the people. Even if patriotic passion had burned
as fiercely as in 1793, it could not have created overnight the
strategists, officers, equipment, arms, munitions needed to
check the Prussian armies. On September twenty-seventh,
Strasbourg capitulated. On October twenty-eighth, Bazaine
surrendered in Metz with the last organized army. He was not
a traitor in the more obvious sense, but a man with a coarse,
petty, shifty intelligence and no moral fiber. Soon Paris was
held in a ring of fire.

There was no hope, for France had no friend. Gladstone
feared European commitments. Italy and Austria had been
ready to rush to the support of Napoleon III, if he had been
victorious; when he fell, they congratulated themselves on
their neutrality. Trochu, in command of a large improvised
army in Paris, was a fussy theorist and martinet, with a deep
distrust of raw levies. Gambetta, the young lawyer and politician, refused to despair. He escaped from Paris in a balloon,
directed the resistance from Tours, raised new armies, sup-
plied them after a fashion; and the generals who led them,
Chanzy, Faidherbe, with their broken swords wrested from
fate a few minor victories. But Paris, unable to break the
circle of steel, famished, bombarded, finally surrendered

(January 28). Bourbaki's army, unaccountably forgotten in the armistice, managed to escape into Switzerland. Only Belfort had stood firm; and the great wounded lion hewn by Bartholdi out of the rock of the citadel served as the symbol of France's unconquerable spirit.

General elections were held on February 8. Alsace and Lorraine voted in the presence of the conqueror; and they sent to the Assembly at Bordeaux a delegation unanimously opposed to their annexation by Germany. Never did any territory more clearly express its self-determination. The attitude of the Alsace-Lorrainers proved that the treaty of Francfort (May 10) was a *Diktat,* not a permanent settlement. In all languages, "Alsace-Lorraine" became the symbol of brutal conquest. Among the hundred and seven deputies who refused to ratify the treaty of Francfort, one survived to see the day of *revanche,* that is to say of justice. His name was Georges Clemenceau.

The country wanted peace; the republicans, led by Gambetta, were still urging a fight to the bitter end. So, at the elections of February 8, the republicans were sharply defeated; Gambetta was branded as a "raving maniac." Bonapartism had vanished after Sedan. The Assembly, meeting at Bordeaux on February 13, 1871, had therefore a strong majority of monarchists.

Paris had stood for national resistance and for democracy; the city felt doubly betrayed. Its spirit had been ardent and stoic, but Trochu had refused to lead. And now a provincial conservative body seemed bent on humiliating the heroic capital. The seat of government was fixed at Versailles, as though eighty years of history were to be wiped away. Paris rebelled. The word *commune,* which the municipal government assumed or resumed, has nothing to do with *communism.* It is the medieval term for chartered cities and had been used again during the Revolution. The insurrection was first of all an explosion of wounded patriotism; secondly, an attempt to defend or restore the democratic republic; in the third place, it manifested a desire for local autonomy—centralization imposed by Paris means freedom, centralization imposed upon Paris is tyranny. In the fourth place, the Commune was the result of many petty grievances: the pay of the national guards was abruptly stopped; their debts, suspended during the siege, were made immediately exigible. When the insurrection openly became a civil war, when the provinces failed to follow the leadership of the capital, the moderate elements which had at first supported the movement gradually withdrew. The Commune thus became increasingly proletarian and cosmopolitan. The bourgeoisie affected to consider it as the work of the "Red Fiend," the Workers' International. Karl Marx recognized it as such. Revolutionary socialism took up the tradition; the bolshevists confirmed it; and now the legend is ineradicable.

The Commune defended itself against the Versailles troops of MacMahon and Galliffet with great stubbornness; at the end, they shot a few hostages in reprisals; many public buildings went up in flames. The insurrection was repressed by the Versailles troops with unexampled ferocity. Seventeen thousand communards were killed after the fighting was over. Adolphe Thiers, defender of the middle class, was in control. He had not forgotten his own fear in the days of June, 1848. He believed that "the vile multitude"—the phrase was his —should be held in subjection, if need be by means of terror.

Victor Hugo, sixty-nine years old, wrote a great collection of patriotic poems called *L'Année Terrible*. The Terrible Year: not on account of suffering, deaths, destruction; wounds are healed, grief assuaged, ruins restored; but because wrongs were inflicted then which remained alive for half a century. Between France and Germany, there could be no gradual reconciliation. Between the bourgeoisie and the working class, there were memories which the years could not deprive of their tragic intensity. No statesman is great who, even in the name of a worthy cause, creates implacable hatreds. In the long perspective of history, both Thiers and Bismarck must stand as disastrous failures.

4. THE OPPORTUNIST REPUBLIC

The royalists had a handsome majority in the National Assembly. But they were divided. The legitimists supported Henry, count of Chambord, in whose favor his grandfather Charles X had abdicated in 1830. The Orléanists had for their leader Philippe, count of Paris, grandson of Louis Philippe.

A compromise had been arranged. The count of Paris had effaced himself before the count of Chambord, who was both his senior and the representative of the senior branch. But the contest was between principles, not personalities. The Orléanists accepted the tricolor flag of the Revolution; the legitimists stood for monarchy by divine right, and the white standard of the Ancient Regime. The count of Chambord was eager to rule, but on his own terms and under his own banner. Even Marshal MacMahon, whom the royalists had picked out as chief executive, realized that modern France would never accept this mystic conception of royal authority: "the guns would go off of their own accord." Chambord had made himself unacceptable; but he stood in the way of an Orléanist restoration. In this deadlock, liberal royalists and moderate republicans agreed in drawing up a constitution of the British, or bourgeois parliamentary, type. It mattered little whether the figurehead be called king or president, so long as the substantial middle class remained in control. The fossil pretender, Chambord, was childless. In the meantime, MacMahon would keep the seat for the count of Paris.

So in 1875 the actual Third Republic emerged, after four years of confused wrangling. The new regime was obviously a compromise. The royalists eyed their own handiwork with misgivings; the radical republicans viewed it with undisguised hostility. Still, the scheme was workable. It stood many crises; if it perished in 1940, it was not because of its inherent faults, but because it was stunned from without and betrayed from within. It has left very little regret; but, if it could slow down progress, it could not arrest or reverse it.

The royalists had been misguided enough, in 1873, to quarrel with their ablest leader, Adolphe Thiers. Rejected by them, he veered toward moderate republicanism. Gambetta, the fiery radical and "bitter-ender," had grown more opportunistic with the years. Their combined efforts proved irresistible; the first general elections, held in 1876, gave the united republicans an unquestioned majority in the Chamber. The conservatives, still in control of the presidency and the Senate, refused to give up without a fight. Marshal Mac-Mahon forced a liberal ministry to resign (May 16, 1877), dissolved the Chamber and, in the next elections, reverted to the pressure methods of the Second Empire. This is what he called the restoration of *moral order*. Wasted efforts: the republican majority returned, barely diminished, and in resentful mood (October 14–28, 1877). MacMahon, this time, had to acknowledge defeat; and for the remaining sixty-three years of the Third Republic, the presidency was reduced to complete impotence. In 1879, the senatorial elections also turned in favor of the republicans. MacMahon remained an isolated vestige of a lost cause. He understood, and retired. He left a renown of great personal bravery, unquestioned honesty, political ineptitude and, in his chance remarks, incurable naïveté. Jules Grévy was elected president chiefly because, in 1848, he had declared that the republic needed no president.

During this first decade (1870–1879), the republic had been slowly conquered by the republicans. Apart from this protracted political contest, France, sobered but undismayed by the disasters of the "Terrible Year," had been working hard, silently, and with excellent results. The territory was liberated and the war indemnity paid ahead of time, thanks to the wealth accumulated under the empire and to the financial capacity of Thiers. The army was reorganized. The Exposition of 1878, without the fevered brilliancy of 1867, made manifest the thorough recuperation of the country.

The next twenty years (1879–1899) were the era of opportunism. The republicans, now in control, had split into opportunists and radicals. The radicals had preserved the program of the republican opposition under the empire: no Senate, separation of church and state, an income tax. The opportunists had two principles: first, no reform until the time is ripe for it; second, the time is never ripe. It was hoped that two definite parties would emerge and alternate in classical fashion, like Tories and Whigs in old England, "resistance" and "movement" under Louis Philippe, or, in more general terms, conservatives and liberals. That ideal dichotomy, the cherished utopia of doctrinaires, could never be attained. The royalists were still strong. There was an occasional flare-up of Bonapartism. Against such a menace, the republicans of all shades had to unite. So most cabinets were coalitions with the key positions in the hands of opportunists. On the other hand, the right center and the left center combined against any aggressive move of the radicals. In retrospect, these half-hearted, ambiguous political squabbles appear dismal. Clemenceau, the most incisive of the radicals, had in those days the reputation of overthrowing one ministry after another: "They are all the same," he said in self-defense.

The opportunist republic had a Louis Philippe quality. It was decidedly bourgeois, and petty bourgeois at that, with cautious, parsimonious, silent Grévy as a perfect symbol. Gambetta, who was vivid, almost flamboyant, masterful, ardently patriotic, never was fully trusted. He reached power under unfavorable circumstances, kept it for a brief season (1881) and died at forty-four (1882). In the absence of vigorous characters and dramatic issues, the chief episodes of the period were scandals. Daniel Wilson, son-in-law of President Grévy, was involved with shady adventurers, who trafficked in the Legion of Honor. The aged president clung tenaciously to his gilded armchair but he was finally compelled to retire; and Sadi Carnot, blameless, wooden and melancholy, the grandson of the great Lazare who had been "the Organizer of Victory," was elected in his place.

There was a sense of dull frustration; grayness spread over all, and it was dirty. The idea of *revanche* was fading away; the republic, so fair under the empire, had turned into a drab, heavy-jowled matron with a flecked reputation. This gave General Boulanger his chance. Like Louis Napoleon forty years before, like Hitler forty years later, he appealed to contradictory sentiments. A soldier, he stood for the army, patriotism, glory, the liberation of Alsace-Lorraine. He was backed almost openly by the conservatives, as a battering ram to destroy the republic. But he also appealed to the masses, as the champion of Caesarian democracy, direct and effective, against the dreary selfish fumbling of party politicians and profiteers. In 1889, he gave the republicans a scare: he was triumphantly elected in Paris, and a daring *coup* might have been successful. But there was no genuine strength in the man; his chief assets were a blond beard, a black horse, and the support of a vaudeville singer, Paulus. The parliamentarians rallied. They frightened him into exile; he never dared to try his luck again; and two years later (1891), he committed suicide in Brussels, on the grave of the woman he loved.

The politicians had their deserved victory; it did not bring them peace. The enemies of the parliamentary republic were soon offered a splendid opportunity. The Panama Canal Company, headed by the builder of Suez, Ferdinand de Lesseps, had encountered unexpected difficulties. In order to issue new loans, it bribed not only many journalists, but about a hundred senators and deputies. In France, the influence of big business upon politics is invariably resented, whereas America takes it for granted. Many sins could be condoned: failure could not. The financial crash and the political scandal came together, each making the other worse. The anti-Boulanger leaders were ruthlessly smeared; even Clemenceau was not spared and it must be admitted that he had queer friends. The Panama affair is a tangled story of honest mismanagement, corruption, and partisan politics. The republic reeled, lurched, and finally righted itself. A less sensitive regime would not even have felt the blow.

But scandals do not wholly fill the annals of the opportunist era. It has two great achievements to its credit. Both are connected with the name of Jules Ferry, the outstanding statesman of the period; both brought France very close to war, civil and foreign. The first was the development of elementary education; the second was the sudden expansion of the French Colonial Empire.

The republicans made elementary education free to all and compulsory for all. It was their principle that public schools, supported out of public funds, should not be under the control of any church. But ever since the Middle Ages, the Catholic church had considered education as her special domain. Secular education was branded as godless, and the republican laws as tyrannical. This conflict forced the republic into an anticlerical attitude. A keen and generous-minded Pope, Leo XIII, succeeded in assuaging the feud. On his advice, a number of Catholics rallied to the republic; and the republican minister Spuller could hail the rise of "a new spirit." This reconciliation, unfortunately, was not deep and did not prove lasting.

In twenty years, the stodgy, stay-at-home republic acquired, almost unawares, vast and dimly known territories in Asia and Africa. This paradoxical growth was not demanded by public opinion. Clemenceau had country and parliament behind him, when he checked Freycinet's hesitant desires to intervene in Egypt. Jules Ferry jeopardized his popularity because of his aggressive policy in Indo-China. The clearest immediate result of this expansionist policy was to create everywhere causes of friction with England. Every advance of the tricolor was considered in London as trespassing. This culminated in the sharp conflict over the control of the upper Nile. When Sirdar Kitchener, at the head of a victorious army, had reconquered Khartoum, he found Captain Marchand, with a handful of French African soldiers, established at Fashoda (1898). The encounter was dramatic. France had to yield: Marchand was recalled. But the humiliation rankled; no wonder the French cheered the Boers a year later.

The diplomatic situation of the republic was not enviable. Bismarck had succeeded in effecting a triple alliance between Germany, Austria, and Italy (1881). England was then manifestly pro-German. It was the time when Anglo-Saxondom was proudly conscious of its Teutonic origins, and when Cecil Rhodes tried to foster spiritual unity among the various members of the family—the Dominions, America, and Germany. In this isolation, France was pathetically grateful to find an ally and a friend. The alliance with tsarist Russia was paradoxical and precarious. Strictly defensive, it did not provide for the recovery of Alsace-Lorraine. It proved costly, for France poured billions into the tsarist sieve. Yet at the time when the French were haunted with fears of decadence, it seemed a healthy tonic.

5. THE RADICAL REPUBLIC: 1899–1914

The consolidation of the republic, the growth of popular education, the resurgence of socialism, were gradually changing the political scene. This evolution was hastened and made dramatic through the Dreyfus case. The affair began simply as an error on the part of a *Conseil de Guerre* (military court). Captain Dreyfus was condemned to life imprisonment for an act of treason which he had not committed (1894). Antisemitism played but a minor part in this miscarriage of justice; the chief apostle of that barbaric creed, Edouard Drumont, was admired as a journalist but even the people who relished the virulence of his *Libre Parole* shrugged away his fanatical bias. At the height of the Dreyfus crisis, not a single antisemitic deputy was returned from metropolitan France.

When the family of Alfred Dreyfus, supported by a few jurists and patriots, began to appeal for a new trial, the general staff stiffened. They believed in passive obedience and the infallibility of rank. To challenge the verdict of a military court was to break down army discipline; and the army was not merely the sword and shield but the very armature of the nation. Soon, spiritual rather than political forces were definitely polarized. On the one hand, the champions of authority and tradition: aristocracy, clergy, social conservatives; on the other, the defenders of freedom: intellectuals, Protestants, freethinkers. There were, however, not a few royalists and Catholics on the Dreyfusist side, and not a few Jews in the conservative coalition (Arthur Meyer). The orthodox Marxian socialists, led by Jules Guesde, were in favor of remaining neutral. But Jaurès, heir to the spirit of "forty-eight," lifted the problem above party lines: "Socialism stands for justice; in seeking justice for a capitalist and a militarist, we are serving democracy."

Jean Jaurès, Emile Zola (*J'accuse!*), Georges Clemenceau, the delicate skeptic Anatole France, the scientist Painlevé, a host of others turned a mere scandal into a spiritual storm which shook the world. The affair itself stopped in 1899 with a compromise. Dreyfus, condemned by a second military court "with extenuating circumstances," was pardoned forthwith;

an amnesty was proclaimed. It was only in 1906 that the victim was fully reinstated, promoted, decorated, on the very spot that had been the scene of his degradation.

But the victory of the Dreyfusists was nonetheless manifest. Waldeck-Rousseau, their political leader (1899–1902), offered the model of a device which many consider as far superior to rigid party divisions: a coalition, as broad as possible, for a definite purpose—in this case to promote justice and restore civil peace. Waldeck-Rousseau, himself a moderate, included in his cabinet General de Galliffet, a picturesque survivor of the Second Empire, and Alexandre Millerand, at that time one of the most orthodox theorists of socialism.

The Dreyfus case had accelerated the trend toward the left and, from 1899 to 1914, the radicals became the dominant party. Although many ardent Catholics were Dreyfusists, clerical-conservative elements had somehow committed the church to the losing side, and the church had to pay. Religious orders, which had enjoyed exemptions and privileges, were placed under the common law. Those that refused to submit were dissolved; but a number which offered to comply were denied recognition. Only a few contemplative and charitable orders were left undisturbed. Emile Combes, chosen by Waldeck-Rousseau to be his successor, was the leader of the anticlerical crusade. But it was not he who secured the separation of church and state, abrogating Napoleon's concordat. This measure (December, 1905), steered through parliament by Aristide Briand, was moderate and statesmanlike. Although it was at first rejected by the Holy See, a compromise was reached in 1924. In the long interval, there had been irritation rather than persecution. Certainly the church, now free within the free state, was revitalized by the new challenge and the new opportunity. The last forty years in France have been a brilliant period in Catholic annals; the names of Paul Claudel the poet and Jacques Maritain the philosopher are sufficient evidence of this great revival.

The radical, Dreyfusist republic reached its summit in 1906, when Clemenceau, then sixty-five, attained power for the first time. But already the sacred union "for justice and truth" had begun to disintegrate. Idealists like Charles Péguy were disgusted when their spiritual crusade turned into a cheap political victory. The anticlerical struggle had many unpleasant aspects, and wounded many delicate souls. The socialists had been ordered by the Amsterdam Congress (1904) not to co-operate with bourgeois governments. The syndicalists were advocating "direct action," an ominous phrase. After battling their way into the promised land of power, the radicals found worse battles awaiting them.

Of these, the very worst was the flaring up of the old Franco-German feud. We shall see that France, genuinely desiring peace, had reached an Entente Cordiale with England; and that Germany, using the Morocco problem as a pretext, attempted to frighten France out of the Entente. French pride rebelled at such brutal dictation. This was the prelude to a new period, the world crisis which officially began in 1914, and the end of which was barely in sight in 1945. In these conflicting, confusing lights, France swayed right and left. On the one hand, the rise of Raymond Poincaré, the conversion of Alexandre Millerand to militant nationalism, marked the resurgence of traditional values. On the other hand, the elections of 1914 were a definite victory for the radicals and their allies the socialists. On the eve of the war, René Viviani, an independent socialist, was premier, in definite opposition to President Raymond Poincaré.

CHRONOLOGICAL SUMMARY, 1848–1914

REVOLUTION, SECOND REPUBLIC, "DEMOCRATIC
AND SOCIAL"   Feb. 24, 1848–1851
   Lamartine, head of provisional government
   Paris Insurrection, repressed by
     Cavaignac   June 23–25, 1848
   Cavaignac chief executive
   Presidential election: Louis Napoleon
     elected   Dec. 10, 1848
   Legislative Assembly; Roman Expedition   1849
   Coup d'état by Louis Napoleon   Dec. 2, 1851
   Napoleon III proclaimed emperor   Dec. 2, 1852

AUTHORITARIAN EMPIRE   1852–1860
   Crimean War, Sevastopol, Congress of Paris   1854–1856
   Exposition   1855
   Gustave Flaubert: *Madame Bovary*   1857
   Charles Baudelaire: *Flowers of Evil*   1857
   Italian War: Magenta, Solferino   1859

LIBERAL EMPIRE   1860–1869
   Mexican Affair   1861–1867
   Königgrätz (Sadowa)   1866
   Exposition   1867

CONSTITUTIONAL EMPIRE   1869–1870
   Emile Ollivier premier; plebiscite endorses
     reform   May 8, 1870

"THE TERRIBLE YEAR"   1870–1871
   Franco-German War declared   July 19, 1870
   Battle and capitulation of Sedan   Sept. 1–2, 1870
   Downfall of empire, republic proclaimed   Sept. 4, 1870
   Government of national defense, General Trochu
   Capitulation of Bazaine at Metz   Oct. 27, 1870
   Paris besieged. Capitulates. Armistice   Jan. 28, 1871

National Assembly, elected February 8, meets at
   Bordeaux   Feb. 13, 1871

ADOLPHE THIERS PRESIDENT   1871–1873
   Commune (Paris Insurrection)   March 18–May, 1871
   Treaty of Francfort   May 10, 1871

MACMAHON PRESIDENT   1873–1879
   Constitutional laws voted   1875
   Republican victory; May 16 crisis   1877
   Exposition (recuperation of France)   1878

MACMAHON RESIGNS; JULES GRÉVY PRESIDENT   1879–1887
   Occupation of Tunis   1881
   Education law ("secular, gratuitous, and com-
     pulsory")   1882
   Death of Gambetta   1882
   Campaign in Far East; Tonkin annexed   1884–1885
   Boulanger crisis   1886–1889

GRÉVY RESIGNS. SADI CARNOT PRESIDENT   1887–1894
   Panama scandal   1892–1893
   Russian alliance   1893–1894
   Madagascar conquered   1894–1896
   Dreyfus Affair   1894–1899–1906
   Waldeck-Rousseau ministry   1899–1902
   Entente Cordiale with England   April 8, 1904
   Separation of church and state   Dec. 9, 1905
   Morocco crisis: William II at Tangier   March 31, 1905
   Algeciras Conference   Jan. 16–Apr. 7, 1906
   Casablanca affair   Sept. 25, 1908
   Agadir crisis   July–Nov., 1911

RAYMOND POINCARÉ PRESIDENT   1913–1920
   Leftist election; René Viviani premier   1914

CHAPTER VIII.

The Two World Wars (1914 - 1945)

1. THE FIRST WORLD WAR

EUROPE has never known a decade of peace. Yet in 1900, the French believed in peace as an immediate possibility. They thought the Hague Conference, convened by the tsar in 1899, was at least the indication of a trend. Léon Bourgeois, the titular head of the Radical party, was devoting all his efforts to the organization of "peace through law." The growing Socialist party was resolutely opposed to war. The *revanche* sentiment had lost its aggressiveness; if France did not accept the arbitrament of the sword in 1871, she no longer thought of redress in bellicose terms. Above all, the Dreyfus affair had fostered a spirit decidedly hostile to militarism. The "honor of the army" had been foolishly set above truth, liberty, and justice; the French had decided that the nation was first of all a democracy, not a service of supply for a fighting caste.

In 1905, the French realized with dismay that war was still a possibility among civilized nations. And the "Spirit Ironical" willed it that the resurgent threat came from a wise and far-sighted move toward peace.

We have seen that the expansion of the French Empire had brought England and France into conflict in every part of the globe. The Dreyfusist republic desired to end a feud which had been the most persistent element in French history: Seeley points out that there were, not one, but three "Hundred Years'

Wars." Edward VII, who had great personal sympathies for France, had the same wish. He dared to visit Paris (May, 1903). Thanks to his personal prestige, he was courteously received; the bitter memories of Fashoda and the Boer War receded. When President Loubet returned his visit in June, London showed itself even more cordial. In April, 1904, an Anglo-French Entente was concluded. A number of minor conflicts were settled in a give-and-take spirit. This appeared a triumph of shrewd, farsighted statesmanship, "realism" of the highest kind.

Unfortunately, there were in the Entente two factors of a less healthy nature. First, and almost incidentally, the Entente implemented, not peace, but imperialism. The two great powers, after the fashion of great powers, "gave and took" what did not belong to them; France renounced her claims in Egypt for a free hand in Morocco. The world has yet to see a secret agreement for spheres of influence and division of spoils that does not foreshadow war.

The second disturbing factor was that the Entente, not openly, not perhaps even consciously, was directed against Germany. The Germany of William II was not reassuring. Every one of its moves seemed a challenge to the vested interests of the replete nations. It was hard to tell whether this constant menace was mere bluff or inexorable purpose. The kaiser was erratic and theatrical. But behind him stood a people of unsurpassed discipline and efficiency. Soldiers, merchants, professors seemed to breathe the same spirit. *Weltmacht* was the goal: "tomorrow the world."

Had Germany been ruled by an Edward VII, the cloud of distrust might have been dispelled. He might have led his people to interpret *Weltmacht* as equality of status among world powers, not as universal dominion. William II was too weak and vain to give his nation counsels of wisdom. There were many civilized Germans; but not one whose authority could balance the weight of the Bismarckian tradition, "Might is right." So that even an urbane and experienced diplomat like Bülow acted in the purest Junker spirit. The German ruling caste understood nothing but force. They tried to frighten France out of the Entente Cordiale with England, and they made the Morocco agreement a test case.

We cannot relate here the details of that protracted quarrel, which lasted from 1905 to 1911: the landing of the kaiser at Tangier (March 31, 1905); the fall of the foreign minister who had negotiated the Entente, Théophile Delcassé, in June, 1905; the Algeciras conference in 1906, the Casablanca affair in 1908; the Agadir incident in 1911: such were its principal episodes. A compromise was reached on November 4, 1911, when Germany withdrew her objections to a French protectorate over Morocco, in exchange for two slices of the French Congo. But for six long years, every threat, every patched-up ambiguous accord, had made distrust and resentment more incurable. No one felt that the settlement of 1911 was the end.

So France, sincerely desiring peace, was dragged into war through the alliances meant to preserve peace. She did not ultimately fight Germany over Alsace-Lorraine or Morocco; she fought as the partner of Russia and England. Men like Poincaré and Millerand did not prepare *for* war: they were preparing *against* war. To the last moment, Jaurès tried, in Berlin, at Basel, as well as in Paris, to rouse the people against the somber madness of the diplomats; but no country has ever conducted its foreign affairs on a democratic basis. The ancient game of prestige, intrigue, deceit, and violence was reaching its inexorable end. Jaurès was murdered by a fanatic (1914), a major disaster, for neither Clemenceau, nor Briand, nor Blum could later fill the place of that wise and generous leader.

The murder of the Austrian heir apparent at Sarajevo was the proverbial spark in the powder keg. In vain did Viviani, the antiwar premier, order French troops to withdraw six miles away from the frontier, so as to avoid outpost clashes. On August 3, 1914, France and Germany were at war.

The first world war belongs to world history. France acquitted herself well. From the first, there was a "sacred union" such as never had existed before. Symbolically, Viviani's reorganized ministry included Emile Combes, the fighting anticlerical, Denys Cochin, a highly respected Catholic and monarchist, Freycinet, the right-hand man of Gambetta in 1871, and Jules Guesde, the leader of the most uncompromising Marxian socialists. The first wave of German aggression was broken at the Marne (September 5–12, 1914), through the monumental calm of Joffre and the daring strategic insight of Galliéni. A desperate German effort to win the war through one great symbolical victory was thwarted at Verdun (February-December, 1916).

The losses, both at Verdun and at the Somme, had been appalling; the results were negative. In 1917, the situation was exceedingly dark. Russia had collapsed; the socialists had lost faith in the war; even in the army there were ominous symptoms of mutiny. The intervention of America restored France's faith in her cause and in the possibility of victory. Clemenceau was called to power as the incarnation of a win-the-war policy. Doubters were suppressed. The Allies found in Foch a commander capable of co-ordinating the efforts of Haig, Pétain, and Pershing. After two frantic lunges of the Germans in the spring and summer of 1918, the great counteroffensive began. Soon Ludendorff realized that the war was lost. The imperial government was spared the ordeal of capitulation; mutinies had broken out at Kiel, a revolution in Munich and Berlin. Resistance had already ceased when on November 10, the kaiser fled to Holland; on the eleventh, the Armistice was signed in the forest of Compiègne. Ten million men had died; the nightmare was over; and it was hoped that the world had learned wisdom.

The sufferings and heroic resistance of France, the prestige of Clemenceau and Foch led to the selection of Paris as the seat of the peace conference. The various treaties bear the names of sundry suburbs of the French capital. The treaty of Versailles, with Germany, is the one the world remembers. It was signed on June 28, 1919, in the Hall of Mirrors where, forty-eight years before, the German Empire had been proclaimed.

In details, the stipulations of the Versailles treaty were justified, and even moderate. But there were in it several fatal weaknesses. There was ample discussion: Wilson was the able defender of his own principles, which had been accepted by the Germans before they acknowledged defeat; but there was no full and free discussion between conquerors and conquered. So a treaty which, more than any other in history, had a substratum of justice, was made to appear a settlement imposed by sheer force, a *Diktat*. Worse still, it seemed based on an assumption of Germany's guilt. Now this, in a sense, was obvious to the Germans themselves, and their revolution implied a disavowal of the kaiser's policy. But no admission of a moral nature can be extorted at the point of the sword. Because the Germans were *made* to say that they were guilty, it became for them a point of honor to believe that they were not. The reparations were not punitive; the Germans themselves had admitted that they were, in principle, legitimate. But the total figure was left indeterminate, a threat of economic enslavement for generations. The creditors refused either to accept a full settlement in kind or to allow the gigantic expansion of German industry and commerce which would have made payment conceivable. Thus a very concrete problem, through confusion of thought among alleged experts, became unreal, menacing, an incubus which would leave Europe no peace.

Finally, the Clemenceau-Wilson compromise had a dynamic quality; it was meant to provide a transition between a world of force and a world of justice. But it needed the active collaboration, the disinterested leadership, the vast reserve power of the United States. When a minority in America blocked the ratification of the Covenant, the League of Nations became "Hamlet without the Prince," and Versailles an incomprehensible blend of harshness and laxity. France had abandoned definite security—the permanent military control of the Rhine—for a mere shadow.

2. THE LIQUIDATION OF THE FIRST WORLD WAR

It was therefore a disenchanted France that woke up from the pleasant dream of victory and peace; the victory was mutilated and there was no health in the peace. The first victim of this frustration was Clemenceau. In 1918, the old man had been "Father Victory," indomitable, caustic, eloquent, a flaming symbol like Winston Churchill in 1940. In 1920, he was induced to be a candidate for the presidency of the republic and a smooth nonentity, Paul Deschanel, snatched that reward away from him. Clemenceau shrugged his shoulders and went into the wilderness, writing his philosophical testament "in the evening of his thought," attempting to warn America— in vain—fighting old battles with the shade of Marshal Foch. He died in 1929.

The twenty years between the two world wars were not, however, a period of unrelieved gloom. In retrospect, we now understand that France and Europe, during the first decade, recuperated to an extraordinary degree. In contemporary affairs, every affirmation is but a hypothesis: it is at least conceivable that the first world war was all but liquidated when a second crisis began. The link between the two may be more tenuous than we had imagined. At any rate, this healthy recuperation was evident in the home affairs of France until 1929; and it was true also, although not so clear, in her foreign relations.

The "sacred union" had left happy traces. The wounds of the Dreyfus case were healed at last; the army and the nation were fully reconciled; the church and the republic had found a comfortable *modus vivendi*. Alsace-Lorraine had returned to France in a fervor of enthusiasm. Its readaptation to French national life, after half a century, presented difficulties; but the loyalty of the region never was in doubt. The Alsatian autonomists wanted a larger measure of home rule but not independence and, least of all, a return to German allegiance. The French language was spreading fast. In a bold program of public works, the French showed themselves more enterprising than the Germans had been. The University of Strasbourg was thriving as never before.

The colonial empire was in full development. The centennial of Algeria (1930) found the country prosperous, eager to play an ever increasing part in the French community. There were comparative failures, in Guiana, Equatorial Africa, Syria, and Lebanon; but on the whole, the success of France's colonial effort was impressive. The finest achievement was the progress of Morocco under Lyautey. In 1912, he had been appointed resident general in a chaotic empire, primitive, medieval and decadent, where the sultan held sway only as far as his raiders could exact tribute. In thirteen years, Lyautey restored order, reviving rather than breaking native pride; and, while respecting local customs, he created in the interstices of Moorish civilization a new Franco-African world—industries, schools, public works, cities. He gave the fascinating country a new, ultramodern note, which harmonized miraculously with its ancient and teeming past. Lyautey's Morocco is a work of art.

In spite of a heavy debt, barely alleviated by German payments, France was prosperous. When the franc had to be stabilized at one-fifth of its prewar value, those with small savings and fixed incomes suffered, in many cases tragically. But industrial workers, agriculturists, merchants easily ad-

justed themselves to the new currency. The reconstruction of
the devastated regions was accomplished with rapidity and
thoroughness. The wrecking of many industrial plants had
not been an unqualified evil. The French had been too timid,
reluctant to scrap obsolete workshops and machinery: now
for the first time since the Second Empire, France's equipment
was strictly up-to-date. The war factories established away
from the occupied regions were turned to the use of peace.
The mines of the Saar served as a temporary compensation
for the destruction of those in the Nord and Pas-de-Calais. The
iron ore of Lorraine gave France a favored position in heavy
industry. Hydroelectric power was developed on a large scale
in Alsace, the Pyrenees, the Central Mountains, the Alps.
Attracted by this prosperity, immigrants flocked in from Belgium, Italy, Poland, southeastern Europe, North Africa.
There even were—a miracle—years in which the national
budget showed an actual surplus.

The international situation offers a less pleasing picture;
yet the worst difficulties had been overcome by 1929. Among
former allies, Russia was considered as the bitterest enemy;
Millerand, before Hitler and Franco, wanted to lead a crusade
against bolshevism. Italy, treated as a poor relation, was resentful because she had not been given enough Yugoslavs to
oppress. England had reverted to the old balance of power
game: *Debellare superbos*, France must be humbled. America,
in order to justify her relapse into isolation, had to believe
that she had been trapped into the war by lying propaganda
and the wiles of ammunition makers. President Coolidge's
comment on the debts incurred in the war to make the world
safe for democracy, was, "They hired the money, didn't they?"

There was no unity within Germany; but the division of
the former allies gave the reactionary elements a chance. The
only people who had fully endorsed Wilson's principles were
the Spartacists and the communists. But the Allies dreaded a
radical revolution; they were relieved when Karl Liebknecht,

Rosa Luxemburg, Kurt Eisner were killed; they applauded Noske with the iron fist. Thus no party was left in Germany that would honestly attempt to fulfill the terms of Versailles. To admit that these terms were just was branded as treason, not merely to the fatherland but to organized society. So *Junker*, industrialists, socialists, liberals, Catholics united for a single aim: to destroy the hated *Diktat*—by evasion so long as no other method was available, by force at the earliest opportunity. Hitlerism and all its works were implicit in the murder of Liebknecht.

Now the Versailles treaty was France's sole palladium. Poincaré and Millerand, the advocates of a sterner peace, wanted to see to it that Versailles be rigorously enforced. Germany's constant, insidious attempts to elude the terms of the treaty must be exposed and suppressed. As so often happens in world affairs, the actual incident that determined the crisis was in itself trifling. After a number of futile conferences among the Allies, Germany was declared in default. On March 8, 1921, the French occupied Düsseldorf, Duisburg and Ruhrort. On January 11, 1923, after further inconclusive haggling, French and Belgian troops occupied the Ruhr district. The German government, unable to oppose force to force, urged passive resistance. It was an *almost* bloodless war, yet one of the bitterest ever waged.

It is easy to understand Poincaré's "stern and realistic" policy; it is harder to condone it. The occupation of the Ruhr roused deeper hatred against France than the treaty of Versailles itself. To carry out its policy of resistance, the German government embarked upon a desperate policy of inflation, which bewildered and demoralized the German people. Poincaré was "victorious"; Germany formally gave up passive resistance; deliveries began to be effected from the Ruhr. But in the process, France had further alienated English and American sympathies; and the French franc was beginning to tumble.

But this sharp crisis had a happy issue. In spite of isolation-ism, America stepped in and offered competent advice in the form of the Dawes plan. Most important of all, the French electorate, on May 24, 1924, turned sharply against Poincaré; and, because he had backed his fighting premier to the ut-most, President Millerand also had to resign (June 11, 1924).

This opened a friendlier and more constructive period in European affairs. On October 28, Soviet Russia was recog-nized *de jure*. Poincaré came back, as a financial expert, to save the franc he himself had imperiled; but the foreign policy of France remained the more generous one of Edouard Herriot and Aristide Briand. This led to the Locarno confer-ence (October 5–16) and to the Locarno treaties (December 1, 1925), in which Gustav Stresemann and Aristide Briand were the protagonists. A free agreement among equals was sub-stituted for the *Diktat*. To be sure, Stresemann's ultimate aim was to destroy every vestige of the Versailles settlement, while Briand considered that every progress should be made within the framework of that treaty. But the two policies could grad-ually be harmonized. Between the two uncompromising at-titudes, total rejection or strict enforcement, the way was open for cautious and legal revision.

The immediate results were most gratifying. On Septem-ber 8, 1926, Germany was admitted into the League of Na-tions, as a great power, with a permanent seat on the Council, and her sponsor was Aristide Briand. Not only the Ruhr, but the whole Rhineland was evacuated ahead of schedule. It was possible (1926) to convene the Disarmament Conference; it was possible for Secretary Kellogg and Aristide Briand to promote the Paris Pact (August 27, 1928) renouncing war as an instrument of national policy. And on September 5–9, 1929, Briand could submit a plan for a European federal union. Frenchmen and Germans met cordially in many inter-national gatherings; German artists and writers were welcome in Paris.

The improvement was manifest also in the economic sphere. Germany had been remarkably successful in recovering from the inflation of 1923–1924, almost unaided, through the creation of the *Rentenmark*. The Young Plan (June 7, 1929) took the reparations problem out of politics, and created at Basel a bank for international settlements. In every field, it may be said that the first world war had been liquidated to a considerable extent by 1929; a very creditable achievement, when we remember the complexity of the problems involved and the virulence of the passions aroused. At that time (elections of May 20, 1928) the nazis had only twelve members in the Reichstag. Hitler, to sober Germans, was a laughing stock, and not "God's answer to the Versailles treaty."

3. DEMOCRACY BEWILDERED

On September 14, 1930, one hundred and twenty nazis were returned to the Reichstag. What had happened during the previous two years to explain such a sudden and sweeping turn? Evidently it was not the Versailles *Diktat* or the invasion of the Ruhr, which had already receded into history. The new factor was a world-wide economic crisis, which first became manifest with the crash of the American stock market, in October, 1929. Of all the major nations, France was the last to feel its impact. For a while, her stability, her freedom from unemployment were universally admired. But she succumbed at last to the universal distress, which was to become the universal tragedy. Long before Wendell Willkie had formulated that simple truth, it was plain that the world *is* one.

No single cause will adequately explain the great economic depression, that "global disease"; least of all, can it be explained by purely local or personal causes. This truth likewise applies to the French crisis. The constitution of 1875, with all its weaknesses, cannot be held responsible for the ills of France; as we have seen, it had weathered repeated crises, the sixteenth of May, 1876, the Boulanger agitation, the Panama scandal, the Dreyfus affair, the first world war. No single individual or party should bear the full blame. In intelligence and character, men like Herriot, Painlevé, Blum, Mandel, and even Daladier were well above the average. On the conservative side, André Tardieu was not lacking in experience and energy; Paul Reynaud had gleams of statesmanship. The run-of-the-mill politicians, of the Camille Chautemps type, were not appreciably worse than their predecessors; and if there was something ominous about the rise of a Pierre Laval to power and affluence, it must be remembered that the "realists" of earlier days, men like Ernest Constans or Maurice Rouvier, had not escaped suspicion. Men who grow rich in the debatable borderland between business and politics are not a special product of the Third Republic.

So we shall not take up the dreary chronicle of political intrigues and shady deals. It will not do to assert that the republic fell because a couple of middle-aged ministers had rather stupid aristocratic lady friends or that the whole democratic regime was rotten because a foreign magician, Stavisky, conjured up a few imaginary millions out of the municipal pawnshop of Bayonne. France retched on February 6–7, 1934, but regimes with a more robust stomach have lived through worse unpleasantnesses. The whirligig of cabinets—on the strong pivot of a permanent civil service—creates a false impression of chaos. Fernand Bouisson's administration lived but "the space of one morning"; it is very faint praise indeed to say that the foreign policy of France in those anxious days was clearer-sighted and more consistent than Great Britain's —or our own.

The world-wide economic crisis struck Germany hardest because her enormous industrial development had a very insecure financial basis. The sole hope of salvation for Germany was an expanding world economy: abundant credits, open markets. The American depression, tackled at first by orthodox means, started the infernal descending spiral. The United States, politically in excellent health, had vast reserves in natural resources and optimism. So the depression was for America a sore trial but not a catastrophe. Germany had only recently recovered from defeat and inflation; she was convalescent and feverish. The depression brought about the state of utter frustration, bewilderment, and despair so well described by Hans Fallada in *Little Man, What Now?* and by Katherine Anne Porter in *The Leaning Tower*. Germany entrusted her destiny to a band of blatant fanatics, in the same way as a man, abandoned by reputable doctors, will swallow the nostrum of any quack. Capitalistic therapy had failed her; she did not trust the rival system, communism. Hitler profited by the crisis, just as Louis Napoleon had done full eighty years before. But, incapable of growth, he was still peddling his antiquated wares of the early twenties, denouncing the *Diktat* and baiting the Jews. In their confusion, the Germans were thankful for those two scapegoats; and so the economic disease assumed the form of a relapse into the old nationalistic frenzy.

Mein Kampf was explicit enough; future generations will marvel at the blindness of the democracies that could not read the warning written in such blazing letters. But the thing seemed too outrageous to be credible; and even when they did feel the menace, the democracies were too muddled in their thought to interpret it aright and to meet it with decisive measures.

One thing was certain: the forward-looking policy of Briand had failed. France turned against this "pilgrim of peace"; in June, 1931, he was passed over for the presidency and he died ten months later, a broken and forgotten man. Freedom from fear through federal union had to be shelved; it was still possible to organize Europe for defense. Louis Barthou, the friend of Poincaré, undertook the task. But he was murdered at Marseilles (October 9, 1934) with King Alexander of Yugoslavia. After Barthou's death, this policy was not seriously revived. England had achieved her end: the balance of power was restored, French "hegemony" on the continent was at an end. Already the Poland of Pilsudski and Beck had made an agreement with Hitler.

For this failure, there was a deeper cause than the selfish "realism" of the old-fashioned diplomats. The conscience of the west was not clear. With the best intentions in the world, liberals (in the broader sense) in England, America, and to a lesser degree France had endorsed Germany's tale of self-pity. They gave their full approval to the disastrous fallacy that Versailles was an error, if not a crime. They became openly anti-French and pro-German. In their opinion, by refusing to abrogate the *Diktat*, France was perpetuating the bitterness of war and standing in the way of genuine peace. France's desire for continental security was ascribed to vindictiveness and pride; through *Einkreisung* (encirclement), she was trying to keep her fallen enemy humble and mindful of death. The perilous leadership which circumstances had thrust upon France was interpreted as imperialism and militarism. We now realize that no fifth column propaganda could have worked more efficiently for Hitler than this attack upon France and the Versailles settlement. It was all the more effective because its apologists were sincere, not in the pay of Germany, and because it contained a sizable element of truth. French opinion was not converted, but it became confused.

From 1934 to 1939, France, discouraged, abdicated. She thought more and more of retiring behind that pitiful *Ersatz* for the inviolate Channel, the Maginot Line; and she allowed England to steer the joint course of the western democracies. Now England's aim was peace but her method was appeasement. Hence the lamentable series of capitulations which nourished the audacity, power, and prestige of the dictators: the Ethiopian imbroglio, the half-hearted sanctions against Italy, so speedily lifted, the nonintervention policy in Spain which gave a free field to fascist intervention, the dismantling, without any vigorous protest, of the whole diplomatic structure upon which European peace was founded, the brutal suppression of Austria, and the crowning shame of Munich. For all this, France has to bear her full share of responsibility; had she spoken with a clearer voice, England might have understood. Still, England was the leading partner; and the official England that was so virulently denounced by Mr. Winston Churchill showed an incredible lack of foresight.

There was a deeper cause for the hesitant policy of the western democracies. Hitler was posing—and he would pose to the last—as the defender of European civilization against communism. The privileged classes in the west dreaded a socialist, proletarian revolution. They dreaded the horrors that had attended the civil war in Russia and its aftermath of liquidations and purges. But above all, they dreaded the end of the bourgeois regime, the only one they could understand, which they identified with order, liberty, decency. Even if communism had advanced by peaceable methods, they would still have fought it with stubborn despair.

Their opposition to Soviet Russia was deeper in the thirties than in the twenties. In its earlier stages, the Russian upheaval had been a horrible example, a salutary warning; in its later developments, it was turning into a tempting model. A series of five-year plans, at the time when the capitalistic system was not conspicuously successful in England or America, was a more effective argument, a greater threat to the established order, than Trotsky's defiance a decade before.

It must be remembered that the Revolution of 1789 had been essentially bourgeois in spirit. It had declared private property a "sacred and imprescriptible right of man." It had threatened with death anyone who should propose a socialist law. Its chief effect had been to multiply peasant proprietors, and to destroy any check on plutocracy. Even though France had been since February, 1848, a democratic state with manhood suffrage as the ultimate authority, wealth and influence had remained in the hands of the bourgeoisie. A few gifted sons of the people had the chance of becoming bourgeois, just as a private in Napoleon's armies had a marshal's baton in his knapsack. So long as the democratic republic did not challenge the social hierarchy, the ruling class accepted it without enthusiasm but without demur. When it was feared that economic democracy might follow political democracy, the self-styled elite throughout western Europe lost interest in so-called "liberal" ideas. Mussolini, the former socialist who had roughly suppressed the communist danger, was a man after their own hearts. Hitler, although less reassuring, stood essentially for the same cause. Repeatedly, Hitler promised the west peace, and the respect of the territorial *status quo;* but he must be armed, and have a free hand, against bolshevist barbarism. There were those who listened to these captious arguments not only as late as Munich but even a whole year later, right up to the sudden attack upon Poland in 1939.

4. A FALSE SPRING: THE *FRONT POPULAIRE*

The riots of February 6, 1934, on the magnificent square so ironically dedicated to "concord," had a threefold significance. On the surface, the outburst was a protest against the collusion between crooked business and professional politics: the official who had repeatedly shielded Stavisky was the brother-in-law of M. Camille Chautemps, prime minister until a few days before. More deeply, intense though hard to formulate, there was the distress and anguish of a people that felt itself drifting away from peace, order, and prosperity, and obscurely believed that "something ought to be done about it." And there was also a definite intention, on the part of conscious and organized groups, to exploit that nameless discontent in favor of their own political aims. Of these, Colonel de la Rocque's Croix de Feu, a veterans' association with confused rightist tendencies, was the most spectacular if not the most dangerous. France realized that she had reached the ultimate prenazi stage, and that the apparently aimless riots might easily have turned into a putsch. French nazism had already adopted as its figurehead the living legend, the glorious memory known as Marshal Pétain.

The putsch of February, 1934, had been premature, and the republic survived. To relieve the irritation, a poultice was applied: the administration of Gaston Doumergue. So eager were the French to see tranquillity restored that "Gastounet" was successful for a few months; that smiling nonentity even learned to frown, and believed himself the providential strong man. As soon as the shudder of February was over, Doumergue disappeared.

The left realized that "it could happen here." The communists had at last learned their lesson. Their violent hostility against bourgeois states and bourgeois parties had admirably served the cause of nazism; now they reversed their policy. The Soviet Union showed itself willing to co-operate with the "pluto-democratic" west and sought admission into the League of Nations (1934). The French communists joined what was later to be known as the Popular Front. The reactionary policies of Doumergue, Flandin, Laval had failed to relieve the situation in France. The working masses were in ferment. A new weapon had been devised, the sit-down strike, which, not necessarily violent, had a definite revolutionary tinge. Albert Sarraut, an excellent radical politician of the traditional type, formed a stopgap cabinet but was unable to cope with the growing unrest. On May 3, 1936, the general elections gave the Popular Front a large majority. The socialists had now become the central party of the leftist coalition and their leader, Léon Blum, became premier on June 5. The cabinet was exclusively composed of radicals and socialists; the communists, with Thorez, had chosen to collaborate from without.

Léon Blum was a scholarly, elderly Jew, well off, but not wealthy. This leader of a working class party had already behind him two oddly contrasted careers. A sensitive man of letters, critic and philosopher, he had written, among other books, a searching study of Stendhal.[1] He had also been an official in the highest administrative body, the Council of state. On forming a cabinet, he proposed at once a series of social reforms: the forty-hour week, vacations with pay, collective bargaining, compulsory arbitration of labor disputes, a democratic reorganization of that fortress of the "two hundred families," the Bank of France, the nationalization of the war industries. Awed by the epidemic of strikes and by the manifest electoral victory of the Popular Front, the very conservative Senate (by that time, *conservative* was spelled *radical*) ratified these swift and sweeping measures. On the whole, there was in the country a resurgence of hope. The masses had come into their own in a constitutional manner, without a bloody revolution. After ninety years, the promise of February, 1848, seemed to be fulfilled: a democratic and social republic.

It was a false spring. The Popular Front leaders were honest and intelligent men; not a few of them had political experience; but in financial matters, they were too conservative. Another devaluation of the franc had become necessary, if the French currency were to remain adjusted to the pound and the dollar; they hesitated a little too long and lost the psychological benefit of the measure. It is now realized that their social reforms were long overdue. But there were three conditions for the success of their program: the hearty cooperation of the employers, an expanding economy, and a

[1] Stendhal (Henri Beyle) 1783-1842, a psychological novelist (*Le Rouge et le Noir, La Chartreuse de Parme*), is one of the engaging enigmas of French literature. Writing in the noontide of Romanticism, a survivor of the eighteenth century, he was not fully understood—as he had prophesied—until fifty years after he wrote. With Dostoevski, he is one of the great masters of the modern novel.

world at peace. All three were lacking. The international situation was growing more ominous. Hitler took the rise to power of a democratic Jew as a personal affront. Mussolini was determined to destroy the Spanish Frente Popular. When Blum wanted to exercise France's right under international law, and sell armaments to the legitimate government of Spain, he received warning that, if this policy should lead to any conflict with the dictators, he could not count on England's support. America, of course, stood resolutely aloof.

Blum, frail of body, delicate of mind, was not lacking in political courage. He faced the situation "realistically," called a halt (*la pause*) to social reform, started a vast rearmament program, and offered to form a new "sacred union," from Thorez the communist to Martin the rightist. For this patriotic attitude Henri de Kérillis, a Nationalist deputy, hailed him as "a great Frenchman," a verdict endorsed by personalities as diverse as Winston Churchill and William Bullitt. But Kérillis was isolated. The conservative policy was summed up in four words, "Rather Hitler than Blum." The *Cagoulards* (hooded ones) were arming against the republic with support from abroad. When their plot was exposed prosecution stopped short; for the conspiracy was traced to men in close touch with Marshal Pétain; and, in the people's mind, the handsome old man was still the hero of Verdun.

Like Herriot twelve years before, Blum found his way blocked by *le mur d'argent,* the breastwork of money bags. The Senate was the instrument of orthodox finance. This is not an accusation of venality. We must never forget André Siegfried's pungent epigram: "The heart of the French bourgeois is on the left, but his pocket book is on the right." Of this combination, the perfect example was Joseph Caillaux who, for three decades, had been considered "advanced" in politics. It was Caillaux who forced the resignation of Blum (June, 1937). After a brief Chautemps interim, Blum returned to power, only to be defeated a second time in April, 1938.

The bourgeois radicals, led by Edouard Daladier, had thus broken with socialists and communists; they now had to seek support from the right. For the last two years of the Third Republic, the coalition in power was definitely hostile to the extreme left. Daladier, a sincere patriot, praised by the general staff as their most efficient agent, had been war minister under the Popular Front and retained that position almost to the end of the regime; with all its faults, the French parliament never stinted national defense. In foreign politics, Daladier followed the lead of Neville Chamberlain. Munich and the full recognition of Franco were dictated from London. On December 6, 1938, appeasement won its most signal triumph; a Franco-German pact was signed in Paris—and was understood to be a lugubrious farce. In home affairs, Daladier, who like Doumergue fancied himself in the role of a strong man, used his best energy against organized labor. And so, in confusion and despair, the fatal year 1939 was reached.

5. THE SECOND WORLD WAR

Up to midsummer 1939, appeasement with Germany was still the rule of the British Foreign Office, France following like a shadow. Promises of generous loans were offered to the nazis; no compromise was reached with the Soviets about the Baltic area; nothing was done to mitigate the anti-Russian bias of the Polish government. Snubbed at Munich, offended by the unconditional recognition of Franco (February 28, 1939), Russia finally imitated America's example, and proclaimed her neutrality. On August 23, a Russo-German pact was signed. The western democracies had abandoned their central European bastion, Czechoslovakia; they had forfeited the support of Russia; they had antagonized their own leftist elements; and yet they had not won the trust and sympathy of the dictators, Franco, Mussolini, Hitler. The "middle road" had led to war in our time and under the worst possible conditions.

So the second world war began on September 1, 1939, with the western democracies in utter moral disarray. The occasion of the conflict was the status of Danzig and the Polish Corridor; and for twenty years, the liberals had repeated that these provisions of the Versailles treaty were indefensible. The masses had deplored the betrayal of Czechoslovakia and Spain; they saw no reason why Poland, with one of the most reactionary governments in Europe, alone should be worth the risk of war. The paradoxical reconciliation between Russia and Germany further confused the issue. The conservatives in power regretted the necessity of fighting Hitler, whom they had preferred to Blum, and with whom they had just signed a pact of "lasting" peace.

On September 1, 1939, the Germans opened their attack: Poland fell in three weeks. The west had a respite of ten months and did not know how to use it. During the "phony war," the utter moral confusion of the Allies was cleverly exploited by enemy propaganda. Morale disintegrated. No one was willing to acknowledge defeat; but there was no enthusiasm, no "sacred union." The democracies felt safe, anyway. The Maginot Line was impregnable, the French army was the first in the world, the British navy controlled the seven seas.

Suddenly, in April, 1940, the great offensive began. Denmark, Norway, then Holland, were swiftly overrun. Reynaud, who had succeeded Daladier as prime minister, attempted to strengthen his government by making Pétain vice-president of the council. Charles de Gaulle, just promoted to brigadier general, was appointed under secretary of war. But this spurt of energy came too late. The Belgian army had capitulated. The eastern front was broken at Sedan. The Franco-British armies in the north barely managed to escape through Dunkirk, losing all their equipment; and Mussolini thought it safe at last to stab France in the back (June 10, 1940).

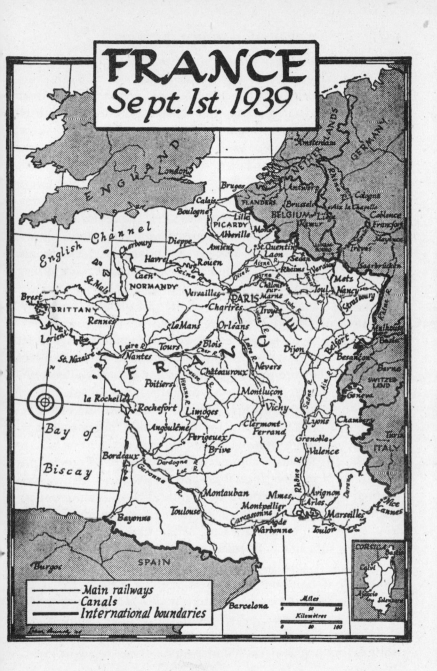

FRANCE
Sept. 1st. 1939

Main railways
Canals
International boundaries

Miles
Kilomètres

The obvious cause of this swift military disaster was military. Although listless during the "phony war," the rank and file had not lost their fighting spirit. It was the general staff that lost the battle, not the common soldier. The blitzkrieg had been met by a fossil army. For twenty years, Pétain and Weygand had given all their care to an instrument that would have been adequate in 1914. The revolutionary methods advocated by Colonel Charles de Gaulle were ignored or derided. Men like Corrap, Georges, Gamelin, Weygand, and Pétain himself were not traitors in the crude sense of the term; they were not even incompetent; they were irrelevant. Ten months after the Polish campaign, they had not yet understood the meaning of mechanized warfare. When their antiquated conceptions collapsed, they thought the world had come to an end.

In the abysmal disaster, half of the ministers, particularly Reynaud and Mandel, wanted to keep up resistance. They were overruled by a tacit coalition—the shady intrigues of Laval, the ingrained defeatism of Pétain, the abdication of parliament. For the parliamentarians knew they would, with summary injustice, be turned into scapegoats; and they tried to beat their fate by relinquishing all power into the hands of Pétain. Was he not the man who had said, "They shall not pass," the incarnation of national pride?

Churchill offered a complete merging of the French and British empires: that dramatic—and mysterious—gesture was ignored (June 17). General de Gaulle, from London, issued his great clarion call (June 18): France is not alone! She has lost a battle, not the war! But Pétain had already publicly offered to surrender. Thanks to his haste, for eight days the Germans were able to round up demoralized French troops by the hundred thousand (June 17–25).

To have agreed to any armistice at all was, we are now certain, a grievous error; to have done so in such a blundering fashion was a crime. But the haste of Pétain and his friends was intelligible. They rushed into surrender as into a promised

land. If they did not fight, the republic alone would be held
responsible for the defeat; and the greater the disaster, the
heavier the guilt. The collapse gave them at last the opportunity of carrying out the counterrevolution that Charles
Maurras had been preaching for forty years. It was their
revenge for repeated electoral failures. So Pétain, who at
Bordeaux and Vichy became head of the state, with the right
to frame a constitution, started a crusade against "the lies that
have done us such irreparable harm"; and the motto *Liberté,
Egalité, Fraternité* disappeared from public buildings and
official documents.

At home, Pétain's plan was to re-create an agrarian, patriarchal France, free from the blight of thought and the curse of
industry. This purified France would find her place—modest,
to be sure—within Hitler's new order. At the Montoire meeting with Hitler (October 24, 1940), a policy of collaboration
was agreed upon.

How did France react? At first, France was stunned. Many
Frenchmen were hoping—absurdly—that the marshal was
playing a clever waiting game. They still thought of him as
the indispensable center of French unity. They rejoiced when,
on December 13, 1940, he dismissed Laval, too obviously the
tool, the willing and sincere tool, of the Germans. But Laval's
successor, Darlan, was just as thorough a collaborationist. He
went to Berchtesgaden to receive his master's orders (May 11,
1941). And the *attentistes,* the wait-and-see people, began to
wonder.

The turning point was the Riom trial (February 19, 1942).
Daladier and Blum, arraigned, turned an avenging light upon
their accusers. Pétain shrank from the contest: he had to ad-
journ the proceedings *sine die* (April 14). Laval returned,
more thoroughly bent upon collaboration than ever. He openly
wished for a German victory. He forcibly recruited workmen
to be slaves in German war factories. Marshal Pétain, in his
usual tone of infallibility, proclaimed, "M. Laval and I are

one." Even before the Germans seized the whole of France (December, 1942), there was but a shadowy distinction between the occupied and the nonoccupied zones. Vichy, the capital of the collaborationists, had openly become a *Kommandantur*.

But the French people, of all classes and parties, had not surrendered. On June 18, 1940, in London, with the assent and support of Winston Churchill, Charles de Gaulle started organizing the Free French, later to be called the Fighting French. Men went through incredible perils to escape from France and join him. Parts of the empire rallied to his Lorraine Cross. France was not a memory and a hope: she had a territory, an army, a navy. Paradoxically, Brazzaville in Equatorial Africa became *ad interim* the successor of Paris. Everywhere in France, spontaneously, little "underground" groups organized themselves for resistance. Through such men as André Philip, their efforts were co-ordinated; and they freely chose de Gaulle as their leader. For men attached to traditional forms, Vichy alone was "legal" and "legitimate"; the resistance movement was merely lawless and futile violence. Those for whom the living past of France was a reality knew that Vichy was but a shadow.

There were hesitations, delusions, plots and counterplots, from the landing of Allied troops in North Africa in December, 1942, to their landing in Normandy in June, 1944. All these intricate and contradictory moves may never be organized into a consistent pattern. Some men played double and triple games; some died without telling their full secret; others will conveniently forget But if the episodes are blurred, the general trend is clear. There were Americans who banked heavily on the *attentistes*. They knew that Pétain was feeble and that Laval was through; but they thought—and perhaps they wished—that the solid classes in France were not at heart with de Gaulle, that the underground and the *maquis* were irresponsible bands of terrorists. The hope of these men was

General Giraud, a devoted soldier, a true patriot, politically inexperienced. De Gaulle, who knew better, would not capitulate to the quasi-Vichyism prevailing in Algiers, of which Marcel Peyrouton was the perfect symbol. As he stood firm, he had to be recognized as the coleader of the French Committee of National Liberation. As soon as de Gaulle appeared in Algiers, Giraud's political star began to decline. Finally, the candidate of the *attentistes* had to give up every shred of power. He retired with simple dignity. Many months later, de Gaulle and Giraud visited liberated Metz together; and de Gaulle paid a generous tribute to his senior officer and whilom opponent.

As soon as Allied troops had broken down the walls of *Festung Europa* and were treading on French soil, every ambiguity was removed. The French Forces of the Interior, under General Koenig, co-operated most effectively with our effort. Everywhere the resistance took hold; and it was seen that it was not composed of hoodlums and anarchists. Paris, unbroken by four years of servitude, liberated itself joyously ahead of our onrushing armies. There was some sniping on the part of the Quislings, the militiamen of Darnand and Doriot, but not even a suspicion of civil war. Vichy and all its works, an unsubstantial pageant, left not a rack behind. There was but one France, and her chosen spokesman was General de Gaulle. Every Frenchman could repeat the words of André Gide: "Blessed be he through whom our dignity was restored."

The most obdurate skeptics had to yield. The provisional government of the French republic was at last admitted to sign the declaration of the United Nations (January 2, 1945). France, ravaged and famished, but unbowed, resumed her ancient place in the councils of the world. At Bretton Woods, at Dumbarton Oaks, at Yalta, in San Francisco, it was in principle acknowledged that her status should be second to none.

CHRONOLOGICAL SUMMARY, 1914–1945

Jaurès murdered   July 31, 1914

WORLD WAR I

War declared	August 3,
Battle of the Marne	Sept. 5–12,
Verdun	Feb.–Dec., 1916
The Somme	July–Nov., 1916
First Russian revolution, provisional government established	March 12, 1917
America declares war	April 6,
Chemin des Dames offensive (Nivelle)	April 16–20,
Mutinies in French army	May–June,
Bolshevist Revolution	Nov. 6,
Clemenceau premier	Nov. 16,
Foch commander-in-chief	April 14, 1918
Allied counteroffensive begins	July 15,
German revolution	Nov. 9,
Armistice (Compiègne)	Nov. 11,
Peace Conference opens, Paris	Jan. 18, 1919
Versailles Treaty	June 28,

INTERWAR PERIOD, 1919–1939

Clemenceau defeated for presidency	Jan. 17, 1920
Millerand president	Sept. 23,
Poincaré prime minister	1922–1924
Invasion of the Ruhr	1923
Leftist elections (Cartel des Gauches)	May, 1924
Poincaré and Millerand resign. Gaston Doumergue president	1924–1931
Locarno treaties (A. Briand)	Oct.–Dec., 1925
National Union Ministry (Poincaré)	

for defense of the franc 1926–1929
Military service reduced to one year .... March 28, 1928
Paris Pact (Kellogg-Briand) .... August 27, 1928
Leftist elections .... May, 1932
Stavisky scandal breaks out .... Dec., 1933
Riots in Paris .... Feb. 6–7, 1934
Coalition Cabinet under Doumergue .... Feb.–Nov., 1934
Barthou assassinated at Marseilles .... Oct. 9, 1934
Elections, Popular Front majority .... May 3, 1936
First Léon Blum Cabinet .... June 5, 1936
Franco rebellion in Spain .... July 18, 1936
Blum defeated in Senate .... June 19, 1937
Cagoulards plot revealed .... Nov. 18, 1937
Second Blum ministry .... March 13–April 10, 1938

Daladier prime minister 1938–1940
George VI in Paris .... July 19–21, 1938
Czechoslovak crisis, Munich .... Sept., 1938
Franco-German Pact .... Dec. 6, 1938
Franco government reorganized .... Feb. 27, 1939
Danzig-Polish crisis .... Aug. 20–Sept. 1, 1939

WORLD WAR II

War declared on Germany .... Sept. 3, 1939
Daladier resigns, Reynaud premier .... March 19, 1940
Great German offensive begins .... May 10,
Italy attacks .... June 10,
Proposed merger French-British empires ...... June 17,
Pétain offers to surrender .... June 17,
General de Gaulle's appeal .... June 18,
Armistice: firing ceases .... June 25,
Mers-el-Kebir (Oran): British destroy
    part of French fleet .... July 3,
Hitler and Pétain at Montoire .... Oct. 24,
Laval dismissed .... Dec. 13,
Darlan at Berchtesgaden .... May 11, 1941
Riom trial .... Feb. 19–Apr. 14, 1942

Laval returns to power	April 18, 1942
Allied landings in North Africa	November 8,
Darlan deal	November 11,
Darlan assassinated; Giraud succeeds	Dec. 24,
Victory in Tunisia; Cape Bon	May 12, 1943
D Day: Invasion of Normandy	June 6, 1944
Paris liberated	Aug. 23–25,
Provisional government signs Declaration of United Nations	Jan. 2, 1945
San Francisco Conference	April 25,–June 26,
VE Day: Collapse of Germany	May 7,

CHAPTER IX

Greater France Today and Tomorrow

1. POPULATION AND WEALTH

I HAVE attempted to trace through the living past of France the trend and the momentum that determined her identity. It is a commonplace to compare history with a symphony: no single note and no single chord—and no dissonance, wilful or accidental—can express the *truth* that is the symphony. Charles de Gaulle is not *France;* the France of 1945 is not *France;* the complex French symphony is still in full development. "Eternal France," said President Roosevelt, appropriating Victor Hugo's famous phrase. Paradoxically, France is eternal because, apart from any particular instant, she exists in the deepening stream of time.

Now we have reached the present, which is already the immediate past. I have no desire to offer any anticipation. Within a short range, anticipations belong to practical politics; within a long range, to utopia; in neither case, to history. A symphony is a constant surprise; yet every new chord is a confirmation. My one hope is to prepare the reader's mind for the next development, which I am unable to forecast. This conclusion is a summing up, not a prophecy.

I have entitled it *Greater France*. The term is capable of many interpretations, from the coarsest to the most idealistic, All have one point in common: they take it for granted that France is still expanding. They are a denial of decadence.

In the eighteen nineties, France toyed, in dilettante fashion, with the idea of decadence. Writers like J. K. Huysmans and Rémy de Gourmont dwelt on the exquisite maturity that immediately precedes corruption and contains a foretaste of it. It was a natural and I dare say a wholesome reaction against the brutalities of naturalism and the crudities of pseudo science, falsely associated with material progress. Decadentism disappeared in the Dreyfus storm. Skeptics took sides, with no lack of simple courage. There was both on the right and on the left a revival of vigorous causes, Catholicism, nationalism, socialism. The vast majority of the French people, anyway, had regarded decadentism merely as a sophisticated paradox. When foreign countries took it literally, the French were indignant. Some forms of art are *fioriture*, mere ornamental notes which do not affect the fundamental tone or rhythm. France decadent because she relished the *haut goût* of Huysmans' *A Rebours?* One might as well consider a palais-royal bedroom farce, or *La Vie Parisienne*, as a true picture of French morals.

Decay is a constant process in life. Certain American ways are manifestly decaying because they are superseded: horses will never mean to us what they meant to our forefathers. There was decadence in the Dark Ages; but the magnificent medieval synthesis was being prepared. There was a decadence of the feudal age in the fourteenth and fifteenth centuries; but it was the seeding time of the Renaissance. There was a decadence of Bourbon absolutism under Louis XV; but it was also the Enlightenment, dispelling chaos. There has been in our lifetime a decadence of that sturdy if unlovely conception of life called bourgeois liberalism. It is being dissolved and resolved into something incomparably richer. Losses are not denied: France may never build another Versailles. But a city of health and harmony is a greater masterpiece than any royal palace.

Greater France! If greatness be taken in strictly material

terms, is it not a fact that the population of France is stationary
and possibly dwindling? The "fact" should be scrutinized more
closely. France reached, ahead of other great nations, the stage
of conscious parenthood. She checked—not by law—the geo-
metric progression forecast by Malthus, which would turn the
world into a solid mass of humanity. This argues no loss of
vitality, no lowering of moral standards. No doubt the health
of France has deeply suffered during the second world war;
the few months that followed the liberation of the country
were the hardest. But the harm is not irreparable; the starved
land and the starved people will be nourished into health and
strength again.

A few French publicists speak in nazi terms of "breeding" in
ever increasing numbers. To what end? In preparation for a
third world war? Or so that France may claim that she is
bursting within her old confines, and is entitled to ampler
Lebensraum? This way madness lies. The ideal of France is the
optimum, not the maximum.

This optimum will be reached through a liberal immigra-
tion policy. I cannot repeat too often that France is not and
has never been a race: France is the epitome of Europe. For
twenty-five hundred years at least, we know that men from
the south, the east, and the north have settled in the propitious
land. The process of infiltration has been practically uninterrupted. It was greatly accelerated at times; between the two
world wars, France, next to America, received the largest number of immigrants. In France as in America, there are many
foreign names in the roster of distinguished citizens. Not all
adopted sons turned into Staviskys.

The population of France depends upon political, tech-
nological, and social factors. Even from the military point of
view, numbers are not the sole consideration. If there are any
more great wars (*absit omen!*), they will again be waged between coalitions. In such groupings, a well-knit, conscious,
satisfied country counts for more than one which, although

much larger, is divided or dispirited; compare the weight in battle of tiny England compared with that of India. It was not numbers that conquered in 1940: England, France, the Netherlands, Belgium, heavily outnumbered Germany. But the nazis were determined, and the western democracies were bewildered.

A decent standard of living for all should be the goal of every sane country, even though the effect were to limit and even decrease the total population. France does not want eighty million people on the barest subsistence level. Unless there were to be a great revolution in technique, a high standard of living could not be attained, in a medium-sized country like France, through *autarky* or economic self-sufficiency. If France attempted to preserve, within the nation, a perfect balance between industry and agriculture, the result would be detrimental to both. Genuine progress in agriculture will mean the abandonment of substandard and marginal land, and a much more intensive use of machinery. Both developments imply a decrease in the rural population. To maintain that population at its present figure through tariffs and subsidies would actually pauperize it; and it would impose upon French industry a handicap which could hardly be overcome. France needs freer trade, with the empire, within a united Europe, and ultimately with the whole world.

The problem is whether French industry will be able to absorb the workers released from the land. Technically, it is a possibility. As we saw in the second chapter, if France is poor in coal and almost destitute of oil, she has other resources, not the least of which is a long tradition of hard work and ingenuity. Large-scale developments will probably have to be of a public or semipublic nature. The bourgeoisie had adopted too cautious an attitude in economic affairs; the people never had any great love for "big business" in private hands. To the average Frenchman, the service of the state offers both more dignity and more security than employment by a capitalist concern. This tendency, deep-rooted and not unhealthy, fits in very well with the pressing necessities of the hour. To clear up the unbelievable confusion created by the nazis and the collaborationists, to reconstruct devastated France, to equip her anew in the shortest possible time and with the least possible waste are tasks so vast that only collective agencies could adequately cope with them. Already new formulas are devised, whereby these agencies will be removed from political influence, and will enjoy a large degree of autonomy. Between universal servitude and *laissez faire* anarchy, there are innumerable shades. It seems certain that we may expect an increase of the socialist sector undreamed of in the timid days of the *Front Populaire*. It is significant that the provisional government was from the first heartily supported both by Catholics and by communists. These strange fellow travelers have at least one point in common: they are not committed to bourgeois liberalism and to the worship of the profit motive.

The prospect is far from discouraging. If by an economic "great power," we mean one which is able to beggar its competitors, France will not enjoy that sinister kind of greatness. America, upon whom greatness was thrust in the decade following the first world war, found that it was not good business to ruin one's customers. We could not afford to be a Rockefeller among nations, if all the rest were reduced to the position of share croppers; and it would give us very little satisfaction to bury the world's gold at Fort Knox. If by economic greatness we mean economic health, comfort for the common man, reasonable leisure, intelligent luxury, then France can be great, and so can Holland, Switzerland or Denmark. France on the whole has been successful in the past. Yet she suffered from a triple blight: the constant threat of war, class antagonism, and bourgeois timidity. There is a fair chance that all three will be greatly decreased.

2. THE NEW FRENCH COMMONWEALTH, "A NATION OF A HUNDRED MILLION"

Greater France is often used as a synonym for the French Colonial Empire. General Mangin liked to assert: "We are a nation-of a hundred million," and General de Gaulle, a man of a different mental caliber, saw fit to repeat that boast, with a 10 per cent increment. The area under the French tricolor is larger than that of the United States. *Statistically*, France is to be reckoned among the giants.

In this rudimentary form, the assertion may be dismissed with a shrug. Belgium is not counted a great power, although her domain in the Congo is four times larger than was Germany. No patriot with a true sense of his country's greatness rejoices because the Sahara is a French desert; and it would be just as well for the country of Descartes, Racine, and Pasteur if the pestilential swamps of Guiana were mismanaged from Rio de Janeiro instead of Paris. Many people—the present writer among them—have no love for the colonial system; the very word empire strikes a coarse and even a vulgar note.

In addition, it is often said that the French have colonies but no colonists; that even if they had colonists, they would not know how to colonize. They apply to the jungle the meticulous care of metropolitan bureaucracy. They export nothing into their overseas dominions except damaged officials; and they import nothing from them except the same officials, worse damaged.

Now this is a caricature which amused the French themselves some sixty years ago. A great part of the empire came into French possession in the eighteen eighties and nineties, almost surreptitiously. The masses hardly knew it, and did not want it. But those days are over. To the French at any rate, their empire is now a very definite reality.

Here we may apply again our familiar concept of *momentum*. The empire is not a venture of yesterday. The French have a colonizing tradition which goes back nine hundred years. In the eleventh century, the Normans—no longer Norsemen, but true Frenchmen—embarked upon daring expeditions. They won Sicily, and they won England—France's most successful achievement in the colonial field. The dynasty, in England, a great part of the nobility, the courts, remained French after 1066 for a longer time than England has ruled India. When England finally asserted her cultural independence, in the fourteenth century, she was no longer Anglo-Saxon, and still less British, but a hybrid with a strong French imprint.

The Crusades were, in certain respects, colonial expeditions and the French played a prominent part in them. The kingdom of Jerusalem was practically a transplanted piece of feudal France. The Latin empire of Constantinople had a strong French tinge. For centuries, all westerners in the Levant were known as Franks, and their commercial Esperanto as *lingua franca*. Nor was the activity of the French limited to the Mediterranean; at the close of the Middle Ages, they were trading with West Africa.

Although lagging far behind the Portuguese and the Spaniards at the time of the great discoveries, they had their explorers and their pioneers. Ango, a shipowner from Dieppe, blockaded Lisbon with his own fleet. There were attempted settlements in Brazil, in Florida, as well as in the West Indies. Coligny had at least an adumbration of a colonial policy. In the seventeenth century, the empire assumed definiteness. The St. Lawrence, the Great Lakes and the Mississippi were linked by daring explorations; Madagascar was loosely drawn into the orbit of France. In the eighteenth century, the empire showed great promise, both in America and in India. It was lost, not primarily through lack of skill or courage, but because France could not, like England, withdraw at will from European commitments and put all her energy into naval warfare. The wars of the Revolution prevented a revival of colonial expansion; the influence of Napoleon was wholly disastrous. By attempting to restore slavery, he lost Haiti; and he recovered Louisiana from Spain only to sell it at once.

By 1815, France had only a few vestigial outposts, in Senegal, in the West Indies, Réunion in the Indian Ocean, five townships in India. But Charles X started the conquest of Algeria, and Louis Philippe, lover of peace though he was, pursued it. Napoleon III extended French rule in Oceania, secured a foothold in Indo-China, preserved the ancient tradition of France's special interests in Syria and Lebanon. It may be added that at all times France had great navigators—Bougainville, La Pérouse, Dumont d'Urville—whose travels entranced the reading public; and that French priests took an important part in the world-wide Catholic missions. The empire of the Third Republic had therefore a checkered, but very long, line of descent. Its origin was not merely a trick of Bismarck to embroil France with Italy and England.[1] There was no doubt something fortuitous about the acquisition of overseas dominions by the stodgy opportunistic republic; but the apparent accident was in fact a return to a very long tradition.

A few of the old colonies strictly follow the pattern of the home government. Martinique and Guadeloupe, for instance, are practically French departments, and the French would no more think of selling them than they would sell Corrèze or Allier. But these are exceptions. On the whole, French administration is extremely diversified. Take for example North Africa, which offers a striking unity from the geographical point of view: the methods followed in Tunisia, Algeria, and Morocco are totally different. In Algeria itself, which is technically an extension of France, there are regions directly under French law, others under a mixed regime, and outposts under direct military rule. A Mohammedan has the choice of coming under French civil law or retaining his native status.

[1] It was Bismarck who encouraged France to take Tunis.

The five states of the Indo-Chinese Union offer even more striking contrasts.

It is not wholly accurate either to say that the French erect an impassable trade fence, of the Smoot-Hawley type, round their colonies. There was some ground for that accusation in Indo-China and Madagascar; and Algeria is simply part of the metropolitan French system. But in the mandated territories, in the whole of Equatorial Africa (as part of the Conventional Basin of the Congo), in the major portion of West Africa, in Morocco, that is to say in the largest French possessions and in some of the most active, equality of economic opportunity is fully preserved. Prewar Morocco, for instance, was one of the few regions in the world where Japan could dump her incredibly cheap and flimsy wares.

Nor are the French guilty of a dog-in-the-manger policy in the matter of population. They do not reserve for themselves vast, rich, and empty territories for which they cannot provide settlers. The parts of the French Empire that are rich are inhabited to their full present capacity. Those that are empty hold no attraction for white men. North Africa, for instance, does not compare in economic resources with our Pacific coast; and it already counts eighteen million people. The problem that the French have to face is not to bring in more immigrants but to find living space for the present dwellers in the land. They will have to plan for active migration within the empire. North Africans, for instance, may be sent to the "new Egypt" which is being created by irrigation in the internal delta of the Niger; perhaps to Madagascar; perhaps even to European France. The teeming populations of the Indo-Chinese deltas might colonize Laos, which is still primitive, or French Oceania. Frenchmen from the old country can only hope to be an elite of administrators, engineers, health officers, teachers. The problem is whether they are qualified to assume such a role.

The record of the last forty years is the answer. British and German observers discovered, before the skeptical Parisian public, that in several places the French were doing an admirable job. Sir Harry Johnston in particular revealed the success of the protectorate method in Tunisia. A few great governors succeeded in putting large dominions "on the map": Paul Doumer in Indo-China, Galliéni in Madagascar, and especially Lyautey in Morocco. The Mandate Commission of the League of Nations recognized that French rule in Cameroun was more humane and also more efficient than that of Germany. Success does not automatically follow the French flag any more than ours: few people are proud of our record in Puerto Rico. Guiana is a blot, Equatorial Africa was long a Cinderella; Syria and Lebanon were political failures unredeemed by economic triumphs. But on the whole, the French Empire has been increasing in numbers, wealth and strength.

What about the spiritual values which, contrary to alleged "realists," are the most real of all? The question is complex. It is a fact that in the hour of France's worst trial, the loyalty of the empire was unshaken. There was no rebellion against a suzerain which, temporarily, had lost all power. The Indo-Chinese could not resist the Japanese, but neither did they welcome them or heartily collaborate with them; until 1945, the invaders had to operate through the Vichy officials. French rule has not been cruel. Individual soldiers, officials or colonists, may have shown themselves brutal; but there was no philosophy, no deep trend of public opinion, to justify their arrogance. It is the supreme asset of the French in the colonial field that, as a nation, they are entirely free from race prejudice. Alexandre Dumas, the quadroon, was not only a popular writer, he was a great favorite in Parisian society. It did not seem a miracle to the French that the very able conqueror of Dahomey, General Dodds, should be colored; that men like Messrs. Diagne and Candace should attain cabinet positions;

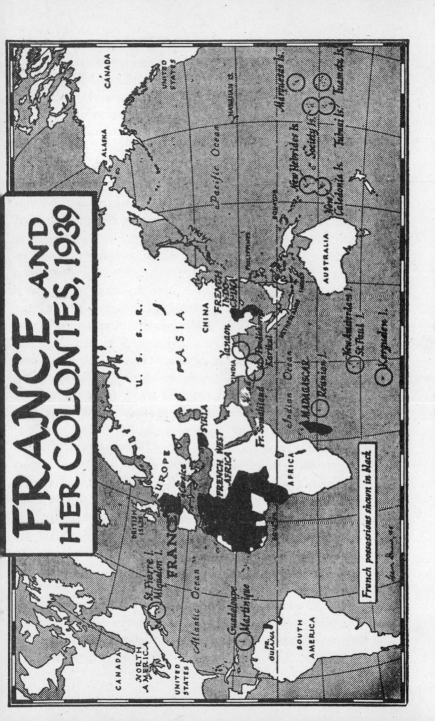

FRANCE AND HER COLONIES, 1939

French possessions shown in black

or that one of the key men in the Free French movement, Governor General Eboué, should be a pure-blooded Negro.

No doubt this refusal to admit fundamental differences between the races had at one time an unfortunate effect. With excellent intentions, the French committed themselves to a policy of immediate assimilation. The result was ludicrous in the case of primitive peoples, and offensive to those who had a civilization of their own. This conception has long been abandoned. For many decades, the prevailing method has been, not assimilation, but co-operation. In North and West Africa, in Madagascar, in Indo-China, the French attempt to revive native arts and native pride. In various expositions between the two world wars, Indo-Chinese and Moroccan handicrafts scored well-deserved triumphs; and there was a veritable craze for the architecture, the sculpture and the music of West Africa. Even with the primitive tribes of the Congo, there is a determined effort not to destroy the surprisingly complex framework of their culture. This was particularly the philosophy of Governor General Eboué, and it was adopted at the Colonial Conference of Brazzaville (Jan. 30 seq. 1944). Its most brilliant success was the revitalization of Morocco under Lyautey.

Yet, while refusing to impose French culture, ready-made, upon the natives, the French believe that the various elements in their empire will not grow further apart but that on the contrary they will steadily be brought into closer unity. They place their hope in *converging evolution*. Material civilization, of course, has an inevitable standardizing effect. But the French are thinking of something quite different. They believe that principles of universal validity will gradually be disengaged from the rich variety of local traditions. They are the heirs of the crusaders, the classicists, the *philosophes*, the revolutionists of 1789, the humanitarians of 1848; their ideal has always been world-wide. In the Greater France that they are shaping, French or Indo-Chinese nationalisms may retain their purely regional character, profoundly dear to their own members, picturesque and attractive to the "sister provinces." It would not be well if Strasbourg, Bordeaux, and Ajaccio were reduced to the same pattern; it would be worse if Hanoï, Antananarivo, and Fez were turned into mere suburbs of Paris. The Greater French community will resist deadly uniformity; but it will remain *French,* if by that is denoted a common effort toward a unifying ideal.

Toward this synthesis, the natives are at times moving faster than their guides. African Negroes insist that they feel themselves French rather than Negroes. They refuse to have cannibalism or fetishism thrust back upon them, under the plea that the continuity of their cultural tradition must be preserved. Both in Indo-China and in Morocco, there are natives who prefer a purely French education to the special and local brand that is offered to them. The cautious policy of Governor General Eboué has its reactionary aspects. Eboué himself, of course, never doubted that he was French through and through.

So "the nation of a hundred million" is not an impossibility. It is at any rate a not unworthy ideal. It will give French culture a richness of harmonics as different as possible from the rigid uniformity of the totalitarians. It is an experiment different from our own, more delicate than the one so magnificently carried out by the Soviets. There are at least indications that the experiment is not absurd. The French do not desire to give it up, and turn the management of their overseas dominions to an inchoate international authority. They want to build up Greater France, not as a chance mosaic cemented by force, but as an organic whole, bound together in terms of liberty, equality, fraternity. The enterprise requires an act of faith and an act of will. It may fail; but it deserves to succeed.

3. THE SPIRIT OF GREATER FRANCE

I am sure the reader understands that by Greater France I mean, not industrial France, and not colonial France, but the France of the spirit. In this domain particularly, it may be confidently asserted that France has not lost the momentum of a thousand years.

It is exceedingly difficult to appraise the living age. We are the victims of two contradictory delusions. The first is a sense of immeasurable superiority over our incompetent fathers. Men of this generation are apt to smile, "with irony and pity," at the worthies of yesterday, Anatole France, Pierre Loti, Paul Bourget, Maurice Barrès, Romain Rolland, Edmond Rostand, and at the *art nouveau* of 1900.

The second delusion is that our own age is one of hopeless mediocrity compared with the great periods of the past. Both are easy to understand. Yesterday is old-fashioned without having yet achieved the quaintness or dignity of a "period." Today is cumbered with the thousand facile and competent successes, with the thousand paradoxes and experiments, that are so hard to distinguish from genuine works of art. Even the keenest of critics, like Sainte-Beuve, cannot see their contemporaries in the perspective of tomorrow. To consider mundane affairs under the aspect of eternity is the privilege of a Spinoza, not of the average man; and Spinoza did not try his hand at literary criticism.

I prefer not to forecast the fame, with later generations, of Messrs. Maurice Dekobra and Marcel Pagnol, two random instances of popularity, perhaps not wholly undeserved. I shall use instead an indirect approach. The France of the Second Empire judged her own literature most severely. Darkness was spreading over all; it was the age of positivism and vulgarity, and industrial methods had invaded the artistic field. Yet, in retrospect, the period seems to us singularly original and vigorous. Apart from glorious isolated survivors like Victor Hugo, apart from critics and historians like Sainte-Beuve, Taine, Renan, Fustel de Coulanges, it was the time of Charles Baudelaire and Gustave Flaubert, whose influence is still felt among us. They protested against the society in which they lived, no doubt. But protest is one of the essential functions of literature; and their protest is now the glory of the generation they denounced.

The example of the Second Empire is no decisive argument. It shows, at any rate, that depreciation is not infallibly synonymous with clear-sightedness. I see no reason to believe that French art and thought, in the dark valley between the two world wars, suffered any permanent eclipse. No catalogue of names would be convincing. It would have to include, in eclectic fashion, both "safe" writers and experimentalists, with no absolute standard by which to select them. I can only bring my personal tribute. Péguy and Proust, who ought to have survived into this age, André Gide, already an "ancient," and more quiveringly alive than fifty years ago, Paul Claudel, Paul Valéry, St. John Perse among poets. Colette, Georges Duhamel, Roger Martin du Gard, Jules Romains, André Malraux, Céline, Aragon, Bernanos, Montherlant, François Mauriac, Julien Green, *j'en passe, et des meilleurs!*, have given me, on various levels, many hours of earnest delight. Once more, this individual testimony has no objective value. Works I have enjoyed may go the way of Octave Feuillet and Paul Bourget; names known at present only among the cliques may rise to a strange eminence, as did in the past Isidore Ducasse, Arthur Rimbaud, Jules Laforgue and even Alfred Jarry.

Our time, as yet, has no name either in France or in America. Perhaps one of its tendencies will emerge with compelling significance; textbooks will have us neatly labeled. Perhaps also pluralism may be accepted at last as a basic truth. But whether we tag it or not, this age does not lack power. It is cluttered with epigoni but it is not ruled by them. I have studied many periods with great sympathy. I like to return constantly to Montaigne, Pascal, Voltaire, Vigny. But I do not believe that at any moment French intellectual life has been more searching, freer, and at the same time more reverent of its instrument than it is today.

It is reassuring to have such a personal impression confirmed by material tests. Serious American criticism devotes more attention to French literature than to any other. For a decade at least, Paris was the literary capital of America. The University of Paris regained between the wars the cosmopolitan splendor of its dawn in the days of Abélard; it contained thousands of foreign students, and its university city was truly international. Nor was this prestige limited to letters. Arts, sciences, techniques kept abreast of the foremost. Even in the industries in which American supremacy is indisputable—aviation, the automobile, the cinema—the French were pioneers and remain in the front line of discovery. In every field, from gastronomy to the most abstruse mathematical physics, the French were competitors not to be ignored. Of this many-sided activity, two symbols caught American imagination: the liner "Normandie" and the French pavilion at the New York World Fair. Both were the fruit of a culture at the same time ancient and ultramodern; daring but with a sense of measure; not afraid of contrasts, for it carried a light that could harmonize them. Such a France did not disappear because an obsolete army lost a great battle.

At the time of the Revolution, French soldiers erected a sign on the left bank of the Rhine: "Here begins the land of liberty." In the realm of the spirit, these familiar words remain profoundly true. It cannot be denied that Germany and Russia have bartered their intellectual freedom for fanatical dogmas—the master-race fallacy, the literal inspiration of the Marxian gospel. France is the outpost of the liberal west.

And this not in the geographical sense only. There are other frontiers to defend, and France is the most alert of the watchmen. Because her destiny has been more tragically checkered than England's or ours, France has learned to question eternal verities that we leave in slumberous peace. We have forgotten the lesson of eternal vigilance. Few sound Americans actively challenge established religions, the profit motive, the party system: France challenges everything. If Blum had been an American, an early book of his would have debarred him from any position of leadership; in France, his daring was a title to respect. According to Matthew Arnold's famous definition, culture does not consist primarily in "getting to know the best that has been thought and said in the world." Its object is "through this knowledge (to turn) a stream of fresh and free thought upon our stock notions and habits." If this be true, France has played and has still to play a major part in the growth of human culture.

Throughout this little book, I have endeavored to show that France was not to be identified with a race, a climate, or a set of institutions. The greatness of France is to transcend all these. France is a collective and age-long striving for human values. She is most French when she is most universal. For her, the world commonwealth of tomorrow will mean not abdication but fulfillment. That world commonwealth can be based only, like France herself, on liberty, equality, fraternity. Any attempt to establish world unity by force, through the might of superpowers, will find France an irreconcilable opponent. She is realistic enough to know that might is might; but she knows also that might is not all. Every Frenchman knows by heart, and repeats as a national prayer, the words of Pascal: "Man is but a reed, the frailest in nature; but he is a thinking reed . . ."

Suggestions for Further Study

THIS BOOK is based to a large extent upon my previous works in French history and civilization from 1913 to 1944. For elucidation of many debatable points, the reader is referred to:

Guérard, Albert: *French Civilization* (I) *from its origins to the close of the Middle Ages*

    French Civilization (II): *The Life and Death of an Ideal* (The Classical Age)

    French Civilization (III) *in the Nineteenth Century*

    Reflections on the Napoleonic Legend

    Napoleon III, an interpretation

    French Prophets of Yesterday

    Five Masters of French Romance

    The France of Tomorrow

and in French:

    Honoré de Balzac et la Comédie Humaine

    L'Avenir de Paris

The greatest history of France by a single writer is that of Jules Michelet (1798–1874), published between 1833 and 1875. His treatment of Joan of Arc and of some aspects of the Revolution remains unsurpassed. But the age of such monumental individual undertakings is probably over.

GENERAL HISTORIES:

Lavisse, Ernest, editor: *Histoire de France depuis les Origines jusqu'à la Révolution, 9 tomes,* 18 vols. Paris, Hachette,

Histoire de France contemporaine (to the Versailles Treaty) 10 vols. Paris, Hachette. Each contributor, as a rule, discusses a period in a "half-tome" or volume. Very scholarly. Good working bibliographies. Moderate republican tendency, "left of center." The work of Lavisse himself (Louis XIV, General Conclusion) is outstanding.

Hanotaux, Gabriel, editor: *Histoire de la Nation Française, des Origines Préhistoriques jusqu'à nos jours (1920)*, Paris, 15 vols. Less conventional in material make-up than Lavisse, a trifle on the showy side. Divided, not into periods, but into special histories (Political, Military, Religious, Economic, etc.). Definitely "right of center."

Funck-Brentano, Frantz, editor: *L'Histoire de France racontée à tous*, translated as *The National History of France*, 11 vols. N.Y., Putnam. The first two volumes by the editor and the three volumes on the Revolution and Napoleon by Madelin are the best known. Very readable but decidedly not free from bias. To the treaty of Versailles.
Briefer, semipopular, for the educated general public.

CONTEMPORARY HISTORY:

Brogan, D. W.: *France under the Republic, 1870–1939*. New York, Harper, 1940. Limited to politics but extremely well-informed, sympathetic without undue bias, keenly intelligent. Indispensable.

The following may be singled out as valid testimonies from various points of view.

Micaud, Charles A.: *The French Right and Nazi Germany (1933–1939)*. Duke University Press, 1944. A scientific demonstration.

Werth, Alexander: *The Twilight of France 1933–1940*. New York, Harper, 1942. Also his earlier *France in Ferment* and

Which Way France? Very intelligent reports by an Anglo-Russian journalist.

Kérillis, Henri de: *Français, voici la vérité!* . . . New York, Maison Française, 1942. A conservative nationalist deputy hostile to Vichy.

Pertinax (Géraud, André): *Les Fossoyeurs (The Gravediggers of France)* I. Gamelin-Daladier-Reynaud. II. Pétain. New York, Maison Française, 1944. A conservative nationalist journalist, long considered the mouthpiece of the general staff, with a unique knowledge of contemporary politics.

Defense of the Front Populaire:

Cot, Pierre: *Triumph of Treason*. Chicago, Ziff-Davis, 1944. A very thorough and very able plea.

Blum, Léon: *L'Histoire jugera*. Montréal, L'Arbre, 1943. Collection of editorials and speeches. The last 75 pages are his masterly vindication before the Riom tribunal. Contains glowing testimonials by William Bullitt and Winston Churchill.

De Gaulle, General Charles: *La France n'a pas perdu la guerre*. New York, Didier, 1944. Proclamations and addresses. De Gaulle speaks for himself.

Aglion, Raoul: *L'Epopée de la France Combattante*. New York, Maison Française, 1943. Convenient.

France Forever: *L'Effort de la France*. New York, Maison Française, 1945. Convenient.

Probably the best presentation of the Vichy Case will be found in the articles of Charles Maurras. The Vichy ideology was the result of the *Action Française* campaign for some forty years. Cf. Roche, Alphonse V.: *Les Idées Traditionalistes en France de Rivarol à Charles Maurras*. Urbana, University of, Illinois, 1937.

Index

Turgot, A. Robert, 161, 163, 180
Tuscany, 197

United Nations, 239, 242
United States, 30, 32, 219, 232, 233, 247, 248; *see also* policy
university, 29, 109; of Paris, 26, 29, 95, 97, 106, 118, 122, 129, 258; Sorbonne, 27; Strasbourg, 220

Valéry, Paul, 257
Vallière, Duchesse de, 142
Valois, the, 87, 92
Vandals of Genseric, 71, 80
Varennes, 167, 180
Vauban, Sébastien, 142, 153
Vendée, 168, 181
Vendôme, Philip de, 152
Vercingetorix, 17, 65-6, 79
Versailles, 26, 142, 164, 165, 201, 244; *see also* treaty
Viau, Théophile de, 137
Vichy, 22, 237, 238, 239, 252
Vigny, Alfred de, 51, 258
Villon, François, 17, 86, 106, 120
Visigoths, 36, 74
Viviani, René, 211, 213, 216, 217
Voiture, Vincent, 152
Voltaire, François, 26, 30, 40, 43, 50, 51, 113, 129, 132, 145, 146, 150, 152, 153, 155, 156, 157, 158, 159, 162, 180, 258

Waldeck-Rousseau, Pierre, 112, 210, 213

Wallonia, 48
war(s), of American independence, 162-3; of Austrian succession, 145, 150; Crimean, 196, 212; Devolution, 149; Ethiopian, 227; Franco-Prussian, 199, 212; first Hundred Years', 36, 93, 94-8, 214; first world, 214, 219-24, 225, 240, 247; La Fronde, 140, 141, 149; Italian, 124-6, 196, 197, 212; of Liberation, 182; religious, 131; of the Revolution, 249; Russian civil, 228; second Hundred Years', 99-106, 119, 214; second world, 233-9, 241, 245; Seven Years', 159, 162, 180; Spanish, 182; Spanish civil, 232, 241; of Spanish succession, 144, 149; Thirty Years', 138; *see also* revolution
Waterloo, 27; *see also* battle
West Africa, 249, 251, 254
Weygand, General, 236
William II, 213, 215, 216, 217
William of Normandy, 87
William the Conqueror, 88 *n*
Wilson, Daniel, 206
Wilson, Woodrow, 218, 221
Workshops, national, 190, 191
writers, French (1914–1945), 257

Young Plan, 224

Zola, Emile, 44, 113 *n*, 209